INDIA'S HISTORY

550 B.C. to 1858 A.D.

INDIA'S HISTORY

(550 B.C. to 1858 A.D.)

An Analytical Review

K.C. Ponnappa

RAWAT PUBLICATIONS
Jaipur and New Delhi

ISBN 81-7033-790-9

Published by
Prem Rawat for ***Rawat Publications***
Satyam Apts., Sector 3, Jawahar Nagar, Jaipur - 302 004 (India)
Phone: 0141 265 1748 / 7006 Fax: 0141 265 1748
E-mail: info@rawatbooks.com
Website: rawatbooks.com

Delhi Office
4858/24, Ansari Road, Daryaganj, New Delhi 110 002
Phone: 011-23263290

Typeset by Rawat Computers, Jaipur
Printed at Chaman Enterprises, New Delhi

This book is
dedicated to the
memory of my parents,
Kongetira K. Chinnappa
and
Kongetira C. Subbavva

Contents

List of Maps

Preface

The history of India is a fascinating one, full of the constant tussle for power of amazingly large kingdoms which endured for long periods. If more effort is expended on archaeological investigations, and research on the masses of scriptures in the Buddhist monasteries, in the Hindu temples and the Muslim libraries both in India and abroad, much more accurate information would perhaps be available to throw greater light on our history. There is a crying need to unearth more of Indian history, because as has been said, a people that do not know their own history can never be a nation.

Meanwhile, whatever is known of Indian history should be objectively presented with correct identification and interpretation of the forces that moved events. Likewise, the state of the country and the people during various important periods should be assessed to the closest degree possible. All this is a major task which would challenge the most dedicated and best historians. The British administration and scholars were the first to put together a reliable history of India from studying archaeological and epigraphical evidence, and by their own researches into the writings of various periods, whether the Upanishads, *Ramayana* and *Mahabharata*, or Al-Beruni's *India*, the *Baburnama* or the *Akbarnama* and from other sources as far back as Greek and Roman writings. But even the best of them could not overcome the tendency to present the actions of the British in softer or rose-tinted lights. Similarly, they could not resist a sneaking admiration for the Muslims, whose physical vigour and decisive actions, as they saw them, they understood better than the involved thinking and convoluted motivations of the Hindus, again as they saw them. Muslim writers on the other hand, even so methodical and objective a writer like Al-Beruni could not free themselves from seeing all actions of non-Muslims, be they Hindu, Jain, Buddhist or Christian, as actions of 'Kaffirs' or unbelievers, as suspect and untrustworthy.

In this book I have sought to present Indian history in a concise manner for the general reader but without omitting important events or tampering with the facts as established so far. In the process, I have attempted to highlight various large kingdoms and dynasties of the ancient period (before 1000 A.D.) and drawn attention to the fact that during the medieval period also, large Hindu kingdoms existed in a state of independence fighting periodically with Muslim kingdoms, allying themselves with Muslim kingdoms in fighting against other Muslim kingdoms, or against the British, throughout the medieval period upto about 1800 A.D. Hindu power was by no means prostrate after the invasion of Mahmud of Ghazni and Mohammed Ghori. There was a major resurgence of Hindu power during the time of the Vijayanagar empire and after the emergence of Shivaji.

Another aspect I was impressed by was the conditioning of religion on the character of actions of kings and commanders. Hindu, Muslim and Christian (Portuguese, British and French) commanders and rulers took actions based on their attitudes which were conditioned by their religion from their earliest years. While discussing this aspect, off and on, at various places in the book, I have discussed it in greater detail in Chapter 3 (Rulership in Ancient India), Chapter 6 (A Discussion of Muslim Rule), and in Chapter 8 (Reasons for British Success).

In Chapter 9 (The Mutiny and After), I have relied on

contemporary despatches by Karl Marx and Frederick Engels to the newspaper, *The New York Daily Tribune* to a great extent, while also having studied the development as given by other authors (British and Indian). I have tried to show, based on my own conclusions, that the mutiny of 1857-1858 was truly a national uprising and not a series of scattered and sporadic events. I have called it the mutiny for the sake of connectivity with earlier histories. I have highlighted the military operations during this struggle, including the capture of Delhi and of Lucknow.

I have tried to write this book in an easy, narrative style to create interest in the general reader and to make him familiar with Indian history in a holistic manner, which he may not have read since his school days. I have tried to re-create the grand scale of our history. At the same time, I have tried to present the social condition of the people, even during the best periods.

I have covered the period from historical times upto 1858 A.D. only, because the period after 1858 A.D. with the whole of India formally under the British Government to my mind needs to be treated with a different approach, as nationalistic political trends emerged very soon after.

K.C. Ponnappa
Lt Col (Retd.)

Acknowledgements

It is my pleasure to acknowledge with thanks the support and encouragement given by relatives and friends in the writing and production of this book: to Mr. Justice P.P. Bopanna, recently of the High Court of Karnataka, for steady encouragement; and through him to Professor Badri Raina of Delhi and his friends for an early evaluation of the historical content and writing style of this book; to Commodore K.M. Acharya of the Indian Navy and Mrs. Acharya for loaning me several books from their excellent library in Bangalore; to Mr. V. Ramnath, I.A.S., for giving me two very useful books from his collection; to Messrs. Oxford University Press, New Delhi, for permission to quote the passage on Discipline from Professor Vincent A. Smith's book, *The Oxford History of India* in the chapter "Reasons for British Success" in my book; to Mr. and Mrs. P.G. Ponnappa and their son, Sharat Chinnappa, for extending their hospitality during my frequent stay in their house in Bangalore in connection with the writing and research periods; for Mr. K.L. Gopi and Mr. K.S. Keshav Kumar of Laser Line Graphics of Bangalore for help in producing the manuscript and floppies in tune with the requirements of format of the publishers; to my wife Kusum for steady encouragement and support. To all of them my heartfelt thanks.

Introduction

Even from Alexander's time in the 4th century B.C., India was known as a rich and fabulous land, exciting the curiosity and interest of the people of Europe, Asia and Africa. Perhaps even from the time of the Sumerians and the early Pharaohs of Egypt, India was known, and attracted sailors and tradesmen from many lands who came to trade with the people of the rich southern coasts. The spices, coconuts and fruits, the rare and attractive timber of the west coast, the pearls, stones and textiles of the south and east were valued materials which sold for many times the purchase price in the lands of Arabia and Persia. Through Arabia and Egypt, through Central Asia and Asia Minor, the Greeks and Romans were in touch with fabled India and established trading colonies in South India. The metal workers of the north were famous for the wonderful bronze and steel articles they produced. Some of the finest swords known to the then civilised world were produced in India.

India during the time of Vedic Aryans was full of forests and deep, perennial flowing rivers, teeming with animal and bird life, a huge sub-continent three quarters the size of Europe (less Russia), cut off from mainland Asia by the highest mountain ranges in the world. Its population which today is over a thousand million was perhaps not more than forty or fifty million including all the forest and mountain tribes. Even during the time of Akbar the Great in the 16th century, more than 2,000 years later, the population was estimated to be about hundred million.[1] There was a lot of space in this rich land, blessed with a reasonably temperate climate, with the potential to sustain human life with a minimum of effort. To the Aryans and other migrating peoples, India must have appeared to be truly a paradise on earth compared to the harsh, stony and windy uplands of Afghanistan and Central Asia and Northern Iran.

With its vast and varied resources, India gave rise to sophisticated cultures and promoted skills and talents among her peoples greatly different from the peoples who were her nearest neighbours in Afghanistan, Central Asia, Persia and Iraq. Her eastern borders with Burma were sealed off by some of the densest and most impenetrable jungles in the world. Her long coastline in the west and east, rich in itself and teeming with fish, was protectively backed up by high mountain ranges which called for special intrepidity and effort on the part of anyone wishing to cross them and penetrate inland. For those early times therefore, India was a geographically protected land, insulated by prohibitively high mountain barriers, dense jungles and vast areas of salt water. Only desperate peoples fleeing from harsh climes and violent enemies, or adventurous and daring peoples of insatiable curiosity could venture to penetrate the physical barriers to find out what lay beyond. The north-west passes from Afghanistan were the easiest (if they could be called easy) approaches to the bountiful plains of north India. However, with forward and backward movement over the north-west passes, word gradually spread to Central Asia, Afghanistan, Iran and Turkey, and through those areas to the Caucasus and Europe, of the great, big, fertile land of India, which had vast spaces and few peoples, and which could accommodate many more people and promise them an easier life.

Presently, there is an increasingly influential school of thought, mainly among North Indians, that the Aryans were

1. Vincent A. Smith, *The Oxford History of India*, p. 715.

indigenous to India, and that they did not migrate into India from outside. This theory is mainly based upon fresh interpretations of Vedic literature and upon the presence of internal fireplaces in some of the houses unearthed in Mohenjo-Daro, Harappa and in some of the other Indus Valley settlements dating from 3000 B.C. to about 2000 B.C. These fireplaces have been called 'fire altars'[2] implying that they were places of worship of the Aryans who worshipped fire. No consideration has been given to the possibility that these 'fire altars' could have just been internal fireplaces which helped the Indus Valley folk to warm themselves inside their houses during the much colder winters (during those times) of the plains of the Indus Valley. By this reasoning, the fireplaces inside the houses of the Anglo-Saxons of Britain could also be called 'fire altars'. However, this theory of the Aryans being indigenous peoples to India is still to be proved against the wealth of evidence accumulated and accepted so far from archaeological, historical and literary sources, and perhaps even from anthropological sources. Meanwhile, for the purposes of this book, it is intended to follow orthodox thought[3] that the Aryans migrated into India from the north-west between about 2500 B.C. and 1500 B.C. and were an 'Indo-European' branch of the Aryan tribes.

Positing from these, so far, universally accepted theories of the migration of the Aryans, the natural process for these pastoral tribes would have been for some tribes to have wandered further afield and entered India almost by accident, and for more tribes to have come later into India by intent,[4] after having heard from returning relatives about the fertility and bounty of the land. There could hardly have been any resistance to them in the initial phase of their migrations. The Indus Valley Civilisation, stretching basically from the Indus

2. "The Kunal Discoveries, Mud, Sweat and Tears", *The Week*, 16 April, 1995.

3. A.L. Basham, *The Wonder That Was India*, pp. 29, 30.

4. Vincent A. Smith, *The Oxford History of India*, pp. 32 and 50.

delta upwards and northwards was spread out in the reverse direction upto about Multan, and had largely spent itself out, either due to successive droughts, or due to cataclysmic changes in the course of the river Indus. In fact, the course of the mythical river Saraswati which is identified somewhat parallel and east of the present course of the river Indus, could have been the earlier course of the Indus which was perhaps changed suddenly due to earthquake, disturbances, or due to major landslides in the northern stretches, or due to unusually heavy floods which change the course of rivers when they debouch from the mountains into the flat plains contiguous to them. The resistance to the Aryans from the indigenous tribes could have developed only after major migrations of the Aryans during the period 1700 B.C. to 1500 B.C. But such resistance could not have resulted in intense conflicts involving heavy loss of life, because it would have been easier for the indigenous peoples to move further east or south, because there was plenty of space, all fertile, to accommodate everyone. It was perhaps only after 1000 B.C. or so when the Aryans pushed forward more aggressively that conflicts of a more serious nature developed, and the indigenous people were pushed into the less attractive hill and forest regions of present day Bihar and Madhya Pradesh, or present-day Kumaon, Garhwal and Nepal.

The Vedic Aryans came into a bountiful land, a beautiful and inspiring land where nature manifested itself in all its different forms, alluring and frightening, attractive and repellent, welcoming and intimidating. The scale, cold beauty and grandeur of the Himalayas contrasted with the warm, humid jungles of the plains. The light, warm drizzles and murmuring brooks contrasted with the torrential rains and furious floods of the gigantic rivers. The cold breezes of the winter contrasted with the searing heat of summer. The soft, multicoloured flowers of the plains and small hills contrasted with the towering trees and dense jungles in the tropical areas. The friendly peacock and the deer contrasted with monstrous elephants and ferocious tigers. They saw dark, rolling clouds and thunder and lightning, and they saw a bright, brilliant sun in a cloudless sky. They saw the silver glow of the moon amidst vast sky of a myriad twinkling stars, and they saw the sky completely hidden by the dense canopy of the suffocating jungle. It was inevitable that they were overwhelmed by nature, and felt that this tremendous universe had been created by a powerful creative force of which the scale and magnitude could not be imagined or defined. It was also the genius of the Vedic man that he tried to speculate on this great creative force and to try and determine his own relationship to this force and to the universe it had created. Thus probably was born the Vedic religion and philosophy which unfailingly relates to nature in its various forms. Later, Vedic man sought to influence his own life in relation to nature, and to master his stupendous environment by meditation, by speculation, by discipline and by inspiration and intuition. Thus were evolved the ritualistic practices of the Hindu religion, closely related to natural phenomena and to the preordained, inexorable movement of the sun, moon and stellar constellations across the sky.

With their aggressive expansion across Northern India and later towards the deep south, the Aryans celebrated their prowess and their success with the great epics of the *Ramayana* and the *Mahabharata* which in due course assumed the character of treatises hardly different from the metaphysically and intuitionally derived Vedas. The stories of heroes and villains endowed with easily identifiable human qualities became the bedrock of the Hindu religion in as far as the general population was concerned. These stories found an easy empathy with the people of the villages who saw their own struggles and successes and failures in terms of the struggles and success and failures of the characters in the epics. The epics were also laced with friendly humour and tolerant attitudes which have imposed their stamp on the character and attitudes of the people who call themselves Hindus.

In time, as population increased and people organised themselves from mere tribes into societies in stable and more permanent locations, the idea of kingship, ministers and council grew and was practiced, in contrast to republican societies of the pre-Aryan peoples.[5] Kingship required standing armies and taxes to maintain them, and involved dominating the local environment for continuation of the kingship. Trade and commerce grew with ease of riverine transport. Along with kingship grew the idea of dynasties and the need for planned protection against competing neighbouring kings. The settled society in areas defined by boundaries gave rise to planned exploitation of the local resources, and development of the talent of people to transform natural resources into more useful forms. Although societies became more competitive, overall conduct was governed by the religious practices of the day which had no creed or dogma. The Hindu religion was adjustable and tolerant, allowing for all the vagaries of human nature, and seeking to reconcile such vagaries to bring about harmony in society. What was frowned upon was excessive indulgence in any emotion or practice, much like the Athenians of the old city-state. These basic characteristics of the Hindu religion seeking to harmonise human activity with nature continue to influence the Hindus even today. They were not forced to follow the teachings of prophets, long since dead, whose supposed infallibility was celebrated and worshipped thousands of years later under conditions far removed from those of their time. There was no theory of original sin under which people laboured guiltily through no fault of their own. There was, of course, the concept of Karma but that was more to regulate conduct than to impose any dogmatic belief.[6] There was no revealed book moulded in cast-iron which had to be adhered to dogmatically on pain of untold and even unimagined retribution. After all, even such dogmatic revealed books were interpreted differently by different people at different periods of history in accordance with their own mental and environmental conditioning.

5. R.C. Majumdar, *Ancient India*, pp. 45, 46.

6. A.L. Basham, *The Wonder That Was India*, p. 322.

INDIAN SUBCONTINENT

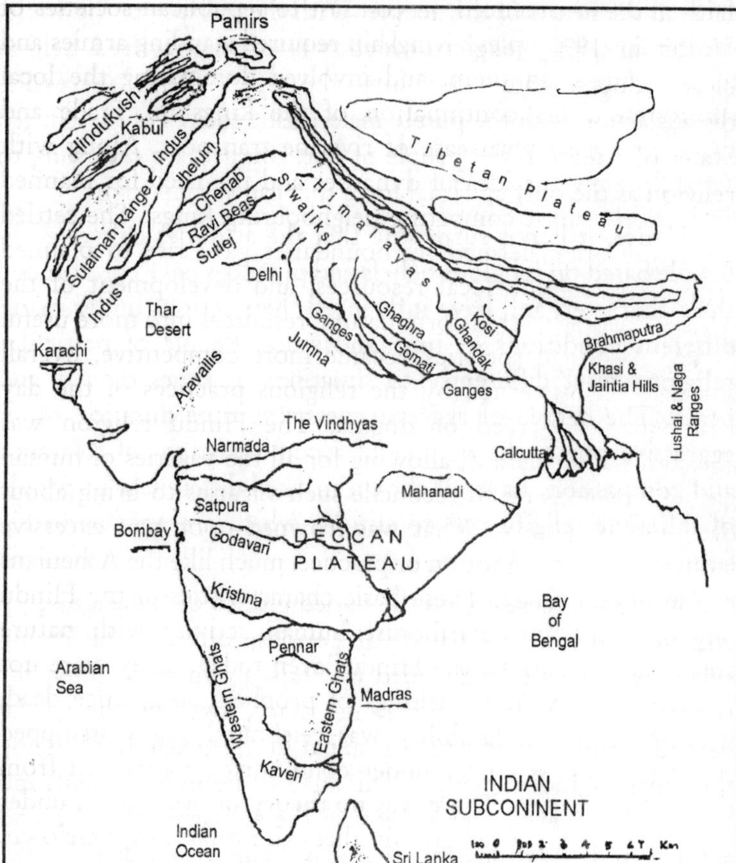

Religion has been the most powerful belief that has influenced man through the ages. Religion may have been an opiate for the people, but the vast mass of humanity has been protected and sustained by religion through every kind of vicissitude. The latest assault on religion by the pure reason of Karl Marx and the resulting communist states has shattered itself on the rocks of human greed, cleverness, exploitation and versatility. An even more persuasive attack by the physical sciences has also failed to reduce the power of religion based on faith in the hearts of the people. With the collapse of the Soviet Union in 1990, religion which was often practiced behind closed doors, came out into the open. With increasing dissatisfaction with the purely materialistic society of the United States of America, the people of that country are returning to religion as the only spiritual force that can sustain them.

Hence, it is not surprising that the attitudes cultivated in people based on religious beliefs and practices have conditioned their character, and have influenced their actions under many different conditions of time and space. People of particular religions react differently to situations in times of war and peace. The degree of aggressiveness, the time duration of an aggressive phase, the degrees of accommodation, of tolerance and compassion, have all shown marked differences in people of different religions in conditions which are approximately similar.

While we recapitulate the varied glories of India's history and highlight certain particular periods; while we justifiably celebrate the vast lands ruled by India's dynasties, often for centuries, we shall also, where necessary, dwell on the crucial decisions and actions which resulted in irremediably changing the course of Indian history. This analysis seems important, and has relevance even today because the selfsame attitudes and actions and reactions occur today which are due to the conditioning of religion and its practice.

Not wishing to make this book a forbidding tome, I have covered the period from 550 B.C., which can be considered as in historical times, to 1858 A.D. when the British Government formally took over the governance of India, in this book. This period seems to have enough instances that illustrate these points.

2

Background Sketches of Ancient India

The Strong and the Weak

What had happened in the 20th century is conditioned, to a lesser or greater extent, by what has happened in the remoter past and in the immediate past. Attitudes and events in the past have always had an influence on the attitudes and events of the present either by a continuity of ideas and policies, or by reaction, violent or peaceful, to those ideas and policies. The wonderful being that is man is always vital and energetic, and is always looking to dominate his environment and to change it for his own benefit. Groups of people, men and women, living in different places and under different conditions, have evaluated their environment, each in their own way, and assessed for themselves what would benefit them most. These assessments would naturally not always be identical or complementary and would therefore lead to conflict. Resolution of differing interests by conflict would depend upon which group is strong and which weaker. The genius of man has been such that he avoided conflict until it was the last resort, when methods of bargaining, persuasion and threats failed. When conflicts were unavoidable, man still closely calculated the minimum force and minimum loss to achieve his objectives. Of course, some groups were less strong or more rash, or their calculations did not prove accurate, and so we have some groups overcoming and dominating other groups and imposing their will and manner of living and culture on the weaker groups. In time, these weaker groups have waited for their opportunity, gathered strength and overcome their conquerors. And so the cycle went on. In spite of modern civilisation, the benefits of science and technology and the coming into being of the global village with its instant audio and visual communication, the struggle between the strong and the weak goes on, assuming different characteristics and methods suited to the times and means available.

Sources for Indian History

The history of India is largely hidden because of the paucity of discovered records -- archaeological, epigraphical and literary. The highly developed civilisation of India which has blossomed at various times and at various places on this large sub-continent, bears comparison in originality and chronology with the ancient civilisations of China, Egypt, Mesopotamia, Greece and Rome. There are obviously many archaeological and epigraphic records waiting to be unearthed and discovered which may throw greater light on its history. However, many epigraphic and literary records suffer from the lack of chronological documentation and objective recording. Still, by cross-linkage, it has been possible to put together a history of India which is basically credible and authentic. It is, however, necessary to give due weightage to the beliefs, persuasion and motivations of the recorders and to discount suitably their personal viewpoints influenced by the conditions of their own times. For the available and largely credible histories of India, we have to acknowledge the efforts of the early British historians like Sir William Jones who mastered Sanskrit and who not only unearthed and studied many records but also cross-checked them from sources as widely separated in time and space as Hindu, Jain and Buddhist scriptures, Greek writers like Megasthenes, literary productions of Kalidasa (5th century A.D.), Vishakadatta (6th century A.D.), and Bhavabhuti (8th century A.D.), from observed accounts of travellers like Marco Polo (12th century A.D.), Fa Hien (5th century A.D.), Hiuen Tsang (7th century A.D.), Herodotus (4th century B.C.), and chroniclers like Pliny the Roman (2nd century A.D.). Muslim observers like Al-Beruni (11th century A.D.) spent time in India, learning Sanskrit and studying the scriptures. Al-Beruni's *India* is a concise and objective study of India and its culture at first hand although it is conditioned by his own attitudes nurtured in Afghan and Muslim social life of the period. Writers like the Mughal emperor Babur (*Baburnama*), biographers like Abul Fazl and historians like the Persian Farishta (17th century) have left accounts which have been integrated into Indian history by historians like Sir William Jones, Professor Sylvain Levi, H.G. Rawlinson, Vincent Smith, Percival Spear, A.L. Basham and many others. So also, accounts by adventurers and courtiers like the French doctor Francois Bernier, the English ambassador Sir Thomas Roe, the Portuguese Domingo Paes and Patrick Nuniz, the Persian Abdul Razak, have thrown light on details of life in the monarchies and empires of India during the middle ages. There are more accurate details of Indian history from the time the French and English entered India.

The Effects of Stability

What emerges from present known history is that the rich and varied climate, geography and resources of India gave rise to highly sophisticated cultures from prehistoric times until the end of the Mughal empire. The fertility and richness of the land and the developed skills of its peoples enabled the rulers to create monumental works of art in buildings, statues, literary works, painting and so on which were uniquely Indian, although influenced later on by Persia and Central Asia. While from even as early as 500 B.C. to as late as 800 A.D. India looked outward also and had extensive political, cultural and trade contacts with Europe, West and Central Asia, Tibet, South-East Asia and Indonesia, and even with China, after that period, the people who exercised power and the intellectual elite of India became inward-looking.[1] They became preoccupied with their own immediate concerns. The wealth of the country on the one hand, and the high state of their own civilisation on the other, were such that they did not feel any need to be in touch with countries outside India. Their quarrels, disputes and wars were more concerned with overcoming local opposition, satisfying local egos. For over 200 years, there had been no invasions or threat of invasions. They had everything they wanted locally in India and did not need to look outside. It was only the southern kingdoms of the Cholas,[2] the Pandyas and the Cheras which looked across the seas, and of these, it was only the Chola power that ventured out and created an empire which stretched from North and North-Eastern Sri Lanka to parts of Malaysia, Thailand, Cambodia and Indonesia. The Pandyas and the Cheras ventured out to northern Sri Lanka, the Lakshadwipa islands and the Maldive islands. Perhaps they also reached and interacted with people in the Seychelles and Madagascar. But, the people of Northern India, Eastern India and Central India had become self-centred and introverted. Like the people of the Middle Kingdom (China), they considered themselves as the elite of the earth and everyone else as barbarians.[3] They regarded the *mlechhas*, outsiders, as uncivilised barbarians who were unfit to be admitted into their society. Hence, they failed to keep in touch with and assess the developments in countries around them.[4] This feeling of being "the salt of the earth" lowered their guard, reduced their vigilance and made them

1. Vincent A. Smith, *The Oxford History of India*, p. 197.
2. Ibid., pp. 160, 161.
3. Al-Beruni, *India*, in Qeyamuddin Ahmad (ed.), pp. 8, 9.
4. Vincent A. Smith, *The Oxford History of India*, p. 197.

vulnerable and easy targets for any invader. Meanwhile, three to four hundred years of relative internal stability had created great wealth.[5] The ritualistic worship of Gods and Goddesses which included the proffering of rich gifts consisting of gold and silver ornaments, often studded with precious stones, made temples the repositories of untold wealth, all tied up in ornamentation and display on important religious occasions.

Major Powers in India: 500 B.C. to Circa 800 A.D.

There should soon come a time when the Government of India and also strong non-governmental organisations should set in motion a major well-coordinated effort to find out more about the history of India during this period. They should, if possible, go further back to trace the history of India from the Indus Valley Civilisation. It is impossible that such major civilisations existed on this sub-continent without clear systems of governance, philosophy and human behaviour and strong social institutions. No doubt, the Vedas, Brahmanas, Upanishads, Puranas and the two epics throw a great deal of light on these matters. But, we need to know more about how empires and kingdoms applied those time-honoured tenets to their everyday governance. There obviously are a great many Buddhist and Jain scriptures written in the privacy of cloistered monasteries, not meant to be shown to any reigning monarch, that have been written objectively as private records. There are also hundreds of potential archaeological sites which may yield conclusive results. Until such time that these mysteries are brought to light, we have to rely on the recognised histories so far compiled.

Videha

The earliest instance of a major kingdom having a strong

5. Ibid., p. 200.

government is that of Videha,[6] north of the Ganga river and east of the Gandak river. It existed before 500 B.C. and its most well-known king was Janaka who reigned some centuries earlier and was presumably the same as king Rama's father-in-law. King Janaka, being mentioned several times in the *Shathapatha Brahmana* is regarded by the historian A.L. Basham as a historical (that is, provable as factual) figure who patronised the wandering holy men and who often had discussions with them about the Upanishads and the Brahmanas. His capital city was Mithila, north of the river Ganga.

Magadha

This was the period, that is, about 1200 B.C. to 500 B.C. when Aryan bands of warrior peasants migrated eastwards in the Gangetic basin and established settlements one of which, Magadha, gradually became an important kingdom south of the Ganga. These warrior peasants although Aryans, did not follow Vedic rites and were called 'Vratyas'. It was only under Bimbisara that Magadha consolidated itself into a major kingdom. South of Magadha, near the present areas of Bhagalpur and Mongyhr, was the small kingdom of Anga. Many tribal republics called 'ganas' ruled by tribal assemblies settled down and consolidated themselves into kingdoms where the king became the supreme ruler. Still, the supreme ruler was being controlled by advisers, by traditional procedure and to some extent by the force of public opinion.[7] The tribes were breaking up and the composition and integrity of communities was becoming more on the basis of geographic contiguity. The rise of kingdoms paralleled the knowledge, not only of gold, copper and bronze but also of tin, lead, silver and iron. The Aryan communities from being a pastoral people had gradually become transformed to an agricultural society cultivating a

6. A.L. Basham, *The Wonder That Was India*, Chapter 2, p. 40.
7. Ibid., pp. 40, 41.

ANCIENT INDIA

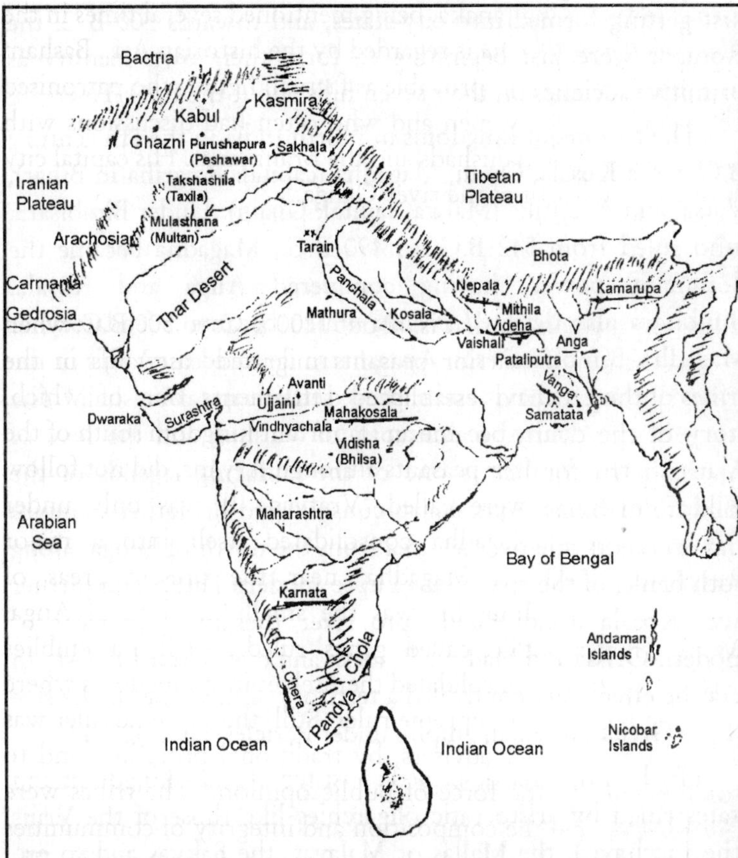

large range of crops and having knowledge of irrigation and manuring. Many specialised trades and crafts were known, thus setting the stage for the growth of urban societies.

About the period of 1200 B.C. to 500 B.C. the Greeks were just getting formed into city-states, and towards 500 B.C. the Romans were just beginning to form their own identity as primitive societies on their seven hills about the river Tiber.

The five major kingdoms in North India in the 6th century B.C. were Kosala, Oudh, Magadha (capital: Rajgriha in Bihar), Vatsa, and Avantika (Malwa, capital: Ujjain). Under Bimbisara, who ruled from 542 B.C. to 490 B.C., Magadha became the dominant power, having conquered Anga and Kosala. Bimbisara also defeated Avanti which became a feudatory to Magadha. Bimbisara's son Ajatashatru defeated the Vrijis or the tribes of the Lichhavis and captured their capital Vaishali.[8] The story of the courtesan Amrapali of Vaishali and the love of Ajathashatru for her is one of the enduring legends of the folklore of Bihar. Ajatashatru consolidated his father's empire and exercised rule over an area from the north of Bengal along both banks of the river Ganga upto modern Patna, and further over Kosala (Oudh) and upto river Jhelum, over parts of modern Orissa and Madhya Pradesh and over Uttar Pradesh. In fact, he effectively controlled a territory almost double the size of the Greek Athenian empire under Pericles, circa 400 B.C.

Much of the area described consisted of small kingdoms and states ruled by aristocratic oligarchies like those of the Vrijis (the Licchavis), the Mallas or Malavas, the Sakyas and so on. The reigns of Bimbisara and Ajatashatru are also famous for the teachings of Mahavira Vardhamana who preached the religion now known as Jainism with its emphasis on 'ahimsa' or non-violence, and of Gautama Siddhartha, the Buddha who taught Buddhism and its eight-fold path of conduct. They were both

8. Vincent A. Smith, *The Oxford History of India*, Chapter 2, pp. 73, 74.

almost contemporaneous between 550 B.C. and 465 B.C.[9] and preached directly to the masses. Both religions spread fast in the Gangetic basin as they could be easily understood in comparison to the sophisticated rituals and scriptures of Hinduism. Buddhism was given a special impetus by the conversion of Asoka who consciously worked for its spread beyond the boundaries of India to Ceylon, South-East Asia, Central Asia, China and Burma. Both religions continue to have millions of adherents both inside and outside India, and remain vital forces.

Ajatashatru's descendants were weak kings under whom the empire was whittled away until the dynasty of the Nandas took over Magadha and also ruled over Mithila, Kosala and Anga.

North-West India

From 540 B.C., the North-West Frontiers and Punjab upto the Indus river formed one of the richest satrapies of the Persian empire, but there is no evidence of any clash between the Persians and the Magadha power.[10]

The Mauryas

After Alexander invaded India in 327 B.C. and set up a number of Greek settlements from Afghanistan to Punjab and in many places down the Indus, these settlements endured and gradually became independent monarchies. This was the period when the Nandas in Magadha were becoming weak and unpopular. The time was ripe for a young adventurer to seize the throne of Magadha and establish probably the greatest and most famous of Indian empires. Chandragupta Maurya was only a few years younger than Alexander and is said to have personally met him

9. A.L. Basham, *The Wonder That Was India*, p. 287.
10. Vincent A. Smith, *The Oxford History of India*, p. 73.

EMPIRE OF THE MAURYAS

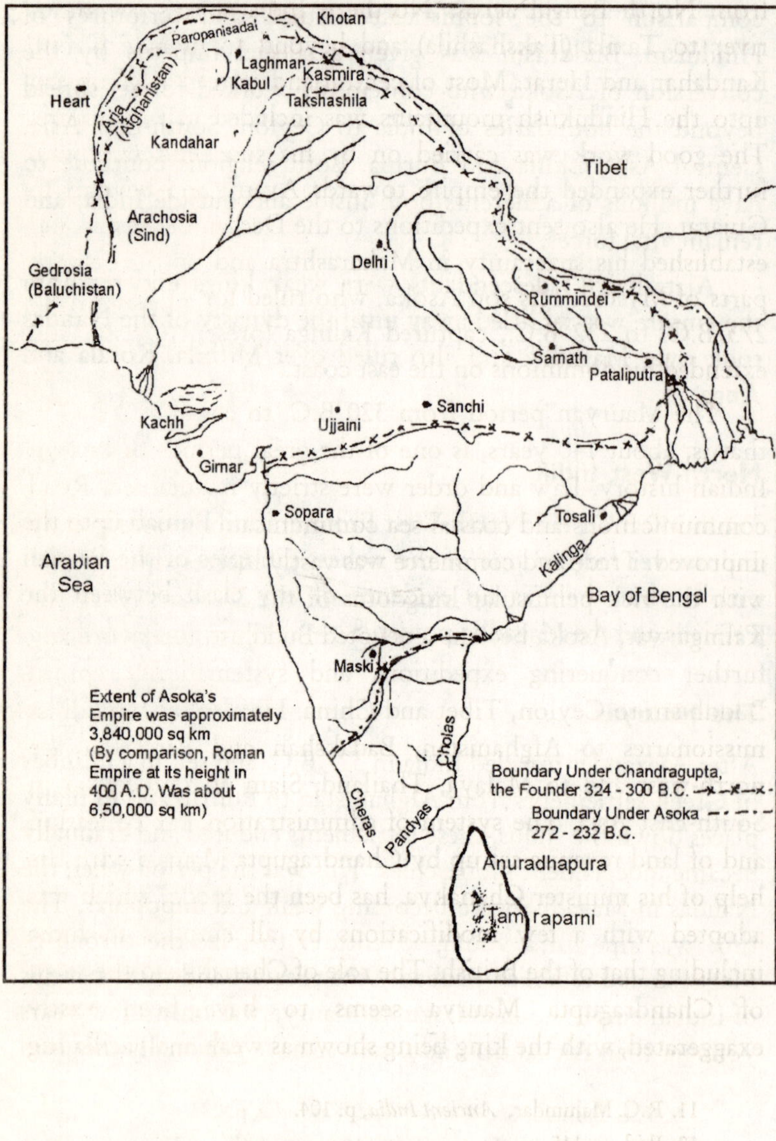

and apprised him of conditions beyond the river Indus. Taking advantage of the weakness of the Nanda king, he usurped the throne[11] in 320 B.C. and by 300 B.C. had expanded his empire from North Bengal across Northern India, across the Indus river to Taxila (Takshashila) and beyond to include Kabul, Kandahar and Herat. Most of central and eastern Afghanistan upto the Hindukush mountains was included in his empire. The good work was carried on by his son Bindusara who further expanded the empire towards Avanti and beyond to Gujarat. He also sent expeditions to the Deccan peninsula and established his suzerainty in Maharashtra and upto northern parts of Mysore. His son Asoka, who ruled for 41 years from 273 B.C. to 232 B.C., captured Kalinga (present Orissa) and extended his dominions on the east coast.

The Mauryan period from 320 B.C. to about 182 B.C.[12], that is, about 140 years, is one of the great periods of known Indian history. Law and order were strictly maintained. Road communications and coastal sea communications were greatly improved. Trade and commerce was vastly increased, especially with the rich peninsular kingdoms of the Deccan. After the Kalinga war, Asoka became a devoted Buddhist, foreswore any further conquering expeditions and systematically spread Buddhism to Ceylon, Tibet and China. He also sent Buddhist missionaries to Afghanistan, Badakshan and Persia in the north-west and to Malaya, Thailand, Siam and Indonesia in South-East Asia. The system of administration, tax collection and of land revenue set up by Chandragupta Maurya with the help of his minister Chanakya, has been the model which was adopted with a few modifications by all empires in India including that of the British. The role of Chanakya in the reign of Chandragupta Maurya seems to have been vastly exaggerated, with the king being shown as weak and vacillating

11. R.C. Majumdar, *Ancient India*, p. 104.
12. Ibid., p. 115.

and with Chanakya being shown as the power behind the throne. The main reason for this projection stems from the play *Mudrarakshasa* or 'the seal of (the minister) Rakshasa' by Vishakadatta written in the 6th century A.D., that is some nine hundred years after the reign of Chandragupta. This highly prejudiced work, obviously written with the flimsiest of historical backing like many other inscriptions, Veerakallus and copper plate records, subtly influences the actual truth in favour of the attitudes or compulsions of the writers or recorders towards their heroes. And writers like Vishakadatta had little compunction in distorting history merely to glorify their hero. In fact, it is historically proved that the *Arthashastra* or the *Art of Politics* as existing today has been the work of three or four writers down through the ages, with Chanakya or Kautilya having provided an intermediate version,[13] and the last writer having embellished it sometime in the late Gupta period. The treatise appears to have been conceived and the first version written during the reign of the earlier Nandas. For example, the *Arthashastra* mentions certain peoples like the Chins in China who could not have been known to the people of Magadha at the time of Chanakya and there are said to be numerous other indications. By writing a quasi-historical play like *Mudrarakshasa* the playwright escapes the disciplined responsibility of the historian to represent the main characters according to the real facts. A recent Kannada publication in Karnataka called *Chickkaveeraraja* written by Masti Venkatesha Iyengar is a typical example. Although it is well known that Chickkaveeraraja, who was the Coorg raja from 1820 A.D. until he was unseated by the Coorgs and the British in 1834, was infact a cunning and cruel despot, a rake and a sadist, he is painted in romantic colours as a victim of circumstances deserving sympathy. If not anything else, the mass grave

13. Vincent A. Smith, *The Oxford History of India*, p. 115.

containing murdered relatives whom he suspected of intriguing to usurp his throne, which was discovered and unearthed by the British near Nalknad palace towards the end of the campaign of 1834 should prove Chickkaveeraraja's character. Hence, the representation of Chandragupta Maurya as a weak king and Chanakya being responsible for establishing the Maurya empire and being the power behind the throne in the play *Mudrarakshasa* is misleading and not true to history. There is no doubt that Chandragupta Maurya was a high spirited man who, with a combination of boldness, tact, diplomacy and well organised force created the empire and ruled it with an iron hand for twenty four years. At best, Chanakya was a talented and loyal minister who implemented and complemented his master's directions faithfully according to the latter's policy.

The Mauryan empire strongly ruled with the help of a centralised and highly trained army[14] and an efficient system of gathering intelligence continued from 320 B.C. upto the death of Asoka in 232 B.C. It was an effective state extending from the Hindukush mountains in the north to Mysore in the south and from Sind to Gujarat in the west to Bihar and Bengal in the east. Later on, until the death of the last Mauryan emperor Brihardatta who died in 182 B.C., the empire, although weakened, continued to dominate north India.

The Sungas of Magadha

The Mauryans were succeeded by the Sunga dynasty established by Pushyamitra Sunga who was a general under the Mauryas. Under his dynasty, there was a resurgence of Brahminical Hinduism. However, the extent of the Magadhan

14. Vincent A. Smith, *The Oxford History of India*, pp. 105, 106. Also see A.L. Basham, *The Wonder That Was India*, p. 132, and R.C. Majumdar, *Ancient India*, p. 107.

empire was greatly reduced. Later dynasties like the Kanvas could hold together only smaller parts of the empire which was eroded by the invasions of the Sakas or Scythians and of the Bactrian Greek powers from beyond Afghanistan.

Kharavela of Kalinga

In the Deccan, Kalinga (Orissa) became a major power during the powerful king Kharavela who at the zenith of his rule had conquered the area from near Magadha to Mysore[15] and from Kalinga to Maharashtra. After Kharavela, Kalinga never again rose to the same heights and played only a relatively small role in the politics of the Deccan. Kharavela ruled during the 1st century B.C., that is after the eclipse of the Mauryas.

The Satavahanas of West-Central India

The Satavahanas on the other hand, ruling from Prathisthana (now Paithan) on the left bank of the upper Godavari in Maharashtra, were an Andhra dynasty. In spite of attacks by Saka powers in early 2nd century A.D. the Satavahanas ruled West-Central India for over 250 years from the 1st century B.C. to about 220 A.D.[16] They had developed trade through their port of Bharuch (Broach) with European countries and east Asia and their kingdom flourished as a rich and strong power. It was known for its precious stones, its textiles and handicrafts. The kingdom was first established by Simukha in 1st century B.C. and consolidated by Krishna, Satakarni and others. The most famous king of the dynasty appears to have been Gautamiputra Satakarni who defeated the Sakas and recovered Malva and Gujarat, but later kings like Vasisthiputra Pulamayi and Gautamiputra Yajnashri also were strong kings.

15. R.C. Majumdar, *Ancient India*, p. 131.

16. Ibid., pp. 132-135.

The Kingdoms of South India

The ancient south Indian kingdoms of the Cholas, the Pandyas and the Cheras remained independent countries since the time of the Mauryas if not from earlier.[17] There are clear references to these kingdoms in Asoka's inscriptions. Even from those times, all the three kingdoms had continuing maritime trade with Ceylon (Sri Lanka), the islands of the south-west Indian Ocean, with Madagascar, and later with incoming Greek and Roman traders who knew of the spices and wealth of India. The Cholas enjoyed maritime trade with the countries of south-east Asia like Malaya, Indonesia, Thailand and Cambodia. Serious wars with the Pallavas, an intruding people from the area of Kalinga who established themselves at Kanchi (Kanchipuram) during the 3rd century A.D.,[18] did not totally eliminate Chola sovereignty. The Sangam literature of the 1st and 2nd centuries A.D. give near historical details of the Chola civilisation of the time, the Sangam being an association of poets, dramatists and literateurs who produced several literary works which they used to discuss among themselves at regular meetings.

The Period after Mauryas: The Kushans

After the Mauryan empire and before the next great empire of ancient India, that of the Guptas, North India was ruled by the Sungas, the Kanvas and others from Magadha. However, the empire was restricted to east of Punjab and upto Bihar. Much of Rajputana and Gujarat, Malva and Avanti were lost to invading foreigners like the Parthians (from Persia), the Bactrian Greeks from Badakhshan (north-west of Afghanistan) and the Sakas from Amu and Syr Darya of central Asia. The Sakas themselves were defeated and displaced from central Asia

17. R.C. Majumdar, *Ancient India*, p. 136.
18. Ibid., pp. 392, 393.

KUSHAN EMPIRE UNDER KANISHKA, c. 125 A.D.

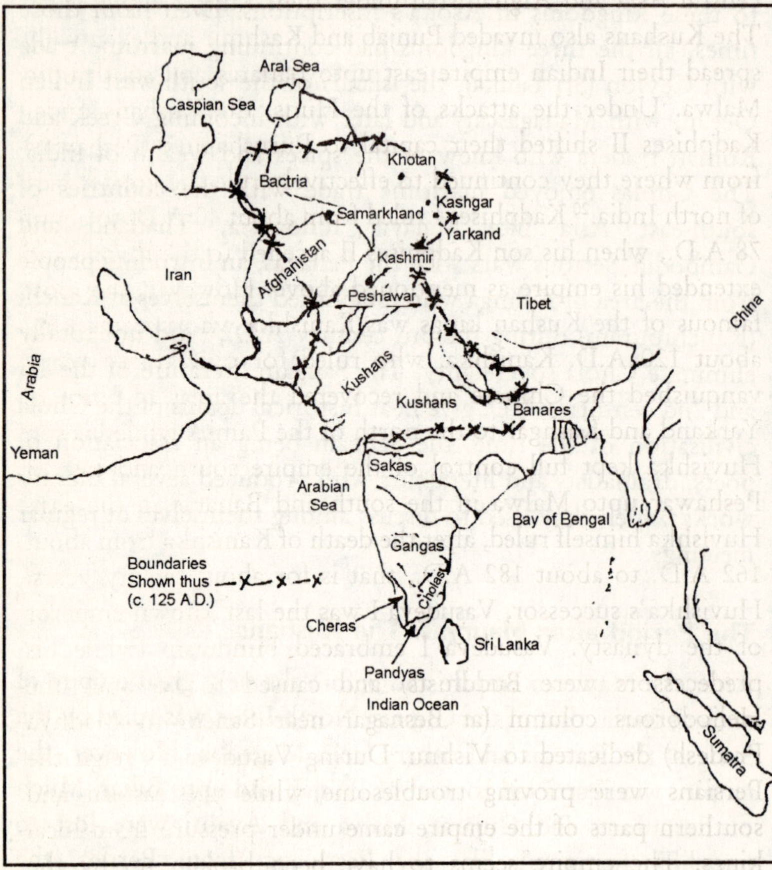

and Afghanistan by the Yueh-Chih people from Mongolia. Soon, the Kushans, one of the five tribes of the Yueh-Chih, established their sovereignty with Kabul as their capital over central Asia and Afghanistan under their king, Kadphises I.[19] The Kushans also invaded Punjab and Kashmir and eventually spread their Indian empire east upto Banaras and south upto Malwa. Under the attacks of the Huns, the Kushans under Kadphises II shifted their capital to Purushapura (Peshawar) from where they continued to effectively rule the greater part of north India.[20] Kadphises I ruled from about 40 A.D. to about 78 A.D., when his son Kadphises II acceded to the throne and extended his empire as mentioned above. However, the most famous of the Kushan kings was Kanishka who became king about 120 A.D. Kanishka, who ruled for over thirty years, vanquished the Chinese and recovered the areas of Khotan, Yarkand and Kashgar to the north of the Pamirs while his son Huvishka kept full control of the empire south and east of Peshawar upto Malwa in the south and Banaras in the east. Huvishka himself ruled, after the death of Kanishka from about 162 A.D. to about 182 A.D., that is for about twenty years. Huvishka's successor, Vasudeva I was the last known emperor of the dynasty. Vasudeva I embraced Hinduism (while his predecessors were Buddhists) and caused to be built the Heliodorous column (at Besnagar near Sanchi in Madhya Pradesh) dedicated to Vishnu. During Vasudeva I's reign the Persians were proving troublesome while the eastern and southern parts of the empire came under pressure from local kings. The empire seems to have been broken up by the Sassanid dynasty of Persia about 220 to 230 A.D., although lesser Kushan kings continued to rule in the north-west for another 150 years when the Huns finally overwhelmed Kushan power.

19. Vincent A. Smith, *The Oxford History of India*, p. 147.

20. Ibid., p. 149.

Kushan history is known mainly from the variety and number of coins discovered, of the period of Kadphises II, Kanishka and Huvishka, Buddhist written records especially during and after Kanishka and Buddhist monuments constructed around Peshawar by the same two monarchies. Although the early kings worshipped Zoroastrian, Greek and Mithraic Gods (Persian sun-Gods), towards the later period of Kanishka's reign, Kanishka became an active patron of Buddhism which had already transformed itself into the Mahayana type with the glorification of the Buddha by statues and busts and with being affected by contact with Greek and Persian concepts and practice of Buddhism. The last major king, Vasudeva I came under the influence of Hinduism, circa 180 A.D. Although the Kushans originally came from east-central Asia, they were Turkic by race and not Mongolian, and were continuously in conflict with Chinese forces in the areas of Yarkand and Kashgar with fluctuating fortunes. Kanishka was particularly engaged in recovering the Kushans' original homelands east of Khotan and achieved his objective by crossing his army over the Pamirs and inflicting decisive defeats on the Chinese forces during the period 140 A.D. to 170 A.D. But later, the Chinese pushed back the Kushans. The approximately 150 years of Kushan rule was characterised by frequent expeditions both towards central Asia and also towards the south, that is Malwa and Gujarat, and towards the east upto and beyond Banaras. At the same time, from the period of Kanishka's rule there was a flowering of art and architecture. The Gandhara school of sculpture, combining Indian skill in stone and wood with Persian and Greek concepts of form, expression and draperies, became very popular. The conquests of Kanishka were largely retained and even enlarged by Huvishka. Buddhism flourished but so did Hinduism and Jainism in their traditional areas of the Indo-Gangetic basin and the Deccan. Kushan rule for about 150 years extended effectively over almost the whole of north India, north of the

Vindhyas, over Afghanistan and over large parts of Central Asia.[21] A conservative estimate of the area would be about 25,00,000 square kilometres. The Roman empire at its height in about 400 A.D. can be estimated to be about 65,00,000 square kilometres. Hence, the Kushan empire was in area about 38 percent of the area of the Roman empire, and it endured as such for nearly 150 years.[22]

After Kushan empire and before beginning of the Gupta empire in about 320 A.D., that is for about 100 years, the whole of north India was ruled by a number of dynasties and kings. The later western satraps (or kshatrapas), the later Satavahanas, the Malavas and the Yaudheyas ruled large slices of the land. Prominent kingdoms in the Gangetic basin were Panchala, Kosala and Vatsa. The Bharasaivas captured power in the eastern part of the present Uttar Pradesh around Banaras. Some Naga kings were ruling at Vidisha (Bhilsa), Kantipura, Mathura and Padmavati (near Gwalior). The Malavas and, further north, the Yaudheyas were republican tribes who were ruled by elected councils. At the dawn of the Gupta empire (320 A.D.), India presented a picture of a number of states, many in conflict with their neighbours, yet each major state exercising power over vast areas the size of France or Italy or Germany.

The Guptas of Magadha

Around 300 A.D., Magadha was a small kingdom ruled by one Sri Gupta who was succeeded by his son Ghatotgaja. But Ghatotgaja's son Chandragupta married a Licchavi princess and acceded to the throne of Magadha in 320 A.D. Within the next 20 years he had extended his boundaries to include most of present-day Bihar and Uttar Pradesh and parts of north-west

21. Ibid., p. 149.
22. The areas are computed from authoritative atlas giving the areas of modern countries and states, then within the empires.

Bengal. He became the successful originator of the Gupta empire which, at its height, included most of north India from Punjab, Sindh and Kathiawar in the west to Bengal in the east, and from Kashmir in the north to the Vindhyas, Kalinga and eastern Andhra in the south, an empire which lasted from 320 A.D. to 550 A.D. that is, for over 200 years. Chandragupta's son, Samudragupta Vikramaditya and grandson Chandragupta II who also took the title Vikramaditya were directly concerned in extending the empire to its maximum limits. Samudragupta is even credited with having led a successful expedition to south India, defeating the Pallavas and occupying Kanchi, and also the Pandyas and Cheras. However, he wisely refrained from trying to directly rule these territories and was content to exact tribute from these powers as they were too far from his base for effective direct rule. The period of the Gupta empire is called by most Indian historians as the 'Classical Age' or the 'Golden Age' because of the enlightened and strong rule of the Guptas which multiplied the energies and abilities of the people phenomenally, and created great wealth. Fa Hien, the Chinese pilgrim who toured the country in the 5th century A.D., that is, during the later part of the reign of Chandragupta II, mentions the light taxes, the liberal administration and freedom of action of the common people. He also attests to the wealth, luxury and the sound economic condition of the common people. Arts and crafts flourished, and there was intellectual and religious revival involving the resurgence of Hinduism and the retreat of Buddhism, and the production of some of the most famous literary works of ancient India. The *Mahabharata* epic was re-written and recompiled in a methodical way, and we owe the present version of the *Mahabharata* to the Gupta period. There was much religious literature and compilation of some of the Puranas. Kalidasa, who is considered to have lived during the period of Chandragupta II and his successor Kumaragupta I, wrote the immortal works *Raghuvamsa*, *Kumarasambhava*, *Sakuntala* and *Meghaduta* besides many other works.[23]

Samudragupta reigned from 340 A.D. to 380 A.D., Chandragupta II from 380 A.D. to 413 A.D., Kumaragupta I from 413 A.D. to about 455 A.D. His son Skandagupta reigned from 455 A.D. to 467 A.D. and is credited with finally subduing the Sakas and the Huns who could not succeed in defeating the Guptas till about 500 A.D. The achievements of Skandagupta in defeating and driving out the Huns so decisively that they could not intrude into India for the next fifty years, could rank as among the greatest military achievements of the period. And this was at a time when the Huns swept everything before them in central Asia, Persia and eastern Europe. In fact, even his predecessor, Kumaragupta I should be credited with keeping out the Huns during his long reign of 40 years.

For the next hundred years, India relapsed into a period of relative instability. North India had a much reduced Gupta kingdom in Magadha, ruling over parts of present-day Bihar, North Bengal and Uttar Pradesh. The dynasty continued until about 550 A.D. Meanwhile, towards the close of the 5th century A.D., the Huns had invaded India once again, and within twenty years had established their sway over western India, that is, Kashmir, Punjab, Rajputana, Malwa, and even parts of Uttar Pradesh under their chief, Toramana, who reigned long enough to issue coins in his own name. Toramana, who was the chief of the Hepthalities or white Huns ruled by terror and cruelty and extracted heavy tribute from the conquered lands. His successor, Mihiragula, outdid Toramana in oppression and cruelty. The rule of the Huns is regarded as the greatest ever scourge suffered by northern and western India.

However, Mihiragula suffered defeats at the hands of

23. "The Classical Age", in Vol. 3 of *The History and Culture of the Indian People*, pp. 304, 305.

Yasodharman of Malwa and Narasimhagupta Beladitya of Magadha when he attempted to expand his territories.[24] But these defeats appear to have been so decisive that Mihiragula did not recover from them. From the records of reports heard by Hiuen Tsang, he had to retreat to Kashmir where he soon died. Hun power faded out soon after under the attacks of Yasodharman of Malwa who had made his kingdom independent of the Guptas and who had embarked upon the enlargement of his territories at the expense of the Guptas, the Huns and sundry other chieftains south of the Vindhyas. The Huns ceased to be a power in India by 550 A.D.

Other Kingdoms

In the wake of the eclipse of the Gupta empire, the Maukharis rose to power in the region of Uttar Pradesh and proved a bulwark against the Huns in the first few decades of the 6th century A.D. They continued in power for the better part of the century. In and around Magadha, there were several Gupta rulers who are collectively designated as 'the later Guptas' as their connection or otherwise with the main dynasty has not been clearly established. In Saurashtra (or Kathiawar) the Maitrakas established themselves with their capital at Vallabhi and expanded their kingdom to the east and south and are said to have been continuously in power for nearly three hundred years, i.e., until about 800 A.D. when they were checked and defeated by the Arab invaders who had captured Sind as early as 712 A.D. This long period of undiluted sway over Saurashtra and adjacent territories to the extent of about 1,00,000 sq km, that is greater than the size of Portugal, and about the size of Bulgaria or Iceland, manifests itself as a mere asterisk or footnote in ancient Indian history, or at best half a page in the more detailed histories of India of the period. It only indicates the lack of knowledge of another of the most enduring

24. R.C. Majumdar, *Ancient India*, pp. 243, 244.

EMPIRE OF THE GUPTAS
320 A.D. TO 647 A.D.

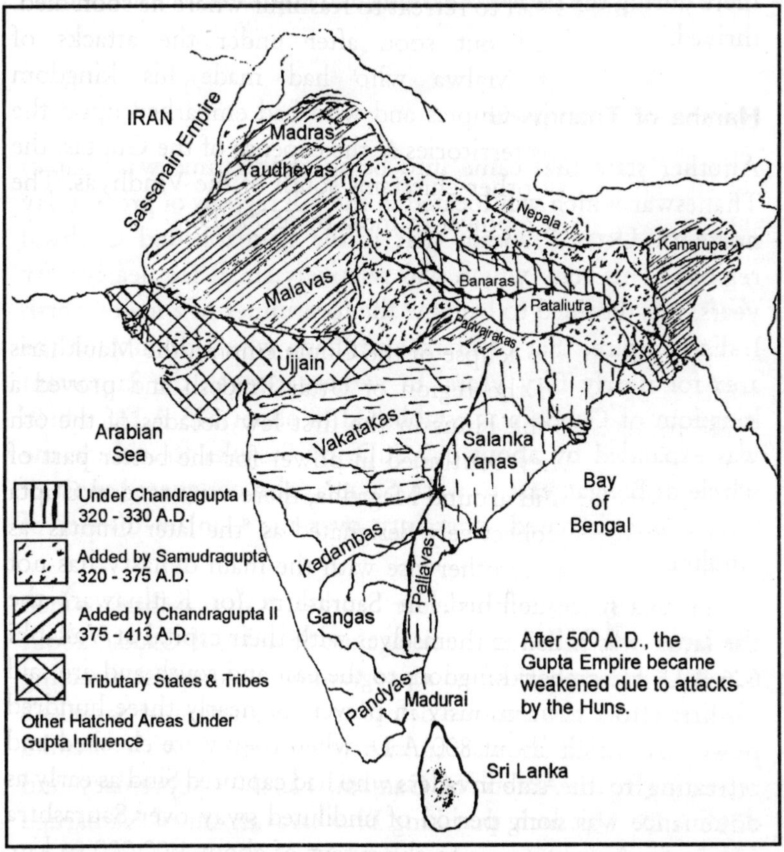

kingdoms of India having a sophisticated existence, for, with the ports of its coastline, and its proximity to Persia and Arabia, it was one of the Indian kingdoms most easily accessible to west Asia and Europe for trade and commerce which flourished there during the period. Learning and culture also flowered and thrived.

Harsha of Thaneswar

Another state that came into being at this time was that of Thaneswar which was located in the hill regions of present-day northern Uttar Pradesh, that is the Kumaon and Garhwal regions. This state which was relatively small for nearly fifty years, was destined to become the forerunner of a major north Indian empire, that of Harshavardhana which dominated the area for nearly fifty years. In western Bengal, the important kingdom of Gauda was established in about 525 A.D., which was expanded by about 600 A.D. by Sasanka to include the whole of Bengal, east to west. Sasanka also conquered most of Orissa and exercised suzerainty over the Ganjam district of Andhra.

Harsha succeeded his elder brother, Rajyavardhana, when the latter was killed in battle against Sasanka of Gauda, about 606 A.D. He embarked on a programme of conquest directing his first effort towards the defeat and destruction of Sasanka's power in which he was eminently successful, with Sasanka retreating to the safety of Ganjam. Harsha's supremacy and dominance was such that king Bhaskaravarman of Kamarupa (western Assam) as also the Maitrakas of Saurashtra acknowledged his superior power. Harsha ruled north India from Saurashtra and Rajputana to Uttar Pradesh, Bihar, Bengal, and south upto the Vindyas. Harsha's empire was held together more by local governors than by any sophisticated system of administration as existed during the time of the Mauryas or the Guptas. Much expenditure was incurred in building of Hindu

EMPIRE OF HARSHA
640 A.D.

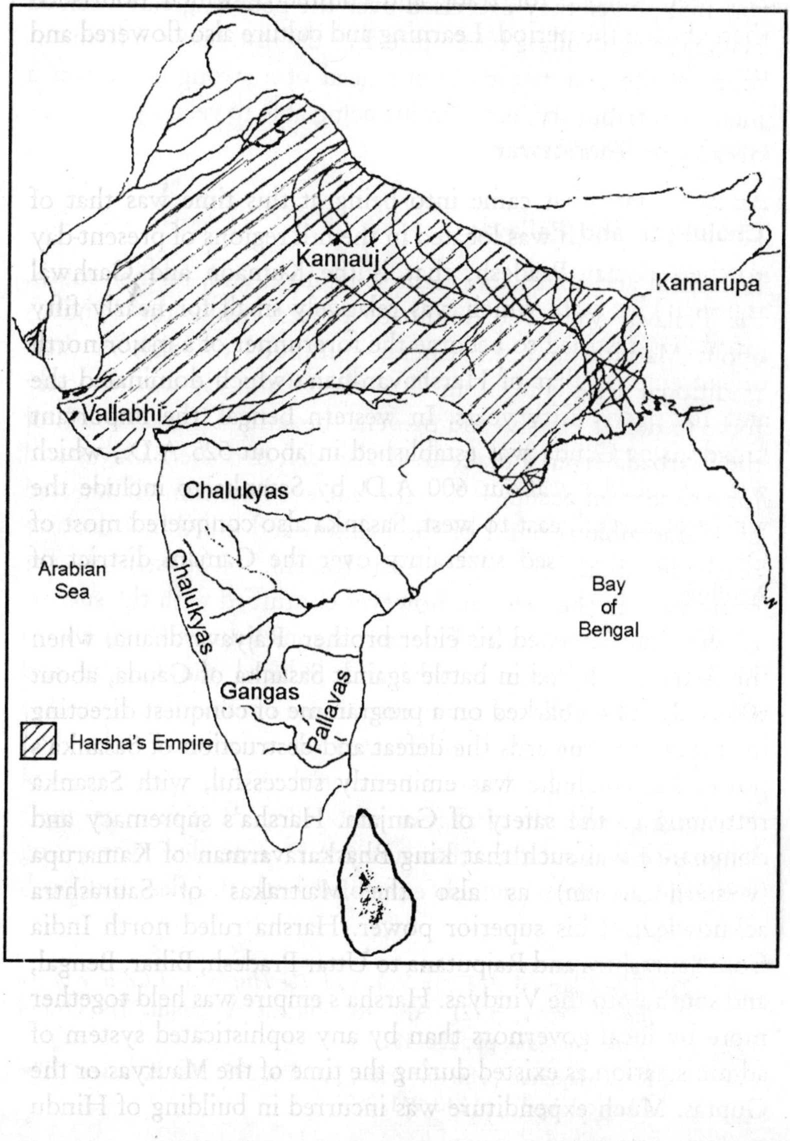

temples and Buddhist monasteries, both the religions being equally favoured. Vast amounts of money were presented to these religious organisations from time to time, so much so that one is led to suspect that the priestly class, and the moral and spiritual power they exercised over the people, greatly helped Harsha in controlling his empire. For the rest, his own frequent tours of the countryside at the head of a strong army was a major contributory factor in his being able to retain power for over forty years.[25]

Chalukyas and Pallavas

In central and south India, the Chalukyas and, further south, the Pallavas were the dominant powers while the Pandyas about Madurai and the Cheras continued to reign in their traditional areas. Pulakesin II of the Chalukyas was the only force to defeat Harsha and prevent the latter's ingress south of the Narbada river. Pulakesin II also defeated the Pallavas and for a time even occupied Kanchi, but was later himself defeated by Narasimhavarman I of the Pallavas and killed in a decisive battle in about 642 A.D. near Kanchi.[26] The struggle for supremacy in the Deccan, however continued with the success of the Chalukyas under Pulakesin's son, Vikramaditya I who once again captured Kanchi and reduced the Cholas and Pandyas. The Pallavas again rose under Parameshwaravarman II and after a long campaign defeated Vikramaditya I and sacked his capital Badami. The wars between the Chalukyas, a tribe of Karnataka, and the Pallavas who adopted Tamil as their language by about the 6th century A.D. extended over a long and ruinous period which enfeebled both peoples. But both

25. "The Classical Age", in Vol. 3 of *The History and Culture of the Indian People*, p.121. Also see Vincent A. Smith, *The Oxford History of India*, pp. 180, 181.
26. R.C. Majumdar, *Ancient India*, pp. 276, 395, 396. Also see, "The Classical Age", pp. 240, 241, 260.

were in power in the Deccan for a long period, the Pallavas from the beginning of the 4th century A.D. to the 9th century A.D. while the Chalukyas reigned from the 6th century to about the end of the 8th century when they were overthrown by the Rashtrakutas.

Other Dynasties

The Rastrakutas in central India, the eastern Chalukyas along the Andhra coast and the resurgent Cholas of the Tamil country reigned as major powers in the Deccan and south India until about 1200 A.D.

After Harsha's death in 647 A.D., his empire fell apart. In the west, the Gurjaras, a people who were an offshoot of the Saka dynasty established themselves under the Pratihara dynasty in the areas of Punjab, Rajputana, Gujarat, Malwa and the western part of Uttar Pradesh. The Pratiharas reigned from about 780 A.D. to 950 A.D., under their kings Vatsaraja, Nagabhatta, Ramabhadra, Bhoja and Mahendrapala. In the east, the Pala dynasty conquered Bengal and expanded their territories to include Bihar, eastern Uttar Pradesh, parts of Orissa and north-eastern Madhya Pradesh. South of the Vindhyas and also north of Narbada in Gujarat and Malwa, the Rashtrakutas dominated all powers for over a hundred years. The period between 800 A.D. and 950 A.D. was characterised by continuous struggle between these three powers on the borderlands of their territories, with weaknesses being exploited to gain more territory and power.[27] All the three powers reigned over areas as large as, or larger than, some of the countries of Europe. The Pratiharas controlled approximately 5,00,000 sq km, that is, double the size of Great Britain and Northern Ireland or 60 per cent of the size of Pakistan. The Rastrakutas controlled about the same area. The Palas of Bengal controlled about 2,75,000 sq km which was larger than the area

27. R.C. Majumdar, *Ancient India*, p. 282.

of Great Britain and Northern Ireland, or of Uganda or, of New Zealand.[28]

The Muslim traveller Al Masudi who visited India during 915-916 A.D. mentions that the Pratihara king was rich in horses and camels and that he maintained four armies in the four quarters of north India, each army being over 7,00,000 strong. Each of these armies therefore was slightly lower than the strength of the whole Indian army of 1965 which was fixed at 8,75,000 by Act of Parliament. However, the accounts of such authorities as Al Masudi, recording his information in all good faith, may perhaps be somewhat exaggerated. But the extent of exaggeration in the case of this outside observer could not perhaps be far off the actual strength. In spite of this strong presence of armed forces, the Rashtrakutas in 917-918 A.D. under the Rashtrakuta king Indra III invaded the Pratihara territories, defeated the Pratihara king Mahipala in a series of battles and plundered and sacked Kannauj, the Pratihara capital city. A further expedition by the Rashtrakutas in 940 A.D. resulted in the capture of the two fortresses of Kalanjara and Chitrakoota, and gradually the Pratihara empire broke up and new kingdoms rose up on the ruins.[29]

The 10th century A.D. saw the rise of several smaller powers who, nevertheless, exercised power over quite large areas. The Chandelas, a Rajput clan, ruled in Bundelkhand with their capital at Khajuraho. The Kalachuris, descended from the ancient Haihaya people, ruled in Chedi near Jabalpur in Madhya Pradesh. This dynasty ruled over a smaller or larger area, depending upon the rise or decline of the greater powers, from the 3rd century A.D. Upto and beyond the 11th century A.D., the Parmaras, a class of Rajputs ruled in Malwa for about

28. Areas are arrived at by correlation of the the areas of empire with modern states, the areas of which are available in authoritative atlases.

29. R.C. Majumdar, *Ancient India*, pp. 288, 289.

200 years until about 1050 A.D. The Chahamanas or Chauhan clan of Rajputs ruled for about hundred years in the 10th and 11th centuries A.D. with their capital at Sambhar near Jaipur. The Guhilots or Gehlots ruled for nearly two centuries from near Udaipur until the end of the 10th century A.D.

3

A Discussion of Rulership in Ancient India

From the available information, largely dependent on epigraphic records or archaeological evidence and on the records of intelligent observers and travellers like Herodotus, Alexander the Great's scribes and writings of Buddhist and Jain monks, it is established as history that several dynasties ruled over extensive areas of India for long periods varying from 100 years to three or four centuries. Some powers like the Kalachuris, the Gangas, the Pandyas and the Cheras ruled in relatively protected Deccan and Peninsular India for eight to ten centuries. The extent of the areas ruled by some of the powers of north India and central India has already been indicated.

During the period 500 B.C. to 1000 A.D., that is for about 1,500 years, the population of undivided India could not have been more than about 50 to 60 million. After the British took over India in 1858, and after they introduced anti-malarial medicines, anti-smallpox and anti-plague vaccines, and after imposition of law and order and systematic governance of nearly a hundred years, the population of undivided India in 1941 was about 330 million.[1] It is difficult to imagine a population of more than 50 to 60 million during the period of ancient India. The country was vast, including within its

1. Vincent A. Smith states it to be 388 million in Chapter 4 of his book *The Oxford History of India*, but this seems to be over stated. During Akbar's time the population was estimated to be 100 million (1600 A.D.), p. 715 for both figures.

recognised geographic boundaries the territories of the north-west frontiers, Punjab, Rajputana, Baluchistan, Sind, Kashmir, Assam, Manipur, Nagaland and Meghalaya, undivided Bengal and the whole of the Indo-Gangetic basin, the Deccan and Peninsular India. Even today, when the population of post-independence India has crossed 1000 million, there are vast tracts of uninhabited or thinly populated land. It is not difficult to imagine that during the period when the land was heavily forested, when water resources were much more plentiful, when the climate was less hot, and when the population was only less than one-tenth of what it is today, the people in India down to the humblest agriculturist or tradesman lived a life of comfort and plenty. The soil was fertile, and the climate conducive to the growth of foodgrains, vegetables and fruit. The land was so vast that chieftains, kings and emperors could not really physically control all the people and land under their rule. They could only establish a rule sufficient to insure their own security, their own well-being under conditions of luxury. The people were reasonably hard-working and talented and produced sufficient food and wealth for themselves and for hordes of soldiers, tradesmen and merchants, for tier upon tier of chieftains, princes, kings, emperors and their entourages and for the proliferating artisan class engaged in production of huge monuments and temples, jewellery, articles of luxury, and so on. The vast priesthood of three major religions, Hinduism, Buddhism and Jainism, lived on the wealth created by agriculturists, traders and artisans. The rulers, if they wanted anything, had only to send their soldiers to command what they wanted from the people. Taxes were generally one-sixth of the produce, but further levies were quite frequent.

The land was also rich in natural resources like timber, wild animals, mineral wealth like precious and semi-precious gemstones, gold, copper, tin and iron. Production of foodgrains, vegetables and fruit was relatively easy as the land yielded in plenty to the least effort. Meat was easy to obtain as fauna of all kinds multiplied themselves many times faster than the people could consume them. Livestock was plentiful. When Alexander's army entered India, Ambhi, the ruler of the area between the Indus and the Jhelum river, supplied him with 3000 oxen and 10,000 sheep for his troops,[2] as Ambhi was feuding at the time with his neighbouring rulers and wished to help Alexander defeat them. Every square kilometre of the land was productive, except for the high Himalayas and the Thar desert which was less in extent than what it is today. It is no surprise that great numbers of chieftains, minor and major kings could exist, supported by standing armies.

The wealth and salubrious climate of the land stood as an open invitation to invading tribes, whether from the north-western passes, through the jungle tracts of the east, or from the sea. However, the dense forests of the east and the long distances to be sailed over the sea severely limited incursions from these directions. Not so in the north-west. Tribes and peoples already acclimatised to the high plateau and cold of Tibet or to the severe mountain regions of central Asia did not find it difficult to cross the Hindukush and the cold, wind-swept regions of southern Afghanistan and enter India. While traffic by small parties of merchants and nomads must have existed as a natural practice since 2500 B.C., invasions by large tribes took place from time to time whenever pressures in Iran, Afghanistan, central Asia and Tibet forced them to seek safer or richer havens. Initially it was the successive waves of Aryans and later the Persians and Greeks. Then came the Sakas and the Kushans, and after them various groups of Persians and Bactrian Greeks. The Huns came in the 5th to 6th centuries A.D. The Arabs at the height of their expansive phase, invaded Sind in 712 A.D. and maintained a presence there and upto southern Punjab for 400 years. Then came the Afghans and after them the Turks and Mughals. There was a lot of space for

2. Vincent A. Smith, *The Oxford History of India*, p. 85.

INDIA IN ABOUT 1000 A.D.

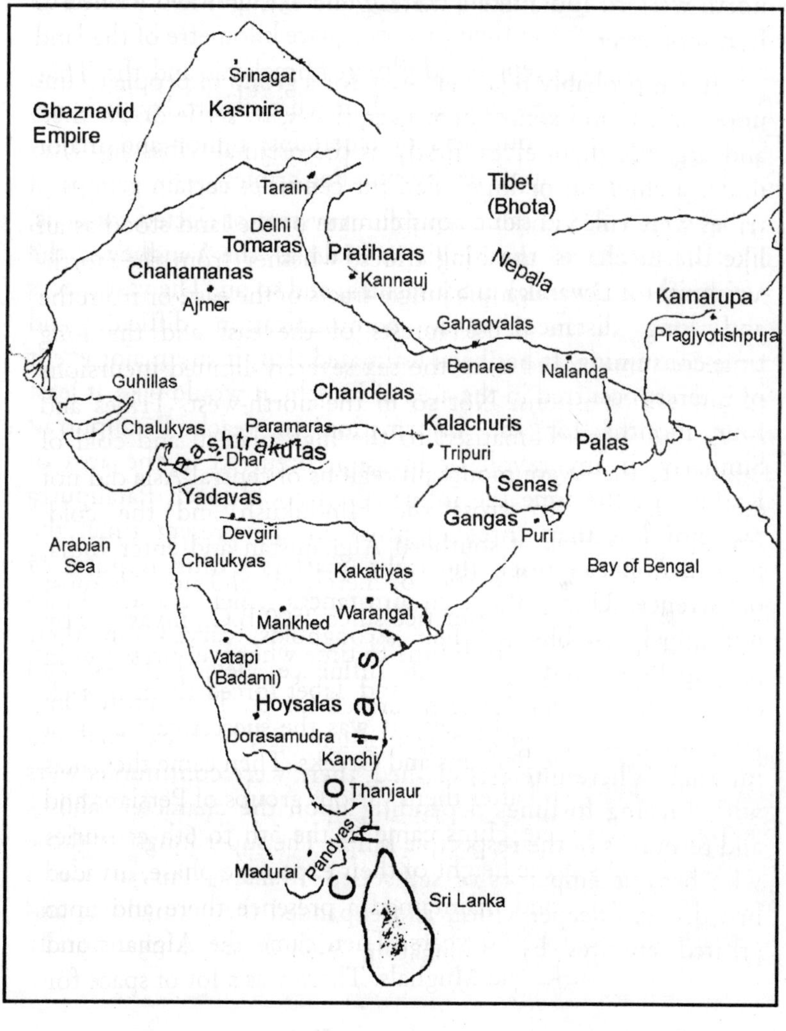

everyone to get in and live comfortably and settle down to the easier living conditions. Yet, every new group was resisted and prevented from establishing itself for two or three centuries or more. The only exception was Alexander who passed through north-western India like a meteor and extinguished himself in Iran soon after.

It was probably relatively easy for a group of people to find unoccupied land somewhere near rivers, to settle down there and organise themselves, firstly as the original tribes and later under a chieftain or king. Yet, for centuries certain groups of tribes were ruled under a republican system of elected councils, like the Licchavis, the Mallis or Malavas, the Yaudheyas, the Vrishnis[3] (of Dwaraka in Saurashtra) and so on. The vast spaces and long distances made communication difficult and time-consuming. It has been estimated that, if any major event of interest occurred in the area of Kanchi, it would take at least four months for the information to reach Pataliputra.[4] Similarly, if any revolt or invasion occurred in the area of Kathiawar, the time the information could reach Pataliputra was not less than three months. At the present time, the information can reach the right quarters within minutes of occurrence. Under these circumstances, chieftains and kings multiplied, established their strongholds, carved out their principalities and areas of influence, levied taxes and commandeered men for their armed forces. They existed in a constant state of vigilance against enemies, both external and internal. Where interests clashed, there were continuous wars with varying fortunes depending upon the character, ability and resources of the respective kings. The super kings, or those who became emperors or self-styled 'Maharajadhirajas' had a broader and deeper vision and expanded their kingdoms and created empires by subjugating such lesser kings, totally

3. R.C. Majumdar, *Ancient India*, p. 71.
4. Computed by the author, considering distance 2000 miles and average rate of movement of 20 miles a day.

eliminating their dynasties in the general proximity of their own kingdoms and installing in their places their own trusted men as viceroys or governors. Where such kingdoms were much farther away making control and communication difficult, they reinstated the same kings and dynasties and were content to exact a generous tribute from them annually. Also, such reinstated monarchs were made to swear fealty and were expected to send their armies whenever required in support of any campaign the emperor was engaged on. It was only the Mauryas and the Guptas who were able to exercise full control on the territories that they captured, and although at some periods they resorted to the two methods of control mentioned above, they were truly able to impose their will on all the territories that made up their empire. On the other hand, the control of Harsha was relatively loose, and brigandage and exploitation outside his control was quite widespread.[5]

It is difficult to find any concrete evidence about the armies of these kings and emperors, and their battle drills, except in vague terms. It is clear from the epics, *Ramayana* and *Mahabbharata*, that the army consisted of infantry, batches of archers and an elephant corps, this latter to march or rush into the ranks of the enemy infantry and strike terror into them. Initially it seems that the archers were employed to shoot arrows en masse and reduce the numbers in the enemy infantry. Soon after, the elephant corps would rush in and scatter them. Infantry, closely following the elephant corps would engage in hand-to-hand fighting and defeat the enemy infantry. The commanders at various levels were either on horseback (junior commanders) or in chariots with easily distinguishable pennants over the roofs of their chariots. The commanders had to be easily visible to the fighting troops in combat. Elephants were often protected by leather armour with tusks tipped with metal spikes. Other than the mahout, the elephant carried two or three men armed with bows, javelins or

5. Hwui Li Shaman, *The Life of Hiuen Tsang*, pp.

long spears. Chariots carried a driver and one to four warriors. However, recourse seems to have often been taken to the system by which a distinguished champion from each side would engage in single combat in a well cleared space between the two armies which were arranged in battle order. It was agreed that the winning champion gave victory to his own side, and all issues were then decided as though the side of the winning champion had won the battle. Thereby, much loss of life and confusion was avoided. This system was said to be often followed in Bhutan which existed in a medieval state until the early part of the 20th century.

Chandragupta Maurya had a well-organised and strongly controlled army. It consisted of sections of ten men grouped in companies of 100 men which in turn were organised in battalions of 1,000 men. A higher formation was one of 3,000 men which probably consisted of three battalions. His army had infantry, archers, chariots (for commanders), an elephant corps and a cavalry contingent.[6] Later kings also had the same kind of organisation. Elephants were plentiful in India, but apparently horses had to be imported.

Fortified Strong Points

During later times, the importance of forts for protection was realised quite early. Pataliputra was fortified from the time of Bimbisara and Ajatashatru by strong timber walls overseen by watch towers. In the hilly areas of the north-west frontier, Himachal Pradesh, in Punjab and Rajasthan and almost everywhere else, strong forts were built on prominent hills having very difficult approaches to an attacker. The fort had to have a perennial water source within its walls. It was common for the besieged to often take the offensive by sallying forth in large numbers to surprise and decimate an unwary besieger.[7] In

6. Vincent A. Smith, *The Oxford History of India*, p. 106.
7. R.C. Majumdar, *Ancient India*, p. 265. Also see A.L. Basham, *The Wonder That Was India*, p. 134.

pitched battles, the two armies were ranged against each other and an archery contest took place between the two sides. The commander of one of the sides took the initiative at an appropriate moment and launched his elephant corps and infantry. Often the fight was decided on the death of one of the commanders in action, when his troops then lost heart and allowed the opposite army to gain the victory. But while the Greeks, the Persians and the Romans followed closely arranged battle drills with weapons designed to suit the roles of each arm, no such drills seemed to have been followed by the kings in India during the ancient period. While individual skills like in archery, horsemanship, swordsmanship, fighting with battleaxes, and so on seem to have been developed by training, specific training does not seem to have ever been practiced to develop roles for masses of cavalry, of infantry, etc. for exploiting their characteristics in pitched battles. The concept of employing armies seems to have been rather confused, with great reliance being placed on the elephant corps which, more often than not, turned back and trampled down their own forces on some of them getting alarmed or injured.[8] In spite of repeated reverses due to this cause, right from the time of Alexander down through the centuries, appropriate lessons never seem to have been learned. Yet, the amazing variety of weapons ranging from daggers of all descriptions to finely tempered swords and scimitars to axes, lances and spears, seem to indicate the knowledge of combat, from assassinations to defensive tactics to cavalry charges.[9] But formal battle drills do not seem to have been developed, although for example, the Sakas were most effective with the cavalry arm. Nothing seems to have been evolved or modified in the light of experience. This is indicative of a subjective approach to these matters, rather than a precise and analytical approach. This tendency to

8. A.L. Basham, *The Wonder That Was India*, p.129.
9. Ibid., p. 133.

automatically adopt a subjective approach exists in India even to this day as evidenced in defeats or victories in cricket or hockey or football matches where team spirit and sustained coordination even in adverse circumstances is of prime importance, but is often lacking.

The Role of Religion

The three religions of Hinduism, Buddhism and Jainism have played a major part in kings and emperors being able to gain and retain power. Of these, Hinduism, paradoxically, has been the one religion that advocates the use of force to subdue enemies as is clear from the *Bhagavat Gita*. The stories of heroes and villains in the *Ramayana* and the *Mahabharata* have kept up a lively interest in martial exploits. Hinduism, justifying the use of force under certain circumstances, sends down mixed signals with its philosophy of renunciation and the subjugation of all desire and with its teachings of tolerance and mercy and magnanimity. This is perhaps the reason why many Indian kings showed lack of decisiveness in battle or war. Also, they often showed mercy or clemency to an enemy who later rose up to defeat them. The belief that what is ordained by God cannot fail to come to pass had often eroded the will and diluted the determination to achieve the objectives. Buddhism and Jainism went overboard in teaching total pacifism. The subjective nature of the ancient Indian people was perhaps due to the influence of their brand of religion which has been a deep influence on their lives since birth and over the millennia. However, good health and a natural vigour, and an instinctive desire to eat and drink and possess, have often been able to counteract the subjective tendencies.

But, there is no doubt that the kings cultivated the priesthood to maintain their power. The vice-like grip of the priesthood and the clergy on the gullible and credulous minds of the general population has enabled many kings to suppress and oppress their people to a degree where the latter have been reduced to the level of mere existence with no will of their own. The priesthood, on the other hand, has generally always been humoured and indulged with many privileges, lands and wealth being conferred on them. These extremely busy kings, busy in fighting each other, had hardly any time to devote to knowing what was happening beyond the borders of India, and were often caught unawares when new enemies invaded India. The kingdoms of India further away from the north-west passes had hardly any interest in combating the new invaders, or going to the help of the kingdoms immediately threatened by invading hordes. This was especially true towards the end of the first millennium of the Christian era. Hence, about 1000 A.D. the map of India shows a mosaic of tribal areas, kingdoms and principalities. But this was only a natural state of things. It would have been difficult to expect these various kingdoms to anticipate an invader and unite to present a solid front. At the most, the kingdoms towards the north and north-west could have done this, but it would have involved the common appreciation of danger from an outside enemy and the willingness to combine together to resist a possible invader. This united action was obviously difficult when such kingdoms were under prolonged and deep rivalries extending to decades if not centuries. But such conditions were not unique to India. As recently as the 18th and 19th centuries A.D., Germany presented a picture of a number of kings, princes and feudal lords constantly feuding with each other until von Bismarck welded them into one nation. Garibaldi did the same in Italy. The closest that was achieved during the period upto 1000 A.D. was the Rajput confederacy, and before that the coalitions of kingdoms which defeated the Huns, under the leadership of Yasodharman of Malwa and Narasimhagupta of Magadha during the period of about 530 A.D. Later there were confederacies under Jayapala of Kannauj to fight Muslim raiders.

Inevitably, however, the climate and fertility of the soil of India made people easy-going and reluctant to train for long and hard campaigns involving an austere and disciplined way of life. There was perhaps little long-term planning to counter threats except during the periods of the Mauryan and Gupta empires. On the other hand, such austerities and discipline were practiced by the scholars and sages who broke much new ground in the disciplines of mathematics, astronomy, medicine, philosophy, literature and drama, and religious speculations, all of which were more highly regarded than martial achievements. To this day in India, achievements in literature and the arts, in mathematics and science, often of indifferent qualities, are greatly appreciated while soldiering and police work are considered to be necessary burdens and are regarded with humour bordering on contempt. It needed the Kargil operations in 1999, and television which brought battle conditions into people's drawing rooms to awaken Indians to an appreciation of the hardihood, endurance and valour which go into the profession of soldiering. It needed the suppression of decades-long terrorist insurgency in Punjab to make Indians appreciate the tenacity, will-power and determination of the army, the police and other uniformed services. Therefore, this reluctance to engage in hard combat and in the physically difficult conditions of long campaigns has been a trait which has come down since generations because of the relatively easy living conditions in the country during those remote times.

Also, during the entire ancient period, and especially so since about 600 A.D., there does not seem to be any evidence of daily training of troops in individual battlefield skills, drills in squads, and discussion and perfection of strategy and higher tactics. Before 600 A.D., the frequent victories of ancient Indian kings against Persians, Bactrian Greeks, Sakas, Huns and others for centuries indicate some attention to training and development of battlefield skills. Later on, armies appear to have been loosely organised masses, control of which could be lost in a moment's confusion. The bigger the army, the more unwieldy it became leading to easy victories by strong, well-disciplined forces, often of much smaller size.

4

Background Sketches: Muslim Entry and Occupation

The Wealth of India

While all the battles and wars were being fought in India from the earliest times, there were always interested watchers in the countries of the north and north-west who invaded India and tried to establish themselves and share in the fertility and productivity of the land. The invaders from Persia and Macedon, from central Asia and Tibet, came and battled their way in and gradually got absorbed in the country, both ethnically and culturally. Some were thrust out, some came back and progressed eastwards and southwards, some were confined to relatively limited areas, and so the process continued for more than a thousand years from 500 B.C. There was always available plenty of information to outside countries of the fabled wealth of India. For example, during the time of Darius I and Xerxes of Persia in 5th century B.C., the satrapy of the north-west frontier and Punjab was only one of the twenty satrapies of the empire, but yielded one-third of all its revenues.[1] During the first Chola period of 1st century B.C. to 2nd century A.D., ships from Greece and Rome frequented the ports of the peninsula to trade[2] in spices, textiles, corals and pearls. So there were always covetous eyes trained on India.

1. Vincent A. Smith, *The Oxford History of India*, p. 173.
2. Ibid., p. 160.

The Life of the People

During and after the period of Harsha, however, there seems to have been a lull in forces trying to invade India, except for the Arabs who invaded Sind in 712 A.D. The north-western marches were relatively undisturbed and the Pratiharas, the Rashtrakutas and the Palas were left to fight among themselves for 300 years.[3] Not to be left behind, the Vakatakas of north Deccan, the Kalachuris of north Madhya Pradesh, the Chalukyas of Gujarat, the Chandelas of Bundelkhand, the Chahamanas of Ajmer, and the Parmaras of Malwa all pitched in at various times and places and contributed to the constant turmoil and chaos. In spite of all this fighting, the general lot of the people pursued their life engaged in agricultural and pastoral activities.[4] When taxes were levied, they paid them. When their people were pressed into military service, they sent them. Where demands were made on them by the priesthood, they acceded to them with fond hope in their hearts. Their life was ordered by the cycle of the seasons, unceasingly and inexorably. They lived day-to-day under the guidance and control of their panchayats, their elected councils of five responsible, elderly and respected men. They rejoiced during marriages, good harvests and festivals with song and dance and simple instruments of pipe and drum. They grieved at the loss of beloved ones through sickness and death, but soon turned again to the business of living, for life was for the living. There was still enough food, and they made for themselves sufficient simple clothing and shelter. They were imbued with tales of yore, of gods and demons and heroes, told sitting around the convivial village camp fire. They invariably stuck to their institutions of marriage and family, of panchayat and orderly society, and to their ideas of good and evil, all of which have helped them survive over the centuries and, astoundingly, have

3. R.C. Majumdar, *Ancient India*, pp. 282, 283.
4. A.L. Basham, *The Wonder That Was India*, pp. 190, 191.

helped adult franchise in India and enabled Indian democracy to operate successfully during the latter half of the 20th century. No doubt, even in the panchayats there were cases in plenty where influential members of the panchayat sought unfair benefits at the expense of their charges.

The Arabs

The Arabs who invaded Sind in 712 A.D. were a different breed of men than the invaders until then, all because they belonged to the new religion of Islam which rapidly won adherents in Saudi Arabia and spread like wildfire over west Asia and north Africa. They were strengthened and fortified by this new religion which had a simple creed of unquestioning faith: "There is no God but Allah, and Muhammed is the Prophet of Allah." By merely declaring this statement, The Shahada, before witnesses and his belief in it, a man became a Muslim or Mussalman, a believer in the religion of Islam, or the religion of those who submit (to God). The divine will of Allah was revealed to Muhammed through the angel Gabriel in the form of the Koran which the Muslims call 'the Book'. All men who believed in Islam were brothers, belonging to the brotherhood of Islam. All humanity was divided into two groups: those who believed in Islam and called themselves believers, and those who did not believe in Islam or who were outside the faith, called unbelievers or 'kaffirs', the most contemptible term of abuse in the thinking of a Muslim. It was the sacred duty of a Muslim to convert unbelievers to Islam, or to "honour them with Islam" and to slay without mercy those who perversely refused to convert themselves to the faith. Image worship or idol worship was prohibited. Those who worshipped idols as representative of God were to be destroyed along with their idols. Among believers there was no caste or distinction or recognition of rich as superior to poor, as all believers were equal in the sight of Allah and of men, and were brothers. This stark, simple religion was shorn of all rituals, imagery and adornment, and belief in its creed was reinforced and hammered into the mind and the soul by the practice of five regular prayers or 'namaz' every day, starting with daybreak and ending with sundown. Wherever a Muslim happened to be, he had to perform namaz these five times everyday with his face towards Mecca, the place in Saudi Arabia where the religion of Islam was first revealed to the Prophet Muhammed. But where possible, he should hark to the call of the Mueddhin to prayer and repair to the mosque or masjid where he could pray together with other Muslims unitedly.[5] This simple creed, understood by all, so easily attainable, by which all men without distinction were equal and were brothers, and by which unity was fostered, attracted hordes of converts in the early years. The believers were proud men who spread their religion by fire and sword and who felt infinitely superior to men outside their faith. Within a hundred years of the 'Hijra' or move of Muhammed to Medina, the Badawi (Bedouin) Arabs and Berbers had conquered lands from central Asia, Syria and Persia in the east along Palestine, Egypt and the North African coast to Morocco, Spain and Central France in the west, and spread the faith of Islam to these countries.

Muhammed went to Medina from Mecca in 622 A.D. and continued to preach and organise his flock. He died in 631 A.D. after going through the battles of Badr, Ohod and the "Ditch" against the sophisticated and skeptical Meccans in 623, 624 and 627 A.D. respectively.[6] Within a hundred years, the Arabs had become a major power and had as their ultimate authority the Caliph, or Khalif, who was the spiritual authority of the Muslims and temporal head of the Arabs.

The Arab Incursions

The Arabs had raided India both by land and sea in plundering

5. Sir Hamilton A.R. Gibb, *Mohammedanism: A Historical Survey*, p.55.
6. Ibid., p. 31.

expeditions, but had not enjoyed much success. In 712 A.D., Hijjaj, the Governor of Iraq, obtained permission from the Caliph at Damascus (or Damishk) to launch an expedition against Sind which was then ruled by king Dahar. The pretext was the capture of a ship in which Muslim women were travelling from Ceylon (Serendip) to Basra, and the expressed inability of Dahar to restore the women on the request of Hijjaj. The expedition, commanded by Ubaidullah, raided the Sind port of Dahal where the captive ship was said to have been taken, but was defeated and Ubaidullah killed. Soon after, another expedition was sent from Oman under Budial which landed and marched towards Debal. King Dahar sent an army under his son Jaisimha which met with the invading force and defeated it in a pitched battle in which Budial was killed.[7]

Hijjaj next made elaborate preparations for another expedition and despatched a large and well-equipped force under his own son-in-law, Muhammed Ibn Quasim, reinforced with 6000 well-armed Syrian soldiers obtained from Caliph Walid at Damascus. Although the small kingdom of Sind did not have the resources to counter this large army, Dahar put up a brave resistance. But Muhammed Ibn Quasim, aided by local treacherous subjects, among them the Buddhists, conquered Dehal, Nerun, Siwistan and many other places, advancing up the Indus. Dahar put up a brave stand before the fort of Raor for two days during which the Muslim army faced certain defeat. At that juncture, however, Dahar's elephant was wounded and rushed back from the battlefield which created considerable panic among his troops. Dahar, although wounded, soon returned to the frontlines of the battle, but the damage was done and the cohesiveness of his force was lost. Dahar continued to fight but was killed.[8]

7. R.C. Majumdar, *Ancient India*, p. 264.

8. "The Classical Age", *The History and Culture of the Indian People*, p.171.

Dahar's queen collected the remnants of the force within the fort and defended it with stubborn courage until provisions failed. She then, along with all the other women, threw herself into a great fire kindled within the fort and died, in the terrible ceremony called 'jauhar'. The menfolk then opened the gates and sallied forth in a great rush on the enemy and fought desperately until all of them were killed.[9]

Jaisimha, the son of Dahar, organised other forces and fortified Bahmanabad and the capital city of Alor. He himself led another force to cut off the enemy from his sea base and to harass him. Muhammed besieged Bahmanabad, defended by Fofi, the second son of Dahar, and took it after a prolonged siege of six months. Then Alor itself was besieged and taken. Muhammed proceeded further to Multan and laid siege to the city which fell after two months. It is said that the residents of the cities of Bahmanabad and Alor were tired of the prolonged sieges and fighting and forced the commanders to capitulate. In the case of Multan, a traitor pointed out the source of water supply to the city and Muhammed cut off the supply forcing the fall of the city.

The Arabs Checked

Muhammed was recalled to Iraq after the death of Hijjaj in 714 A.D. and of Caliph Walid in 715 A.D. The new Caliph Sulaiman and the new governor of Iraq were enemies of Hijjaj, and hence Muhammad Ibn Quasim, along with other adherents of Hijjaj were killed. But the Arab presence in India was continued in the area of Sind and southern Punjab for another 300 years. Further expansion does not seem to have occurred because of the strong resistance offered by the Pratiharas, the Gurjaras and the Chalukyas who were able to stem the tide of Arab ambitions in spite of the successes gained by them in the expedition of 725 A.D. when they conquered Cutch, the

9. R.C. Majumdar, *Ancient India*, p. 265.

Kathiawar peninsula, northern Gujarat and attacked Malwa. The Arabs were stopped and confined to Sind and southern Punjab until they were defeated and displaced by the expedition of Mahmud of Ghazni in the early 11th century.[10]

This first establishment of Muslim rule in India is given in some detail as it is the first major conflict between adherents of the vital new religion of Islam and the old dynasties of Hindu, and possibly Buddhist and Jain, princes. The pattern of resistance, failure and success, seems to have continued largely unchanged for the next eight to nine hundred years. The bravery of the ancient Indian kings and princes and their followers cannot be questioned, but their military organisation and skill together with the lack of identity of interests between them and the troops and subjects under their rule seem to have failed them time and again. The Muslims of the Arab and Persian lands, reared against the background of experience of Persian, Greek and Roman organisation and battle drills, practiced to near perfection, and strengthened spiritually by a vigorous new religion which preached unity and equality of the believers, were a different kind of enemy. They were sustained by inflexible determination and the justice of their cause as understood by them. The Muslims were adept in the use of cavalry which enabled them to range far and wide in front of their main armies for gathering information, and to deliver a crushing blow at the decisive moment in actual battle. The flexibility and rapidity of their cavalry movements and the impact of their cavalry charges were undoubtedly crucial factors in their victories against numerically superior forces.

Mahmud of Ghazni

The era of planned and effective Muslim invasions, which later on led to the progressive occupation of India by the Muslims,

10. "The Classical Age", *The History and Culture of the Indian People*, pp.173, 174.

really began with the expedition of Mahmud of Ghazni, after he succeeded his father, Sabuktigin, in 997 A.D.[11] Ghazni lying to the west of Peshawar, between Kabul to the north and Kandahar to the south, had been a small principality just fifty years earlier as a vassal area of Persia. But Sabuktigin expanded his territory to the east and to the west at the cost of other such principalities, and soon came into conflict with the Shahi king Jayapala who ruled the northern Punjab, parts of Kashmir, the north-west frontier including Jalalabad in Afghanistan. Jayapala recognised the danger of an expanding Muslim state on his northern and western borders and invaded Ghazni to curtail Sabuktigin's expansion. However, he was defeated and had to sign a treaty undertaking to pay reparations. On returning however, he broke the treaty terms as a result of which Sabuktigin raided and plundered his border lands. Jayapala organised a confederacy of other powers including Kannauj, Ajmer and Bundelkhand to attack Sabuktigin and break his power, but the allies were defeated and Peshawar was captured by the Muslims. After Mahmud succeeded Sabuktigin, he inflicted a crushing defeat on the old Jayapala who committed suicide rather than survive the humiliation.[12]

His son Anandapala organised a large confederacy including the kings of Kannauj, Gwalior, Ujjain, Delhi and Ajmer, the whole force being under the command of raja Visala-deva Chauhan of Ajmer. The allied army was much larger than that of Mahmud and as they faced each other, Mahmud decided not to attack but to remain in a defensive position so that the allied army could waste itself on attacks. For forty days no action took place but, immediately thereafter, Anandapala's army launched a furious and tumultuous attack in which about 4000 Muslims were killed and Mahmud's army faced a break-up of the defence and

11. Vincent A. Smith, *The Oxford History of India*, p. 205.
12. R.C. Majumdar, *Ancient India*, p. 307.

defeat.[13] At that crucial time, the elephant carrying Anandapala, perhaps either being wounded or frightened, turned and ran back. Just on seeing this, the confederate forces were confused and broke. Mahmud immediately launched his 10,000- strong cavalry reserve to charge the enemy force which was routed and pursued with 20,000 being slaughtered and immense booty being captured.

After this disaster to the Indians, Mahmud invaded India time and again, in all about 17 times[14] until he died at Ghazni in 1030 A.D. Each time he succeeded in plundering the treasures of hundreds of temples. He destroyed them, captured thousands of prisoners whom he took to Ghazni as slaves and converted to Islam. He was able to invade at will, with no resistance to speak of, except during his raid in 1024 A.D. on the temple of Somnath on the coast of Kathiawar. There was a desperate defence with the defenders dying to the last man, in all about 50,000 men. The treasure and booty was said to be fabulous.

Mahmud of Ghazni had no ambitions to conquer for himself an empire in India, but was content with his plundering raids which enriched him immeasurably, with destruction of the temples of those whom he regarded as idolators, and with the conversion of thousands of unbelievers to the faith of Islam.[15] The north-west frontier and Punjab which remained under his rule were good buffer areas which enabled him to concentrate his attention on domestic squabbles until he died. After his death, for the next 60 years, there was no great threat to the kingdoms of north India. The kingdom of Kannauj expanded and prospered under the Gahadvala dynasty, Delhi was ruled undisturbed by the Tomaras, and the Rajputs under the Chauhans and other tribes held sway over Rajputana. There

13. Ibid., p. 308.
14. Vincent A. Smith, *The Oxford History of India*, p. 208.
15. R.C. Majumdar, *Ancient India*, p. 311.

were always minor raids and skirmishes from Punjab borders, but they posed no threat to the kingdoms mentioned and north India as a whole.

Muhammed Ghuri

By 1170 A.D., however, Ghazni came under attack from the Ghuzz Turkmans and later from the dynasty ruling Ghur, a small territory to the south-east of Herat. In 1175 A.D. Muhammed, Sultan of Ghur, and known in history as Muhammed Ghuri or Ghawri, attacked and captured Multan. He proceeded further and captured Sind but met with a serious defeat when he attempted to capture Gujarat. King Bhimder II of Patan repulsed his attack and defeated him with heavy loss in 1178. But Muhammed Ghuri deposed the Ghaznavid king Kanaru Malik and captured Punjab, having captured Sind earlier. Muhammed Ghuri was now in possession of the area west of the Indus and well placed to attack the rich kingdoms of the Gangetic plain.

In 1191 he organised a powerful army and invaded across the Indus. The various kingdoms, recognising the danger, organised themselves into a major confederacy with troops from most of the kingdoms of Rajputana and the Gangetic plain. The overall leader of the allied host was Prithviraj Chauhan of Ajmer. The two armies met on the battlefield of Tarain, located between Karnal and Thanesar in the present district of Karnal.[16] The battlefield was close to the traditional battlefield of Kurukshetra and just 30 miles north of the future battlefield of Panipat where three decisive battles which decided the fate of India were to be fought. The account of the battle is somewhat vague, but it seems that Muhammed Ghuri engaged the brother of Prithviraj Chauhan in single combat and was severely wounded. In the battle which followed, Ghuri's forces were defeated and routed and he had to beat a hasty retreat. But

16. Vincent A. Smith, *The Oxford History of India*, p. 234.

Prithviraj does not seem to have realised or understood the opportunity that came his way to pursue the invading forces and to capture Muhammed Ghuri and massacre the enemy. He seems to have been content with the victory and did not exert himself to follow it up to destroy the enemy forces.[17]

In 1192, Muhammed Ghuri returned with another army and met with the Indian forces, again organised as a confederate army under the leadership of Prithviraj Chauhan on the same battlefield of Tarain. But this time the unwieldy confederate army was decisively defeated, and Prithviraj Chauhan, who tried to escape, was captured and killed. His brother fell on the field of battle. This battle, the second battle of Tarain, may be considered to be the decisive battle which demolished the psychological and material defences of India and laid bare the routes of invasion to the alien culture and peoples of the Muslim nations of Afghanistan, Turkey and Persia. After this battle, the concept of India as a nation resisting the Muslim invader vanished. Henceforward, it was only the tale of Muslim invaders being resisted by several different kings, each according to his particular interests, his individual power and strength and his quarrels with his neighbours. On the other hand, the Muslims for the next three hundred years, until the arrival of Babur the Mughal, ever remembered that they were Muslims whose greatest duty for ensuring an after-life in paradise, was to kill unbelievers or convert them, to destroy their temples and idols, and to plunder and devastate their land and their people. The organised society of Hinduism, together with its sophisticated philosophy, and its confident belief in its own greatness, was a perennial challenge to these crude and simple Muslim invaders who believed in the creed of force and strength unrelieved by any ideas of humanitarianism or of enlightened administration. The Hindus, with their conceit and pride in their own religion, were different kind of peoples from

17. R.C. Majumdar, *Ancient India*, p. 347.

the pastoral peoples of Turkey, central Asia and Afghanistan. The latter's sense of satisfaction in defeating Hindus and in defiling their temples was infinitely more gratifying than their victories over people outside India. The Indian kings, however, were too inured in their own traditions of war and peace to be able to react effectively to counter their foe inspite of their bravery. The Muslims had mastered the art of warfare and were then united against people of a different culture. Once they had gauged the weakness of the Indians in regard to battle psychology, to organisation and to steadfast discipline, it was relatively easy for them to gain victories over the Hindus.

After this period, there were a series of campaigns after which the Turks and Afghans gradually came to occupy the land and become genuine denizens of the country. The attractions of the fertile land of north India and the wealth of its natural resources made it easy for these Turks and Afghans to leave their own lands and settle permanently in India, establishing their mosques and their madrassas, and adopting many cultural practices of locals.

The Slave Kings

Muhammed Ghuri went back to Ghur, leaving his general, Qutubuddin Aibak, in charge of his Indian provinces. Qutubuddin headquartered himself in Delhi and pursued campaigns against Kannauj, Banaras and Ajmer which fell to him. Another general, Muhammed Bhaktyar Khilji, attacked the king of Bengal and conquered North Bihar. Qutubuddin also attacked the Chandelas of Bundelkhand and defeated them. By 1200 A.D., Qutubuddin had conquered a great part of north India. The only powers which still maintained a strong independence were those of the Parmaras of Malwa, the Senas of eastern Bengal, the kings of north Bihar (or Tirhut), and the Chalukyas of Gujarat. Muhammed Ghuri was himself killed in

1206 by a famous tribe of Jats called the hill Khokars, after which the annexations in India passed into the hands of Qutubuddin Aibak who declared himself Sultan.[18] The period 1173 to 1206 A.D. was characterised by extensive massacres of the local population and the appropriation of their wealth.

Qutubuddin ruled only for four years as he died in an accident in 1210. Having been a slave, the dynasty started by him is known in history as the Slave Dynasty. After a short period of difficulties, he was succeeded by his son-in-law, Iltumush who ruled from 1211 until 1236 A.D. Iltumush's reign is important because he consolidated the Muslim rule, not only by recapturing Bengal, Gwalior and Sind which had broken away, but by adding Malwa and by subjugating rival Muslim chieftains. He was known, like his predecessor, as a great builder of mosques and tombs and is credited with having completed the building of the Qutub-Minar which was conceived by Qutubuddin, and of which the latter had built the basement.

Iltumush was succeeded by his daughter Razziya Begum, a romantic figure in the history of the period, who led her forces in battle not only against Hindu kings but also against Muslim rebel chieftains who thought they could take advantage of what they felt would be the weak rule of a woman. But in 1240 A.D., after four years of a disturbed reign, both she and her husband were killed. A talented and brave lady, she could not survive her turbulent times. After the usual succession quarrels, Nasir-ud-din, a younger son of Iltumush became sultan, but the power behind the throne was his father-in-law, Ulugh Khan Balban. Although Nasir-ud-din ruled for twenty years until he died in 1266, Balban conducted all affairs of state, and finally succeeded to the sultanate when Nasir-ud-din died. Throughout the period, there were Hindu rebellions both south of Delhi and in the Ganga-Jumna area necessitating frequent

18. Vincent A. Smith, *The Oxford History of India*, p. 237.

campaigns.[19] The way prisoners were dealt with, that is, by frying alive, by casting under elephants' feet, and by chopping them up, did not deter new rebellions.[20] Also, Mongols who had penetrated down to, and occupied the area around Lahore frequently raided neighbouring provinces and had to be dealt with. These Mongols were offshoots from Chingez Khan's passage across central Asia and Afghanistan to Persia.

Balban succeeded to the sultanship of Delhi in 1266 and continued his reign until he died in 1286. The terrible toll he took of his enemies, characterised by fearsome tortures, killings and public hangings helped to some extent to keep order in his territories, but nevertheless, as mentioned above, there were no dearth of rebellions both by Hindus and by outlying Muslim governors like those of Bengal, Bihar and Sind. He could subdue these uprisings by having an efficient system of espionage, and by sending armies from the central pool, under the command of officers loyal to him, to fight the rebels. He sent large contingents of Muslim troops to clear the Doab, that is the Ganga-Jumna basin, build a series of forts and to settle down there in strength to keep the Hindu chieftains in check.[21] He never employed any Hindus in his government. A major source of worry for him was the threat of large-scale Mongol invasions, which however, did not materialise although raids were frequent. But, in spite of his long stewardship and reign of more than forty years, he could not add to the conquests of Qutubuddin and Iltumush. He merely held on to the areas already conquered, precariously, because of the regular uprisings among the Hindus, the rebellions of his unruly governors and the constant irritants of the Mongols.[22] Bengal was merely formally under his suzerainty and Hindu chiefs

19. Ibid., pp. 237, 242.

20. Ibid., p. 240.

21. Ibid. Under para "Sultan Balban", p. 241.

22. Ibid., pp. 241, 242.

remained in a state of quasi-independence in the Doab, in Malwa and Gujarat. Muslim control existed only in Punjab, parts of Uttar Pradesh and Bihar, and that only with the continuous expeditions sent to subdue unruly peoples. This was the situation which continued until the end of the Slave Dynasty in 1290 A.D.

The Tughlaks

Ghazi Malik ascended the throne of Delhi in 1321 A.D. under the title Ghiyas-ud-din Tughlak Shah. He had been governor in Punjab and one of the more successful of the commanders who fought the Mongols on the north-western approaches and in Punjab. Son of a Turkish slave of Balban and a Jat woman, his record of achievement won him the approval of the nobles for the sultanate after the last sultans of the Slave Dynasty, Qutub-ud-din Mubarak and Khusru Khan. Apart from guarding against the inroads of Mongols, he despatched his son, Juna Khan (later, the Sultan Muhammed-bin-Tughlaq) to reduce Hyderabad and Warangal which Juna Khan succeeded in achieving in his second expedition, the first having failed disastrously. Ghiyas-ud-din meanwhile marched to the area of Dhaka in east Bengal and restored order among the factions competing for the governorship of the province. During his return, he campaigned against Tirhut in north Bihar and annexed it. Bengal and north Bihar, however, remained practically independent, although nominally a vassal state paying tribute. Ghiyas-ud-din built the fort of Tughlaqabad near Delhi.

Ghiyas-ud-din Tughlaq Shah was murdered by Juna Khan, his son, in 1325 A.D. The murderer ascended the Delhi throne under the name Muhammed-bin-Tughlaq and reigned until he died of illness in 1351, after a rule of over 25 years. Muhammad's reign has been more reliably and closely documented by Ibn Batuta, the African traveller who stayed at his court for several years, and by Zia-ud-din Barani who was an official at Muhammed's court. Although Muhammed-bin-Tughlaq followed the tradition of earlier sultans in being extremely cruel and despotic, massacering thousands of enemies, mostly Hindus, he was an effective ruler in his earlier years, and brought within the ambit of his empire many of the Deccan kingdoms like Warangal, the areas of Kanchi and Madurai. The only kingdom not fully conquered was the Hoysala kingdom of Vira Ballala III in western Karnataka.[23] However, there were many rebellions in Multan, Sind, the Doab, and later on, in eastern Deccan and in Bengal.[24] These rebellions were not a little due to Muhammed's practice of levying heavy taxation which finally impinged on the Hindu peasantry who had to pay taxes often in kind. These taxes in turn helped Muhammed finance his punitive expeditions and also, later, his ambitions of conquering his enemies in the north-west frontier and in Afghanistan.

Muhammed was a learned man and fancied himself a patron of the arts and sciences. He had a good memory and had studied logic and philosophy, mathematics and the physical sciences, and took considerable interest in medicine. He established schools and poor houses, abjured wine and followed high standards of morality in his private life. He thought himself a just man, but his punitive justice especially when applied to Hindus or Mongols, was indescribably cruel and took the form of wholesale slaughter, inhuman tortures like skinning them alive and pouring boiling oil on them. In this, he felt that he was only practicing the codes laid down by his religion. Yet, overall, he is considered to have been a secular king, in that he ignored the ulemas and dealt with people according to his own ideas of right and wrong. But his flawed judgement, which often passed the bounds of rationality, resulted in the break-up

23. Vincent A. Smith, *The Oxford History of India*, p. 250.

24. K.M. Panickkar, *A Survey of Indian History*, pp. 149, 150.

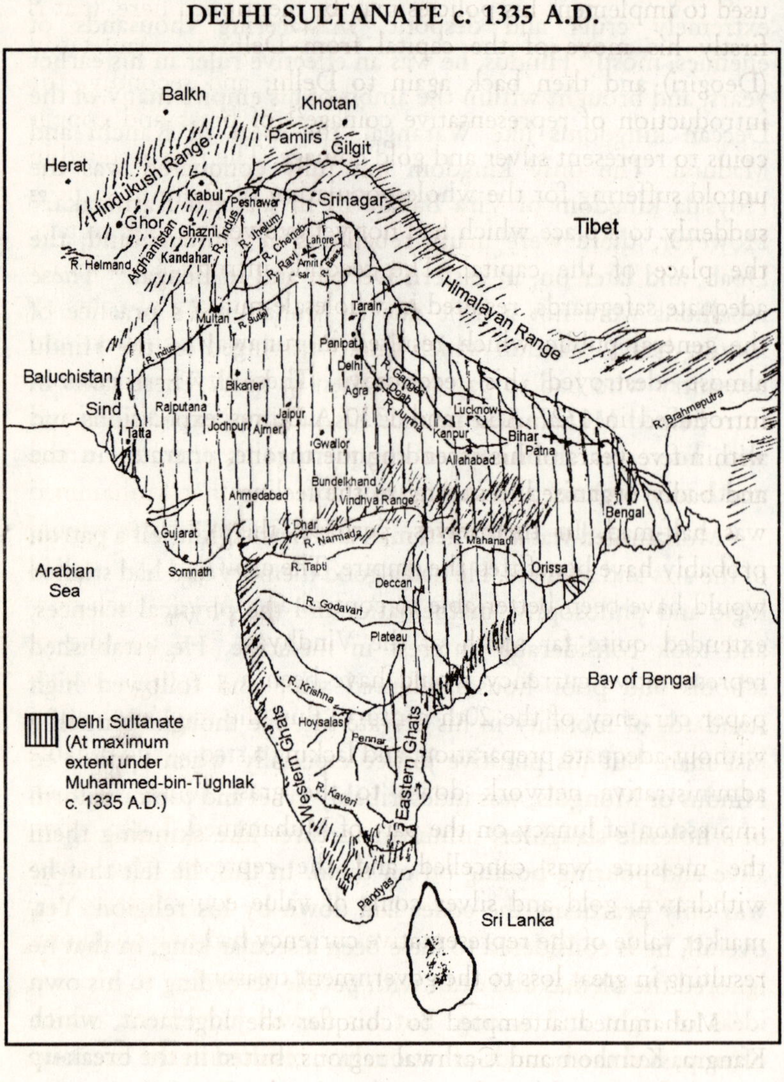
DELHI SULTANATE c. 1335 A.D.
Balkh
Khotan
Pamirs
Gilgit
Herat
Hindukush Range
Kabul
Peshawar
Srinagar
Tibet
Ghor
Ghazni
Afghanistan
R. Indus
R. Jhelum
R. Chenab
Lahore
R. Ravi
Amritsar
R. Beas
R. Helmand
Kandahar
Himalayan Range
Tarain
Multan
R. Sutlej
Panipat
R. Indus
Delhi
R. Ganges
Doab
Baluchistan
Bikaner
Agra
R. Jumna
Sind
Rajputana
Jaipur
Lucknow
R. Brahmeputra
Jodhpur
Ajmer
Kanpur
Bihar
Tatta
Gwalior
Patna
Allahabad
Bundelkhand
Ahmedabad
Vindhya Range
Bengal
Dhar
R. Namada
Gujarat
R. Mahanadi
R. Tapti
Arabian Sea
Somnath
Orissa
Deccan
R. Godavari
Plateau
Bay of Bengal
R. Krishna
Western Ghats
Hoysalas
Eastern Ghats
Delhi Sultanate (At maximum extent under Muhammed-bin-Tughlak c. 1335 A.D.)
Pennar
R. Kaveri
Pandyas
Sri Lanka

of his empire during the later years of his reign.

Two examples of his flawed judgement and the methods he used to implement his policies may be mentioned here, that is firstly his move of the capital from Delhi to Daulatabad (Deogiri) and then back again to Delhi; and secondly, the introduction of representative coinage[25] of brass and copper coins to represent silver and gold coinage. The first resulted in untold suffering for the whole population of Delhi in shifting suddenly to a place which had not yet evolved enough to take the place of the capital. The second, introduced without adequate safeguards, resulted in wholesale minting of coins by the general public which resulted in runaway inflation and almost destroyed his economy. These two measures, introduced in 1327 A.D. and 1330 A.D. respectively, that is within five years of his ascending the throne, proved ill-timed and badly organised, resulting in the feeling that Muhammed was half-mad. In themselves, perhaps, the measures would probably have benefitted the empire. The capital at Daulatabad would have been better able to control an empire which now extended quite far south of the Vindhyas. The minting of representative currency would have been a precursor of the paper currency of the 20th century. But, the implementation without adequate preparation, and lacking a strong and reliable administrative network down to the grass roots, gave an impression of lunacy on the part of Muhammed. Later, when the measure was cancelled and the representative coins withdrawn, gold and silver coins of value equivalent to the market value of the representative currency had to be paid out, resulting in great loss to the government treasury.

Muhammed attempted to conquer the highlands of the Kangra, Kumaon and Garhwal regions, but suffered excessive losses of men, although Nagarkot in the Kangra area was

25. Ibid., p. 149.

captured in 1337.[26] But although he had conquered territories in India to a greater extent than any of the earlier sultans, in the absence of a strong administrative control, and with his governors always looking for opportunities to shake off his control and delay paying taxes or tributes, his empire started breaking up. Furthermore, his arbitrary methods and ruthlessly vindictive cruelty, instead of deterring revolts, actually promoted them. The eastern Deccan or Coromandel coast broke free in 1334, and Bengal revolted successfully in 1337-38. Multan, Gujarat and the Deccan were revolting repeatedly. It was during his last expedition to quell a revolt in Gujarat that Muhammed fell ill and died. This was in 1351 A.D.

Meanwhile, a Hindu kingdom, that of Vijayanagar had grown and established itself south of the Krishna river under a Karnataka chieftain named Harihara and his brother Bukka in 1336. Soon after, in 1347, Hasan Gangu, an officer of the sultan had rebelled and founded the Bahmani Muslim kingdom with its capital at Gulbarga.

Muhammed-bin-Tughlaq was succeeded by his first cousin, Feroze Shah, who was elected by the overwhelming support of the nobles as sultan in 1351. However, not being as ruthless as Muhammed, and lacking his qualities of generalship, Feroze Shah suffered defeat in his attempts to re-establish authority in Bengal and the Deccan. Sind and Gujarat also proved intransigent, and although a victory of sorts was gained in Gujarat, it was not possible to consolidate the hold of the sultanate in these territories.

While Feroze Shah continued to retain power and control in the territories around Delhi, in Uttar Pradesh, Malwa and eastern Rajputana, his power waned in the outlying territories, but he was content to rule in Delhi without much effort to re-establish his authority in the quasi-independent areas. On the other hand, he occupied himself with construction of buildings,

26. Vincent A. Smith, *The Oxford History of India*, p. 251.

reservoirs and canals,[27] and in repairing and restoring the tombs and palaces of his predecessors. He was sober in his habits, and was liberal in his general outlook, especially in regard to lessening the tax burden on his subjects and promoting agricultural and commercial activity. He abolished the sophisticated systems of torture and mutilation practiced by the previous sultans. However, he encouraged his provincial governors to capture slaves during their exercises in maintaining law and order, and to send the best to his palace at Delhi which had in its environs about 1,80,000 slaves employed as guards, artisans for building and as attenders.[28] All these slaves were converted to Islam and looked after well by the sultan, for he was a firm Muslim who believed in propagation of his religion, in observing its beliefs, principles and laws, and in the utter infidelism of all other religions and also of all other sects of Islam other than the mainstream Sunni form of Islam.[29] He was intolerant of all other faiths than his own, and had no compunctions about destroying Hindu temples and idols and Mongol places of worship, and building towering mosques on the selfsame sites. He genuinely believed that, by these actions, he was fulfilling the desires of Allah and adhering to the teaching of the Prophet, and was thereby ensuring for himself the grace and mercy of Allah and well-earned place for himself in Paradise. His excusing of the oppressive Jizya tax on non-Muslims, provided they converted themselves to the faith of Islam, attracted thousands of converts.[30]

This liberal monarch, Feroze Shah Tughlaq, was therefore a creature of his times, and what we call religious intolerance was, for a Muslim king, the natural order of things whereby it

27. K.M. Panickkar, *A Survey of Indian History*, p. 150.

28. Vincent A. Smith, *The Oxford History of India*, p. 258.

29. Ibid., pp. 258, 259.

30. Ibid., p. 259.

was the duty of every Muslim much more so that of a powerful emperor, to convert the infidel or to slay him. It was his duty to Allah to destroy every vestige of the corrupting and pagan influence of non-Muslim religions, their idols and places of worship, and their priests and practitioners. However, the much greater, and increasing population of the Hindus, Jains, Buddhists and Mongols, the strong roots struck into the soil by the enduring hold of these religions which the vast majority of the population refused to give up even in the face of heavy taxation, violation of their places of worship, and the general persecution, scorn and intolerance of the Muslim rulers, largely defeated the sustained efforts of such rulers as Muhammed-bin-Tughlaq and Feroze Shah.

Feroze Shah Tughlaq died in 1388 after a chequered reign of 37 years. His dynasty and the previous one, were imbued with, among others, the intolerant and forcible proselytising aspects of the religion of Islam, and unrelieved by the gracious urbanisation (helped by contacts with European and other countries) that was a feature of the rule of the Mughals (except for that of Aurangzeb).

For the next ten years no claimant could seize the sultanate, and rival groups among the nobles put up their own candidates, none of whom could consolidate his position. Under these conditions of chaos the provincial governors exercised independent control to a greater or less extent.[31] These governors were themselves beset by factional fights and revolts by chieftains within their provinces and were hard put to impose their authority on their subjects.

Timur

The times were ripe for the invasion of India by Amir Timur, monarch of Samarquand. Born in 1335 as the son of a Turk

31. K.M. Panickkar, *A Survey of Indian History*, p. 150.

converted to Islam, Timur became king of Samarquand in 1369. He conquered central Asia, Afghanistan and large portions of Persia and Turkey. The chaos in northern India and the stories of the fabulous wealth of the country were natural inducements to invade for a rampaging king of the temperament and abilities of Timur. His forces defeated the governor of Punjab and sacked Multan in May 1398, preparatory to his crossing the Indus. In the same year he launched himself across with a strong cavalry component of 90,000. He sacked the towns on the approaches to Delhi, slaying thousands of people. He occupied Delhi, had himself proclaimed king and allowed his people to plunder the city and appropriated the wealth which he carried to Samarquand.[32] He went back via Meerut and Hardwar carrying back treasure and wealth, slaves and booty of all kinds. His path back was marked by killing, burning and rapine, and by the trail of destruction of temples, and by willful atrocities. Delhi, Punjab and western Uttar Pradesh took years to recover from the effects of his ferocity.[33]

The Lodis

Unsettled conditions prevailed in the area until 1415 A.D. when Khizr Khan established his authority in Delhi, and together with his successors, who called themselves Sayyeds (or the pure descendants of the Prophet), imposed control on Delhi and some of the surrounding areas. They launched regular expeditions to impose control over Punjab and the Doab and to collect whatever revenues they could, but towards 1450 A.D., their rule became feeble. In 1451, the Afghan governor of Punjab, Buhlul Khan Lodi, captured Delhi and got himself proclaimed Sultan. The Lodi dynasty started by him remained in power until April 1526 when Babur, the king of Kabul was

32. Gascoigne Bamber, *The Great Moghals.*
33. Jawaharlal Nehru, *The Discovery of India*, p. 234.

invited by Daulat Khan Lodi to come and take over as king at Delhi, as Daulat Khan could no longer manage the fractious nobles.

Buhlul Khan Lodi reigned at Delhi until 1489, a period of 38 years during which he reduced the kingdom of Jaunpur and re-established the authority of the Delhi sultanate over the Doab or Ganges-Jumna basin. He also re-conquered Malwa and Bundelkhand, besides firming up his control over Punjab. However, these achievements and efforts continued throughout his reign. For example, Jaunpur was not finally brought to heel until about 1476, that is nearly 25 years into his reign. Besides, the Hindu chieftains of the Doab were causing continuous ferment and needed frequent forays of the sultan to be kept under control and to be made to pay regular tribute.[34] But Buhlul Khan has to be credited with re-establishing the control of Delhi over these regions for the first time after Timur's invasion in 1398-99, that is, after a power vacuum in north India lasting more than 50 years.

Buhlul Khan was succeeded by his second son, Sikandar Lodi, the one most favoured by the Afghan and Turkish nobles at the court. Sikandar Lodi had a hard time keeping his control over the areas over which his father had restored authority. His only notable achievements were the banishing of his brother, Barbak Shah, from Jaunpur and imposing direct control over that kingdom. Sikandar Lodi died in 1517.

After the usual turmoil over the succession after the incumbent's death, Sikandar's son, Ibrahim Lodi became sultan. He finally abolished the kingdom of Jaunpur. His major military achievement was the investing and capture of Gwalior whose Rajput ruler, Man Singh, had recently died. Ibrahim Lodi was also continuously at loggerheads with the Afghan nobles, but his tendency to wreak cruel vengeance on those nobles and their families whom he overcame resulted in a group

34. Vincent A. Smith, *The Oxford History of India*, p. 262.

led by Daulat Khan Lodi inviting Babur, the king of Kabul, who later became the first Mughal emperor to take over the throne of Delhi and relieve the nobles from the despotic rule of Ibrahim. Babur, after much hesitation, decided to intervene and entered India in late 1525 and met Ibrahim Lodi's forces in early 1526 on the field of Panipat. In the ensuing battle, Ibrahim Lodi was decisively defeated and slain in the field.[35]

Thus ended the sultanate of Delhi, the first Muslim rule in India which lasted with fluctuating fortunes from 1206 A.D. to 1526 A.D., a period of 320 years. During this period, most parts of India, except the deep south of the peninsula, saw the appointment and rule of Muslim governors and kings, all supposedly subordinate to Delhi and paying tribute, but, infact, largely independent. The land spaces were extensive and, except when the sultan personally approached with a large army, like Muhammed-bin-Tughlaq or Allah-ud-din Khilji before him, the local Muslim governors barely acknowledged their subservience to the sultanate and paid tribute only when it was unavoidable. For all purposes they were independent, the more so the further away they were from Delhi.[36] However, the policy of destruction of temples, the conversion of non-Muslims to the faith, the exacting of as much revenue from the Hindu chiefs and peasantry continued unabated. The general population were all Hindu under Hindu rajas and chiefs. Hence, although the control of Delhi was for the most part nominal, the oppression of the huge majority of the Hindu, Jain and Buddhist population went ahead without respite.

The sultans and their provincial governors had a passion for building. Although nearly all of them were bigoted Muslims inclined to demolish temples and convert or slay non-Muslims, such action was not always a continuous activity but became

35. Ibid., p. 263.
36. Ibid., pp. 262, 263.

manifest when temples and religious practices were obtrusively demonstrative, and also when building material was needed to build mosques or tombs. Otherwise, destruction of buildings for the sake of destruction was less frequent. It is not easy to bring down and break up huge structures built over many years. After all, these sultans and governors were eminently practical folk who would not deploy manpower to demolish massive stone structures without any immediate practical advantage. They only looted the wealth, the gold ornaments studded with precious stones, and broke up the idols. The exception was when they wanted to demonstrate their power, or eradicate the very vestiges of non-Muslim religions for political purposes or for the purpose of revenge.

The rule of the Delhi sultanate was more in the nature of suzerainty, including the collection of taxes and revenue, both in kind and in cash, for which the individual governors and appointed kings were held responsible.[37] The Muslims were still too few in numbers, and also followed a simple policy of extracting taxes and services from the people. The entire burden for payment finally fell on the merchants and the peasantry, and this burden kept increasing so that they were reduced to a state of mere subsistence, a state in which they could only multiply to continue their own life to produce more wealth for the rulers. This state was not anything new, as the merchants and the peasantry fulfilled the same role for the Hindu kings and chieftains before the Muslims entered India. But the invasion of Timur and his carrying away money, jewellery and precious goods on a scale, perhaps greater than that of Mahmud of Ghazni, left North India totally drained and impoverished. It took a long time before the process of wealth creation reached tangible levels.

The Afghan and Turki Muslims who invaded India right from the time of Mahmud of Ghazni were bold and intrepid

37. K.M. Panickkar, *A Survey of Indian History*, pp. 158, 159.

adventurers. Not only were they physically strong and enduring, but also they were adept at the art of warfare as known in the area during those times. They had a strong sense of discipline and fought unitedly under a single overall commander whose plans and orders they obeyed implicitly. Furthermore, they had everything to gain by invading India, that rich and fertile land which contrasted so much with their own stark, barren and chilly, windswept homelands.[38] When once established in India, they too became slothful and self-indulgent in their habits, and were often content to ride the peasantry to obtain their needs which became more luxurious, the longer they stayed. But they continued to be greatly strengthened by the single idea that they were followers of the faith of Islam and that they were fighting people who they felt were idolaters. The attraction of plunder was also a strong motivating force.

The Hindu kings of the period had large standing armies which had not developed systematically the art of fighting in battle. They seem more to have been good at withstanding a siege for long periods shut up within forts. Otherwise, they do not seem to have practiced regularly the art of deploying and commanding large bodies of troops. The discipline of the troops was generally poor, as they usually broke and fled when their commander was killed or when his mount was injured or frightened and turned back. They were also vulnerable to the massed cavalry charge which they often did not know how to resist, and against which they had not developed any scientific battle formations. Their repeated reliance on elephants in great numbers to trample down their enemies often failed the elephants actually trampling down their own troops when, for one reason or other, they fled back.[39] But then, this mobilisation of elephants may have been because in the India of

38. Vincent A. Smith, *The Oxford History of India*, pp. 264, 265.

39. Ibid., p. 265.

those days, elephants were available in large numbers whereas horses were not. Horses, in fact, were foreign to the land.[40] The people of the countryside never displayed much support for their kings as they were always being taxed and plundered by various grades of chieftains and kings, and had nothing to be grateful about. The kings by means of force, and the priestly class, whether Hindu, Buddhist or Jain, by means of creating hope and fear in people's minds fleeced the people to the last degree of subsistence. But above all, the imprecise, cloudy and subjective nature of the thought processes of the rulers in understanding and appreciating various situations and their reactions, overlain by vanity and ego nurtured since birth, were the greatest factors in their being defeated time and again. The noble efforts of king Jayapala and, later, king Anandapala of the Shahi dynasty of Kashmir in organising allied armies against Sabuktigin and Mahmud of Ghazni failed because of the uncoordinated actions of the allied commanders and for some of the reasons mentioned above. Again the coalition that fought against Muhammed Ghuri at the first battle of Tarain seventy years later, could not exploit their victory by pursuing the fleeing enemy and annihilating him. The same coalition failed next year in the second battle of Tarain where Prithviraj Chauhan was killed.

The Hindus did not lack of bravery, as they continued to be restive and continued to rebel repeatedly for the next three hundred and fifty years, especially in the Ganges-Jumna Doab, in Gujarat, in Rajputana and Bundelkhand, and in Malwa. But they could not develop a coordinated force any more. The uprisings continued to be local. The masterful abilities of the Mauryas and the Guptas were not repeated by their successors. The stratification of caste after the period of the Guptas, and the ramifications of ritual religious practices inevitably took

40. A.L. Basham, *The Wonder That Was India*, p. 130. Also see Jawaharlal Nehru, *The Discovery of India*, p. 234.

their toll on the fighting abilities of the people, and on the purposeful, clear-headed thinking of the kings and leaders.

The Bahmani Kingdoms and Vijayanagar

Hasan Gangu, an officer of Muhammed-bin-Tughlaq, being in command of the fortress of Daulatabad (Deogiri) declared himself an independent monarch in 1347[41] while Muhammed was busy putting down rebellions in Malwa, Gujarat and Sind. Claiming descent from the Persian king Bahman (although he is said to be an Afghan), he adopted Bahman as the name of his family and called himself Alla-ud-din Bahman. The kingdom he founded extended from the west coast near Nasik to the boundaries of Warangal in the east, and from Berar in the north to the Krishna river in the south. A little earlier, in 1335, two brothers Harihara and Bukka who were officers of the Kakatiya king of Warangal, fled after that kingdom was attacked by Muhammad-bin-Tughlaq. They established, as mentioned earlier, the small principality of Vijayanagar on the banks of the Tungabhadra near Anegondi.[42] Taking advantage of the several revolts against sultan Muhammad, and his dwindling control over the parts of his empire, Harihara became king and extended his territories eastward and southwards. After Harihara's death, circa 1354, Bukka became king and is credited with expanding Vijayanagar to include the Andhra areas of Gooty (Gutti), Udayagiri and Pennukonda. However, until he died in 1377, Bukka had to frequently fight the Bahmani kings and he succeeded in checking them at the Krishna river. Meanwhile, Hasan Gangu, now calling himself Alla-ud-din, conquered parts of the central Deccan up to the sea in the west, including Goa and Dabhol which were thriving

41. K.M. Panikkar, *A Survey of Indian History*, p. 176.
42. B. Suryanarayana Rao, *A History of Vijayanagar: The Never to be Forgotten Empire*, p. 150.

port areas. On the east, he extended his dominions upto Bhongir, about 60 km east of Hyderabad. Alla-ud-din I was succeeded by Muhammad Shah I who reigned from 1358 to 1373 and fought continuous wars with the Hindu kingdoms of Vijayanagar and Warangal (Telangana), resulting in heavy loss of life on both sides not only in battle but by the wholesale killing of captives, until at last, both sides agreed to refrain from killing prisoners and massacering the general population.[43]

The Bahmani kingdom and its five successor sultanates existed contemporaneously with the Hindu kingdom of Vijayanagar for 230 years, and the fortunes of these states were so interlocked with each other throughout this time, that these short sketches of their history are treated in this book almost together.

Harihara I the first king of Vijayanagar, and Bukka I, the second were brothers and sons of Sangama. Hence their dynasty of fourteen kings is called the Sangama dynasty which reigned from 1336 to 1486, that is for 150 years.[44] Harihara I and Bukka I and their two brothers who were chiefs are not treated in history of royal rank, but the next ten rulers are considered royal. However, the fact is that this dynasty established Vijayanagar and held it in spite of constant wars with the Bahmani kingdom. Harihara II, who ruled from 1377 to 1404, was able to extend his territories and consolidate his control over the whole of south India, and north and north-east up to the Krishna river. On the west he captured Goa, Dabhol and Chaul. On the south he conquered Kanchi and Trichinopoly (Thiruchirapalli).[45] Under Devaraya I some territories were lost in the north-east to sultan Feroz Tughlaq

43. Vincent A. Smith, *The Oxford History of India*, p. 282.

44. Ibid., p. 306.

45. B. Suryanarayana Rao, *A History of Vijayanagar: The Never to be Forgotten Empire*, p. 198. Also see Vincent A. Smith, *The Oxford History of India*, p. 305.

but were recovered during the reign of Devaraya II (1426-1446 A.D.), who also conquered north-eastern areas upto the Godavari river at its delta town of Rajamahndry, and who established suzerainty over the whole of Kerala. But he lacked cavalry and archers and had to recruit Muslim troops to supplement his resources in these two arms.

Meanwhile, after the death of Muhammad Shah I in 1373, there were five more sultans of the Bahmanis who reigned for short periods only. They were succeeded by Feroze Shah who ruled from 1397 to 1422 and was able to recover the areas of Goa and Dabhol and extend his southern frontiers beyond the Krishna upto the Tungabhadra river by defeating the forces of Vijayanagar in 1406 during the reign of Devaraya I. But in 1420, he suffered a decisive defeat at the hands of the same king and had to give up the territories he had conquered. He was succeeded by his brother, Ahmed Shah I (1422-35) who murdered Feroze Shah and his son to usurp the throne. Ahmad Shah embarked on warfare with Vijayanagar, adopting the tactics of plundering[46] and despoiling the countryside and killing however many of the general populace he could, but not confronting the main forces of Vijayanagar or the capital city, but soon had to enter into a peace treaty with Vijayanagar as he had to fight his enemies in Gujarat, Malwa and the Konkan coast.[47] Ahmed Shah shifted his capital from Gulbarga to Bidar as he considered Gulbarga unlucky. He was succeeded by Ala-ud-din II (1435-57), a weak sultan who suffered defeats in the Konkan, and during whose reign there was constant factional fighting between various groups of Muslims. His son, Humayun (1457-1461) was a man of tremendous rages and was noted for his cruelty towards those he suspected of disloyalty. His rule was characterised by inhuman torture and massacres on a large scale. The next sultan, Muhammed Shah III, was

46. Vincent A. Smith, *The Oxford History of India*, p. 283.

47. Ibid.

VIJAYANAGAR KINGDOM AND BAHMANI SULTANATES

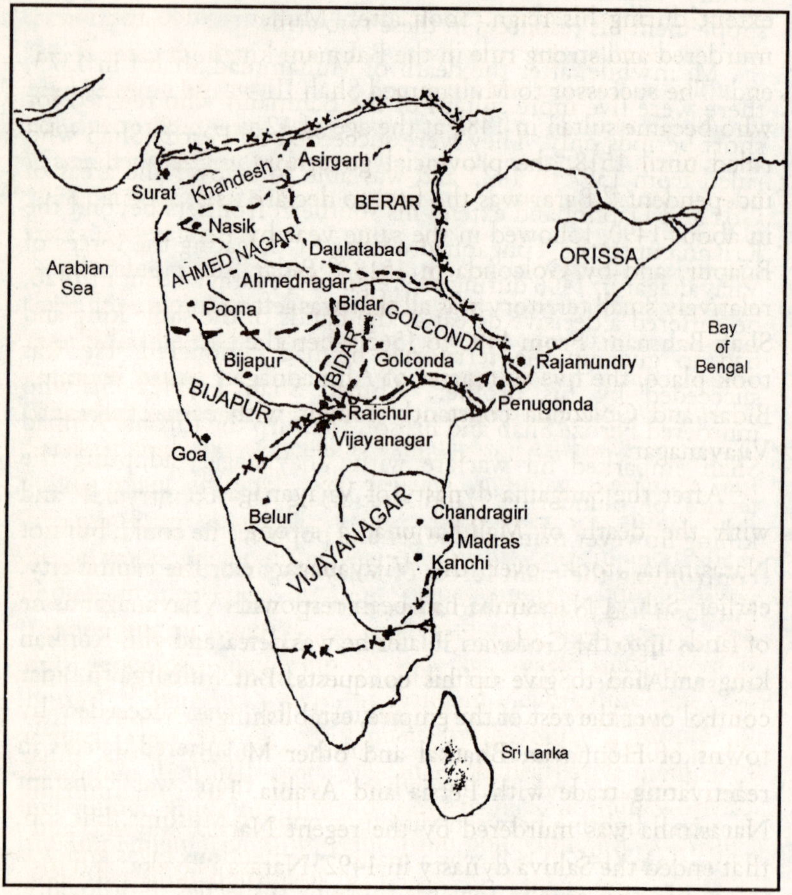

served well by his minister Muhammed Gawan who recovered Goa in 1472, and captured Belgaum in 1473. Muhammed Shah raided Kanchi and obtained much wealth from the temple city in 1481, as a side expedition during his campaign against Vijayanagar.[48] The Bahmani kingdom reached its greatest extent during his reign. Soon after, Muhammed Gawan was murdered and strong rule in the Bahmani kingdom came to an end. The successor to Muhammed Shah III was Mahmud Shah who became sultan in 1482 at the age of 12 years. Although he ruled until 1518, the provincial governors gradually became independent.[49] Berar was the first to declare itself independent in about 1490, followed in the same year by Ahmadnagar and Bijapur, and by Golconda in 1518.[50] Bidar, surrounded by a relatively small territory was all that was left to sultan Mahmud Shah Bahmani. From 1490 to 1565 when the battle of Talikota took place, the five sultanates of Ahmadnagar, Berar, Bijapur, Bidar and Golconda constantly fought with each other and Vijayanagar.

After the Sangama dynasty of Vijayanagar ended in 1486, with the death of Mallikarjuna, a strong minister, Saluva Narasimha, took over the Vijayanagar empire. Although earlier, Saluva Narasimha had been responsible for reconquest of lands upto the Godavari,[51] later he was defeated by the Oriya king and had to give up his conquests. But he still restored control over the rest of the empire, establishing garrisons at the towns of Honnavar, Bhatkal and other Malabar ports, thus reactivating trade with Persia and Arabia. His son, Immadi Narasimha was murdered by the regent Narasa Nayaka, and that ended the Saluva dynasty in 1492. Narasa Nayaka, and his

48. Ibid., p.286.
49. Ibid., p.287.
50. Ibid., p.287.
51. B. Suryanarayana Rao, *A History of Vijayanagar: The Never to be Forgotten Empire*, p. 337.

son Vira Narasimha, ruled until 1509.[52] During this period there were constant campaigns to regain control of the ports of Goa and Dabhol and to recover the Raichur Doab against the sultanate of Bijapur. Narasa Nayaka's dynasty is known as the Tuluva dynasty.

Vira Narasimha was succeeded in 1509 by Krishnadevaraya, generally acclaimed to have been the greatest king of Vijayanagar. In 1509, he defeated Mahmud Shah of Bidar and Yusuf Adil Shah of Bijapur, and besieged Raichur. He also attacked Bidar and Gulbarga and secured his northern frontiers. By 1517, he had conquered Mysore in the south and in the north-east had advanced beyond the Godavari river by defeating the Oriya king.[53] He finally captured Raichur in 1520 and temporarily occupied Bijapur which was partially destroyed by his soldiery. He also captured Gulbarga and destroyed the city. Vijayanagar reached its maximum extent both north and south, east and west, under Krishnadevaraya. He died in 1529.

Meanwhile, the Bahmani sultanates of Ahmadnagar, Bijapur, and Golconda flourished. Berar and Bidar were lesser states which, nevertheless, continued to be independent. Apart from Bijapur, Bidar and Golconda fighting with Vijayanagar frequently, the sultanates fought with each other as often. The Adil Shahi dynasty of Bijapur, the Imad Shahi dynasty of Berar, the Nizam Shahis of Ahmednagar, the Barid Shahi kings of Bidar who were the descendants of the original Bahmani dynasty, and the Qutub Shahi dynasty of Golconda continued to rule those states, until Berar was absorbed by Ahmadnagar in 1574, and Bidar by Bijapur in about 1619. Golconda was a thriving state until about 1611 when it was broken up by the Mughal expansion to the south, and was annexed to that empire by Aurangazeb in 1687. Ahmadnagar was in the direct line of

52. Vincent A. Smith, *The Oxford History of India*, p. 306.

53. K.M. Panikkar, *A Survey of Indian History*, p. 173.

Mughal progress to the South, and after considerable efforts in resistance to the Mughals in the north and to the depredations of the Mahrattas in the west and south, was finally taken over by Shah Jahan in 1637. Bijapur remained a strong sultanate and survived attacks both from Vijayanagar side and later from the concerted attacks of Ahmadnagar, Bidar and Golconda and continued as an independent sultanate until it was annexed by Aurangazeb in 1686.[54] The great achievement of these sultanates was the alliance of Bijapur, Bidar, Ahmednagar and Golconda against Vijayanagar which they defeated at the battle of Talikota in 1565 and that broke the Hindu power which had resisted Muslim expansion to the south for over 200 years.[55]

After the death of Krishnadevaraya in 1529, his brother Achyutaraja ascended the throne but had to contend with the covert opposition of his minister Ramaraja, a Saluva of Udayagiri. With considerable difficulty he managed to remain in power until his death in 1542. But during his reign, he lost the fortresses of Mudgal and Raichur to the Bijapur monarch Ismail Adil Shah. Achyutaraja was succeeded by Venkata, who was murdered by Sadashiva, but throughout this time Ramaraja, the Saluva minister remained the effective ruler. Ramaraja made it his policy to interfere in the quarrels and wars of the Bahmani sultanates. In 1543, Ramaraja allied Vijayanagar with Ahmadnagar and Golconda against Bijapur which was attacked and nearly destroyed. In 1558, he entered into an alliance with Bijapur against Ahmadnagar which was defeated and its countryside devastated by the Hindu forces.[56] But Ramaraja's arrogance in his dealings with his Muslim allies convinced them that the power of Vijayanagar had to be destroyed. Only six years later, the alliance of the four

54. Vincent A. Smith, *The Oxford History of India*, p. 300.
55. K.M. Panikkar, *A Survey of Indian History*, p. 177.
56. Vincent A. Smith, *The Oxford History of India*, p. 308.

sultanates was formed which met Vijayanagar on the field of Talikota near Raichur in 1565 and inflicted a decisive defeat on the Vijayanagar army. The sack and destruction of the capital of Vijayanagar followed over a period of 5 months.[57] Vijayanagar never recovered from this battle, and although existing as a small state with its capital shifted south-east to Chandragiri, never again posed any threat to the Muslims. Hindu power in the Deccan was subdued effectively until the rise of Shivaji and the Mahrattas in western India, a hundred years later.

Whether it was the Bahmani kingdoms or the Vijayanagar empire, the kings and their countries enjoyed immense wealth.[58] So also the governors of the provinces. They were surrounded by nobles, officials, attendants, courtesans, priests, artisans and flunkies who contributed little or nothing to the kingdom. Standing armies were usually about 1,00,000 (more in the case of Vijayanagar) which along with elephants, horses and so on, had to be fed and looked after. When campaigns had to be fought, the governors and chieftains had to provide regular contingents of troops. In the case of the sultanates, nearly all the soldiers were Muslims, either originally from Afghanistan or Turkey or Uzbekistan or Persia, or from the ranks of converted Hindus who were already in millions. At the battle of Talikota in 1565, Ramaraja's army had been estimated to be between 5,00,000 and 10,00,000 and the army of the Bahmani alliance was estimated to be about half of that strength, but reinforced by 600 artillery pieces.[59] At the siege of Raichur by Krishnadevaraya in 1520, his forces were said to number 7,03,000 infantry, 32,600 cavalry and 551 elephants. Obviously, such forces in the field of battle could not be closely controlled,

57. Ibid., p. 309.

58. B. Suryanarayana Rao, *A History of Vijayanagar: The Never to be Forgotten Empire*, p. 312.

59. Vincent A. Smith, *The Oxford History of India*, p. 308.

especially as most of the soldiery were ill-trained and merely dragooned into making up the numbers. They were of such quality that they would avoid actual conflict and merely put up a show to satisfy the commanders who had the power of life and death over them. The soldiery, from the ranks of the peasantry whose whole lives and families had been exploited and terrorised throughout their living memories, obviously had no motivation to fight determinedly and tenaciously for either the Muslim or the Hindu kings. The battles were actually fought and won by small and strong contingents within the armies who had loyalty of some sort to their own individual commanders. Furthermore, during the actual battle, it would have been difficult for the overall generals of the forces to transmit orders to the bodies of troops under them to meet the quick-changing situations. The personal experience of battle and the talent of the Count Leo Tolstoy could be the only sort of qualities which could describe what actually happens on the field of such battles. Tolstoy's descriptions of the battles of Austerlitz and Borodino[60] against Napoleon in his novel *War and Peace* faithfully represent what happens in the actual field of battle, and how extraordinarily difficult it is to get bodies of troops to act together in obedience to the general's orders, conveyed through loyal, faithful, determined and intelligent aides-de-camp. He illustrates how the situations justifying those orders could change drastically by the time the aide-de-camp reached the local commander to deliver the general's orders. And all this, in the case of far smaller armies and dedicated troops and officers organised in famous and proud regiments! It is not surprising that some historians refer to the armies of the sultanates and Vijayanagar as approximating more to armed mobs! Yet, huge masses of men and animals were moved to the

60. Tolstoy, Count Leo, *War and Peace*, Translated by Constance Garnett, The Modern Library, New York, Publishers Random House, Inc., Austerlitz, pp. 253-265. Borodino, pp. 745-765.

battlefield and deployed for battle with some plan of action, and after considering the terrain and the strengths and weaknesses of the enemy forces and commanders. But once the battle was joined anything could happen. However, the "armed mobs" of the Muslims were "a little more efficient" than those of the Hindus, according to Vincent Smith, and hence had the better of the exchanges, although over 230 years of co-existence, fortunes fluctuated.[61]

The lifestyles of the kings and their more important nobles were lavishly extravagant. Muhammed Shah Bahmani III in 1474, according to the Russian merchant and traveller, Athanasius Nikitin, quoted by Vincent Smith, had a standing army of 2,00,000. Another noble maintained an army of 1,00,000 and most of the Khans kept armies of 20,000 to 10,000. While the general lot of the people in the countryside was most miserable, living almost naked and in hovels, the nobles were opulent. When the sultan went hunting, he had a train of 10,000 men on horseback and 50,000 infantry. There were 200 elephants, 100 horsemen, 100 dancers and 300 common horses splendidly decorated, 100 monkeys and 100 concubines, the last of whom were all foreign. The king and the nobles were carried on silver beds.[62]

According to B. Suryanarayana Rao, in his book, *A History of Vijayanagar, The Never to be Forgotten Empire*, and also quoting contemporaneous Portuguese and Persian travellers, the city of Vijayanagar was about 60 miles (100 km) in circumference with seven rings of fort walls, one inside the other, with the innermost ring being 7 to 8 miles in diameter.[63] This innermost ring contained the palaces and temples and

61. Vincent A. Smith, *The Oxford History of India*, p. 289.
62. Ibid., pp. 288, 289.
63. B. Suryanarayana Rao, *A History of Vijayanagar: The Never to be Forgotten Empire*, p. 6.

bazars whereas the next three rings were full of shops and the dwellings of the merchants. The last three rings had cultivated fields and the dwellings of the farmers. The king kept at all times 900 elephants, 20,000 horse and 1,00,000 men who were regularly paid by him. There were 3,000 more elephants in the outer rings of the city along with another 50,000 soldiers. The palace and outbuildings contained 6,000 of the king's special bodyguards, 12,000 maid-servants well-dressed and wearing costly ornaments, 2,000 artisans, smiths, washermen and workers, 200 cooks and innumerable male attenders. When Krishnadevaraya besieged Raichur in 1520, his camp followers included 20,000 dancing women. There were the same number or more in Vijayanagar at the same time. The trading population, catering to the king and his 12,000 wives (during the time of Devaraya II of the Sangama dynasty), the hundreds of nobles, military commanders and their retinues, and dealing with articles of all kinds of luxuries including gold and jewellery, was immense. There were 4,000 temples inside Vijayanagar alone with a huge community of priests.[64] The population of Vijayanagar is estimated to have been at least five lakhs.

The wherewithal to feed this whole population had to come from the people of the countryside who, at final count were said to be forced to give away nine-tenths of what they produced to the hierarchy of rulers upto the king.[65] These continuous demands on the peasantry ultimately left them in a condition of miserable poverty. The annual expedition, fighting, and the building of huge temples, palaces and forts, drawing thousands of able bodied peasantry from their fields resulted in the land becoming despoiled and barren over 250 to 300 years. These lands have still not fully recovered their productivity inspite of improved irrigation, development

64. Ibid., p.11.

65. Vincent A. Smith, *The Oxford History of India*, p. 313.

works, and governmental investment over 50 years of independence in the second half of the 20th century. The 30 per cent to 40 per cent of the people in these parts still below the poverty line exist today in hardly a better state of livelihood than they did during the period of the Bahmani kings and Vijayanagar. A different kind of exploitation has taken the place of the medieval monarchs.[66]

The undivided Bahmani kingdom, judging from the authoritative maps available was about 4,30,000 sq km, or slightly smaller than the size of Iraq. The Vijayanagar kingdom at its height, during the time of Devaraya II in 1470 and of Krishnadevaraya in 1525 was approximately the size of continental France, that is about 4,60,000 sq km.[67] Whereas the European countries of the time had a well-entrenched feudal system which forced the king to pay heed to, and take counsel with the nobles, rulership in India, both among Muslims and Hindus, was extremely arbitrary and despotic. While the Delhi sultanate and the Bahmani sultanates had some system of election of kings by the nobles, in the case of the Hindu kingdoms, succession was often by murder and violence. The priestly class exercised sufficient influence to safeguard their interests by a combination of unctuous flattery and the threat of calamity if the gods were not adequately propitiated. Otherwise, both Muslim and Hindu rule was absolute, and differences were resolved by assassination, murder by poisoning, capture and imprisonment with blinding of the eyes as an added insurance, and so on. In the case of the Hindus, the ruler had a kind of divine status whereas in the case of the Muslims, the ruler had a temporal status.

In the case of the Bahmani sultans, there was quite free employment of Hindu officials on the administrative and

66. The author's own observation during the course of many travels spread over 40 years between 1956 and 1999.

67. The author's computation from authoritative atlases.

revenue sides. In the case of the kings of Vijayanagar, there was increasing use of Muslim contingents and commanders from the time of Devaraya II, especially in the cavalry arm and for archery. In fact, it is mentioned by some authorities that, at the battle of Talikota in 1565 which rang the death knell of the Vijayanagar empire, the entire cavalry of nearly 60,000 horse who were Muslim, and commanded by a Muslim under Thirumala, the brother of Ramaraja who commanded the left wing, deserted and went over to the Bahmani confederation late in the afternoon of the 23rd January, the day of the battle. And so ended the Vijayanagar empire.

5

The Mughals

The history of India under the Mughals is generally quite well-known and will be only briefly dealt with in these pages.

Mughal rule started with the enthronement of Babur at Delhi in 1526 after he had defeated Ibrahim Lodi on the field of Panipat. It effectively ended with the death of Aurangazeb, the last of the six 'Great Mughals' in 1707. After 1707, the Mughal emperor at Delhi became increasingly weak, and although recognised as the emperor for political purposes by all the powers of North India and Central India, and by the burgeoning new British power, exercised little sway except around Delhi and that by the grace of his immediate nobility. The formal end of the empire came in 1858 when Bahadur Shah II, the last Mughal, was pensioned off by the British and banished to Rangoon (Yangon) in Burma (Myanmar) for his passive, not to say, helpless part in the 'Mutiny' of 1857-58.

All the Great Mughals upto and including Shah Jahan were enlightened rulers and generally adopted a pragmatic policy in ruling their subjects. They toned down the uncompromising policy of the Delhi sultans towards the Hindus, and did not unnecessarily kill and slaughter Hindus for the sake of winning a favoured place in the paradise of Allah. Looting and destruction of temples were greatly reduced. However, it was Akbar, the third Great Mughal, who followed a carefully constructed policy close to secularism by encouraging Hindus in martial service to the emperor, by abolishing the highly discriminative 'jiziya'[1] or poll tax which non-Muslims had to pay the administration, by encouraging inter-marriage with Hindus, by taking an interest in the religions and cultures other than Islam for the purpose of understanding them, and so on. He was especially successful in being able to win the support of powerful kings of Rajputana. He himself married a Rajput princess whose son, Jahangir, succeeded Akbar.

Akbar

Akbar could not read and write and was almost illiterate,[2] although his father Humayun and grandfather, Babur were highly literate and learned men. Humayun excelled in writing poetry. Babur's autobiography, the *Baburnama* written during his last years from the regular diary he maintained, is said to be a masterpiece of objective thought and elegant prose. Due to the chequered career of Humayun who was defeated and hunted by Sher Shah Suri of Bengal, the Afghan who later ruled in Delhi for five years, Akbar as a child had to stay with one uncle or another.[3] It was only after Sher Shah was killed in 1545 in the siege of Bundelkhand[4] that Humayun could return with the help of the Shah of Persia and regain his throne of Delhi in 1555. Probably, Akbar's education was somewhat neglected. However, it is thought that he suffered from dyslexia, a frailty due to which he had abnormal difficulty in reading and spelling.

Humayun died due to a fall down the stairs of his library in the same year, 1555. Akbar, a boy of 13 years under the tutelage of the loyal noble Bairam Khan, was fighting Sikandar Shah of

1. Gascoigne Bamber, *The Great Moghuls*, under "Akbar".
2. Ibid.
3. Ibid., under "Humayun".
4. Vincent A. Smith, *The Oxford History of India*, p. 325.

Punjab when Humayun died. Akbar was crowned king immediately, right in the field, and proceeded to expand and consolidate the Mughal empire throughout his reign of 49 years. Not only was he a wise ruler, but also a daring and brilliant commander who led his forces in the field by personal example. About 5 feet 7 inches in height, he was physically very powerful and could ride hard for days and himself participate actively in battle. His empire over which he had closer control than either of his predecessors, extended from Kabul and Kandahar in Afghanistan and Kashmir in the north to the Vindhyas, Khandesh and Berar in the south, and from Baluchistan, Gujarat and Sind in the west to Bihar, Bengal and Orissa in the east. He personally led the expeditions for the conquest of Mewar in Rajputana, and the reduction of its principal fort, Chittor. He also led the expeditions down the Ganges from Allahabad to defeat the Afghan prince Daud Khan whom he drove from Patna and Hajipur. He pursued Daud and defeated him at Tukaroi and Rajmahal and completed the conquest of Bengal in 1576. By 1586, he had brought Kabul and Kashmir directly under his rule. In 1599, he crossed the Narmada and occupied Khandesh, the province located east of Surat. He besieged the strong fortress of Asirgarh and captured it in 1601 by stratagem after a siege of eight months. He acquired the three new provinces of Khandesh, Berar and Ahmadnagar, although Ahmadnagar regained its independence soon after Akbar went back north to deal with the revolt of prince Salim (his eldest son, later the emperor Jahangir). Apart from these conquests, Akbar had to regularly put down revolts from time to time, especially in Bengal and Mewar. In his battles, in addition to the Muslim forces under his command, he had strong forces provided by the Rajputs especially of Amber (Jaipur), Ajmer and Marwar. The Rajputs of these states were a valuable addition to the strength of his armies. However, Mewar never surrendered, Rana Pratap, in fact recovering many of his territories although he could not recover Chittor.[5]

Although Akbar did not formally renounce Islam even until his death in 1605,[6] his faith in Islam was considerably eroded by about 1580. The schisms in Islam made him feel that the religion was not as clear to him as before. The arguments of the ulemas representing these schisms, although conducted frequently in his presence, could not satisfy his questioning mind. Comparative religion greatly interested him, and he lent a receptive ear to the arguments of Jesuit priests, Zoroastrians, Hindu savants and Jain monks to try and understand for himself the differences in philosophy and faith. In 1582, he started propagating a new religion of his own called 'Din-e-Ilahie' or the 'Religion of God', with he himself becoming the head of the religion. In support of this new religion, he introduced various laws which contravened the basic beliefs and practices of Islam and which amounted to blasphemous actions, and sent tremors in the world of his Muslim subjects. These actions sparked revolts in Bihar and Bengal and were considered by the uneasy Muslim clergy of all denominations, as giving way to, and encouraging, the practices of idolators of the Christian, Hindu, Jain and Buddhist faiths. Although the new religion got hardly any converts, except for a palace coterie led by Abul Fazl, Akbar persisted in it until his death.

Akbar may be considered as the true founder of the Mughal empire which at his death in 1605 was approximately 26,60,000 sq km, or more than 40 per cent of the extent of the Roman Empire at its height.[7] His control of this vast empire was close and sound, but still considerably dependent on his commanders and governors and their officers for collection of revenue,

5. Vincent A. Smith, *The Oxford History of India*, p. 342.
6. K.M. Panikkar, *A Survey of Indian History*, p. 191.
7. The author's own computation based on areas given in authoritative atlases.

MUGHAL EMPIRE, c. 1600 A.D.

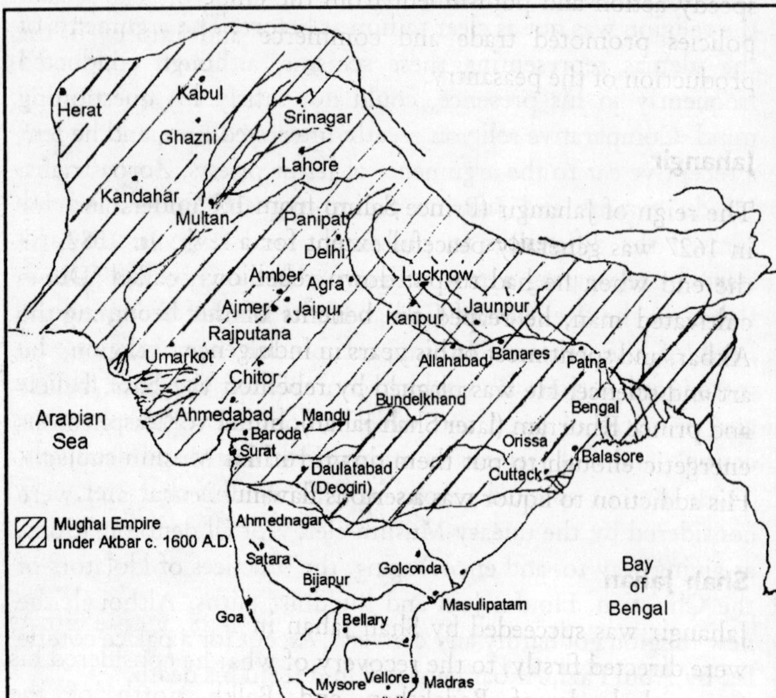

maintenance of law and order, and the efficient maintenance of communication within the empire. However, his firm control over them ensured that his policies were executed faithfully. They understood that any serious departure would invite speedy action and punishment from the emperor. His secular policies promoted trade and commerce and improved the production of the peasantry.

Jahangir

The reign of Jahangir (Prince Salim) from 1605 until his death in 1627 was generally peaceful except for a few years towards the end when he had to put down rebellions by his sons. A cultivated man, he reaped the benefits of the strong rule of Akbar, and spent most of his years in indulgence of his taste for art and science. He was plagued by rebellion of prince Khusru and prince Khurram (later Shah Jahan), but nevertheless he was energetic enough to put them down ruthlessly and decisively. His addiction to liquor was a serious flaw in his character.

Shah Jahan

Jahangir was succeeded by Shah Jahan in 1628, whose efforts were directed firstly, to the recovery of what he considered his ancestral lands of Badakshan and Balkh north of the Hindukush, of Kabul and Kandahar, and secondly, to the defeat and acquisition of the Bahmani kingdoms of Ahmadnagar, Bijapur and Golconda. He failed in conquering the northern areas, losing even Kandahar to the Persians, although his sons Aurangazeb and Dara Shukoh, in all besieged Kandahar three times. In the south, however, he succeeded in conquering Ahmadnagar where the Nizam Shahi monarchy was finally crushed, and in concluding favourable treaties with Bijapur and Golconda. But by 1658, the continuous feuding among his sons ended with the defeat by Aurangazeb of Dara Shukoh the eldest, and of Murad Baksh and Sulaiman Shukoh the second and fourth sons of Shah Jahan. Aurangazeb imprisoned his father and Murad Baksh and executed Dara Shukoh. Sulaiman died after his defeat.

For the first time since the early years of Akbar's reign, a policy was initiated to curb the Hindus who had shown a resurgence in their religious and social activity.[8] Shah Jahan ordered that no new Hindu temples were to be built in the empire, and that those temples which were under construction were to be dismantled.[9] However, he did not destroy any temples already constructed or which were already in existence.[10] Furthermore, he did not reimpose the pilgrim tax and the jiziya, and continued to enjoy the support of the Rajputs. Except for his own military activities which were mainly aggressive against the north and south, there was no threat to him from internal rebellions or external intrusion. He was, however, unable to curb the rivalry between his sons, and in fact, became a participant by specially favouring his eldest son, Dara Shukoh against his third son Aurangazeb. He ended his days in eight years' captivity in Agra fort. Shah Jahan has a special place in Mughal history as a builder of magnificent buildings which are distinguished for their stateliness grace and delicacy of execution. The Taj Mahal, the Jumma Masjid in Delhi, the Red Fort (or Lal Qila) are regarded even today as masterpieces of architecture and building along with the best in the world.

Aurangazeb

Aurangazeb, the last Great Mughal, ascended the throne in 1658, although his formal enthronement was in 1659 as he had to

8. Vincent A. Smith, *The Oxford History of India*, p. 380. Also see Gascoigne Bamber, *The Great Moghals*, under "Shah Jahan".
9. Ibid.
10. Ibid.

dispose of Dara Shukoh, his eldest brother and first claimant to the throne, by defeat and execution. This man, gifted with a clear, calculating brain and a cool head, should be considered as the ablest of Shah Jahan's sons. He was also bold and able in war, although his early military career was marked by two unsuccessful sieges of Kandahar which he could never capture. But he was successful in his campaigns against Bijapur and Golconda both of which he was able to annexe to the empire by 1687. He was helped in his campaigns by a capable general, Mir Jumla, who later on carried the emperor's arms not only to Bengal but also to the hitherto untouched territory of Assam. Cooch Behar in the Duars was conquered and the campaign proceeded forward with the defeat of the Ahom king and the capture of Gauhati. Mir Jumla captured more territory, driving the Ahom king out of his capital, but he had then to return to Bengal where he died.[11] The emperor's uncle, Shaiysta Khan, was also successful in maintaining Mughal control of Bengal, Chittagong and the western districts of Assam (1666). Meanwhile Aurangazeb had to put down rebellions by Rajputs in 1678-81 and the Jats in 1681.[12] Later, the same year, Aurangazeb himself proceeded to the Deccan where he remained until he died near Daulatabad (Deogiri) in north-western Maharashtra in 1707.[13] This campaign resulted in the annexation of Bijapur and Golconda and large territories of the latter state to beyond the Krishna river including the territories of Andhra Pradesh and Karnataka upto beyond Chandragiri. The territorial extent of the Mughal empire was greatest under Aurangazeb,[14] but these achievements amounted to something akin to a Pyrrhic victory, as the control of the

11. Vincent A. Smith, *The Oxford History of India*, p. 405.
12. Gascoigne Bamber, *The Great Moghals*, under "Aurangazeb".
13. Ibid.
14. Ibid.

emperor over these territories was greatly weakened because of his actively anti-secular policies, and his suspicious nature which could not command willing loyalty. These factors were further compounded by the rise of the Mahrattas under Shivaji whom he could not subdue in spite of over forty years of effort.[15]

Aurangazeb was a devout Muslim who was personally exemplary in character, abjuring wine in accordance with the principles of his religion and being a devoted husband and father. In trying to observe to the letter the teachings of his religion, he proceeded to abrogate all the secular policies of Akbar and his two successors, reimposing the poll tax and the jiziya. He demolished the Kasi Vishwanath temple at Banaras and built a mosque near the site, towering above, which stands to this day. Within another year, he destroyed the Keshava Deva temple at Mathura, reputed to be a magnificent structure, down to the ground without a trace, and erected a huge mosque on the site. He reduced the power and importance of the Rajput princes and nobles, members of a proud race who gave their support on the basis of friendship and honour, and never out of fear. He persecuted the Sikhs who were until then a harmless religious group as followers of their Guru Nanak, a Hindu sufi type of preacher who sought to eliminate the complicated system of brahminical rituals and to think of God as a Being who could be directly prayed to with faith and devotion. During Aurangazeb's time, their tenth guru, Arjun Singh, made the Sikhs, the khalsas or the pure, into a martial community which became a thorn in the side of the emperor. The Mahratta lands were buzzing with rebellions. His conquests in Assam, and eastern Bengal, in Sind and in the Deccan territories south of the Krishna river, soon fell away with local kings and governors acting as independent monarchs paying little more than the most perfunctory respects to the

15. K.M. Panikkar, *A Survey of Indian History*, pp. 200, 201.

Great Mughal. The powerful Rajput kingdoms which had been defeated many times from the time of Babur had never really been subdued fully and now revolted. Those Rajput kingdoms like Ajmer and Marwar which had been won over by Akbar's policy of conciliation and which had given their support on the basis of honourable status and partnership to Akbar and his two successors, now became alienated. Mewar, of course, had never even given that support but had acted as an independent state whenever it could. Now it became totally independent.[16] The Muslim governors of Gujarat acted in support of Aurangazeb's son Akbar, who had revolted against his father. Towards the end of his reign, most of the empire was in a state of turbulence and the various provincial governors squeezed the peasantry to a progressively greater extent to meet the growing demands for the armies and the wars.[17] Much of the accumulated treasures in the vaults of Agra fort and Lahore were used up for the campaigns, and where possible replenished from the treasures of Ahmadnagar, Golconda and Bijapur.

The Mahrattas

The period 1640 to 1680 saw the rise and consolidation of the Mahratta state under Shivaji. Shivaji was a Mahratta whose father, Shahu, was an officer in the service initially of Ahmadnagar, but later of Bijapur under whom he enjoyed a 'jagir' or an extent of landholding free of taxes, but with the proviso that the landholder had to bring an appropriate fighting force in the service of the sultan when required. Shivaji's mother, Jijabai, had considerable influence over him and may be said to have moulded his mind from an early age. But there is no doubt that Shivaji was a natural leader of men with a vigorous mind. Born in 1627, he had become a guerrilla leader

16. K.M. Panickkar, *A Survey of Indian History*, p.197. Also see Vincent A. Smith, *The Oxford History of India*, p. 420.

17. Vincent A. Smith, *The Oxford History of India*, pp. 404, 427.

of his native Mahratta hillmen by the age of 16, and a leader with a force that could not escape notice of the Bijapur sultan. By concentrating on the capture of the hill forts in the difficult country of the western ghats between Poona (Pune) and Bombay, and by dominating the Konkan coast, Shivaji established a Mahratta state which defied successfully not only Bijapur but the Mughal empire which was at the height of its power during the period.[18]

Shivaji not only improved the forts he captured but also built new ones, and by the time of his death in 1680[19] at the early age of 53, had extended his control from near Surat and west Khandesh in the north to Satara and Belgaum in the south, and from the Konkan coast in the west to Sholapur in the east. He extracted from the villages 'chauth' or one-fourth of the taxes they were liable to pay the sultans as his own share, and although this measure entailed a harsh policy on the villages, he compensated for this by respecting all places of worship, Hindu or Muslim and by ensuring that his soldiery respected women. Also, apart from this extraction of 'chauth', he did not harass the people. On the other hand, he protected them from the oppression of the jagirdars and zamindars. The forces that this hill chieftain had to contend with were immense, that is, against the established sultanate of Bijapur, and later, against the might of the Mughal empire reinforced by the determination of Aurangazeb to annihilate the Mahratta troops and to capture Shivaji.[20] His personal courage, daring and audacity, and his leadership of his Mahrattas, who revered him and loved him to a man, enabled him to establish the Mahratta state. The institution of an effective system of rule through a council, and good government enabled the Mahratta state not only to survive and endure after his death, but in fact, to expand and

18. Ibid., pp. 405, 406.

19. Gascoigne Bamber, *The Great Moghals*, under "Aurangazeb".

20. Vincent A. Smith, *The Oxford History of India*, pp. 406, 407.

overrun many of the Muslim states until, by 1760, the Mahrattas had captured Lahore and Delhi in the north, crossed the borders of Bengal in the east, and established strong governorships in the Deccan and peninsular India upto Jinji and Kanchi.[21] The Mahratta horsemen, with their battle-cry of "Har Har Mahadev" carried all before them in that fantastic period of fifty years after the death of Aurangazeb. Their progress and the consolidation of their conquests can best be compared to the rapid conquest of West Asia, North Africa and Spain by the Arabs[22] in the hundred years after the death of Muhammed, the Prophet, although the territories conquered by the Arabs were far more extensive. But then those areas were much more thinly populated and the terrain relatively easier. The Mahrattas conquered areas much more densely populated with a hundred established potentates spread all over, and which consisted of the most varied terrain criss-crossed by a hundred rivers, big and small.

The English

The Mughal empire saw the first serious approaches by the English to obtain trade concessions for the newly formed East India Company (1600 A.D.), which had ambitions to enter the spice trade in India where the Portuguese had already established themselves, mainly in Goa, Daman and Diu on the western coast. Later the English were to expand their operations to control the opium trade from China. The Portuguese effectively countered English efforts at the Mughal court in 1608, their influence mainly being due to their superiority at sea by which they could interfere with the trade of the Mughal empire with the Arabs, and with the pilgrim traffic to Mecca and Madina. The Mughals had never been able to appreciate the importance of developing a naval presence,

21. Ibid., p.409.
22. K.M. Panikkar, *A Survey of Indian History*, p. 139.

were ignorant of naval matters and hence had to tolerate the demands of the Portuguese both on the west coast and in the Gangetic delta.[23] However, after they inflicted a series of naval defeats on the Portuguese in 1612, the English won the agreement of local Gujarat governors to trade at Surat at the mouth of the Tapti river.[24] This sanction was confirmed by Jahangir in 1613.

The success at Surat was followed up by the English by sending a formal embassy under Sir Thomas Roe in 1615 to the court of Jahangir. He stayed for three years at the court and secured several concessions that enabled the English to set up later trading stations at several places on the west coast, and at Madras (Fort St George) in about 1640 A.D., and Calcutta (Fort William) in 1696. Thus, in the 17th century were established, at Surat, Madras and Calcutta the first fortified settlements of the English trading stations which eventually developed in the 18th century into the Presidencies of Bombay, Madras and Bengal[25] (Calcutta).

After Jahangir, the succession to the throne of Delhi could only be achieved by venomous fratricide struggles. Murders by execution and poisoning, capture and long imprisonment and blinding were the norms. Even after Aurangazeb, two of his sons and three grandsons were murdered before Bahadur Shah I, under the title Shah Alam could ascend the throne. After him, in the remaining 53 years of Mughal rule, which could be considered only as titular, four kings were murdered and one deposed. Only three kings died under peaceful circumstances.

Inevitably, this atmosphere of intrigue for the succession generated factions supported by one or other of the royal family, with powerful commanders switching loyalties depending upon the inducements of positions and wealth held

23. Geoffrey Moorhouse, *India Britannica*, p. 28.
24. Ibid., p.29.
25. Vincent A. Smith, *The Oxford History of India*, pp. 333, 334.

out to them. Personal vendettas also found expression in these factional struggles. Control of the different parts of the empire became loose giving rise to semi-independent principalities whose rulers assumed powers and titles of kingship. The disintegration of the empire, which had already started thirty years before the death of Aurangazeb in 1707,[26] progressed rapidly, assisted by the exploits of the Rajputs, the Mahrattas, the Sikhs and the English, until by about 1800, the Mughal emperor became only a nominal ruler whose influence hardly extended beyond the walls of the Red Fort at Delhi. In the south, from 1760 to 1799, Hyder Ali and his son Tipu were independent monarchs ruling over the considerable state of Mysore. At Hyderabad, the Nizam-ul-Mulk, ostensibly the viceroy of the emperor in the Deccan, was for all purposes an independent monarch. And so the Mughal empire which gave India 300 years of rule, of which about 160 years were truly distinguished, considered as one of the great empires of the world in the second millennium of the Christian era, gradually petered out.

26. The acquisition of Assam and Chittagong were lost. Control of Bengal was lost. The alienation of the Rajput states of Amber and Marwar resulted in their active hostility. Control over Gujarat, Sind and Baluchistan was lost. The Mahrattas had seized the western Deccan. See Vincent A. Smith, *The Oxford History of India* and Gascoigne Bamber, *The Great Moghals.*

6

A Discussion of Muslim Rule in India

The Role of Climate

The Muslims who invaded India with Mahmud of Ghazni and later under Muhammed Ghuri, were hardy men accustomed to long marches and long periods in the saddle. The cold, thin air of the plateaus and mountains of central Asia, of Afghanistan and Persia contributed to their physical strength and endurance. In their internecine wars, and with the traditions and methods handed down from the days of the Persian empire and of Alexander the Great, they had acquired and practiced military skills and battle drills which proved superior to the age old methods of kings then in the sub-continent. Their tribal obligations and discipline helped them maintain strong discipline in war. In addition to these factors, they were fired with the strength and confidence of a new and vigorous religion which made them feel superior to people of other religions. The intrinsic preaching of the Quran that unbelievers or kaffirs should be either converted or killed, and it was the duty of every Muslim to do so, and that idol worship should be ended and idols destroyed, gave the Muslims a sense of mission. The priceless gems and gold in huge quantities in these temples made their destruction a rewarding task, and proved the greatest incentive to the invaders. The climate and the rich and varied resources of India, and its rich soil, attracted these denizens of the difficult and barren regions of the north.

In time, the sultans of the Delhi sultanate became affected by the warm, languorous climate and the superfluity of conveniences both human and material, and began to lead slothful lives, as did their nobles and tribal chiefs. Indulgence in heavy drinking was a common failing. The harems were filled to overflowing. There was a proliferation of courtesans and dancing girls.[1] These developments eroded the self-discipline and efficiency of the rulers. Every noble who was in charge of a province or a district liked to be left alone so long as he sent to the capital his obligation of taxes and any other remissions. He could then amass wealth for himself, build comfortable and secure palaces and forts and enjoy an undisturbed existence. When ordered to proceed to battle with their prefixed contingents of 5000, 10,000 or more men, they did so often in a half-hearted manner. The climate and cultural atmosphere of India had begun to take its toll on the hardy adventurers.

Features of Muslim Rule

Within these conditions, however, most of the abler sultans like Qutubuddin Aibak, Ala-ud-din Khilji and Muhammed-bin Tughlaq and his father Ghiyasuddin Tughlaq Shah, maintained a strong central presence and were constantly endeavouring to put down rebellious elements by leading forces directly under their command against them.[2] They made constant efforts to extend their territories, ably helped by loyal and good generals like Malik Kafur who raided south India right up to Madurai, the ancient city of the Pandyas. They built large forts to keep control of the countryside and as part of their mission to spread the religion of Islam, built large mosques, often with material from destroyed temples. Along with the mosques, the ulemas followed. Large numbers of people from the captured territories were made slaves, converted to Islam and used for

1. K.M. Panickkar, *A Survey of Indian History*, pp. 149, 210.
2. Ibid., pp. 147-150.

their extensive construction works,[3] or to supplement the ranks of soldiery. The expeditions against rebellious princes continued, as the Rajputs, the Hindus of the Doab, the Princes of Bundelkhand, some Muslim governors of Gujarat, Sind and Bengal, continued to be intractable.

All these activities had to be financed by extractions from the land. The temples continued to be a source of wealth. The peasantry continued to till the soil and produce food. But they came under increasing pressure from the governors and chieftains of the sultanate to pay more in taxes.[4] So also did the trading communities which were almost completely Hindu or Jain.

The number of Muslims coming from across the Khyber and Bolan passes was still small, although several came to seek military service under the sultans or to obtain land on which they could settle down. Hence, the military ranks had to be replenished with locally converted Muslims, and the clerical or accounting posts had to be filled with Hindu munshis.

Justice was rough and ready, being meted out mostly by the local governors in accordance generally with the Shariat or Muslim law, but it was common for such local governors to add imaginative refinements of their own like, for example, causing offenders to be buried alive upto the neck near an anthill, or to be flayed alive, or to be half-immersed in boiling oil, or to be deprived of hands and legs by cutting them off and leaving them to bleed to death. In these matters, they may have copied the practices of Hindu rulers who were equally cruel and inhuman.

The Delhi sultans remained largely primitive, probably because of the state of their society at the time, but managed to

3. Vincent A. Smith, *The Oxford History of India*, p.258.
4. Ibid. Alla-ud-din Khilji passed rules for grinding down the Hindus and for depriving them of that wealth and property which fosters rebellion. p. 246.

retain continuous control of Punjab, Uttar Pradesh, Bihar, Sind and some parts of Malwa, throughout the rule of the slave kings, the Khiljis, the Tughlaqs and the Lodis. Rajputana, Gujarat and Bengal were, more often than not, outside their full control, although owing nominal allegiance. Remitting of taxes was often delayed, and became prompt only under the threat of a punitive expedition by the reigning sultan.

The Mughals Contrasted with the Delhi Sultans

The Mughal emperors, however, were of a different nature. Proud of their Timurid ancestry and their cultural affinity with the Persians, they were urbane, gracious and sensitive admirers of art and literature. Babur took pleasure in laying out beautiful gardens and preferred to stay in a tent in their midst rather than within the confines of even the best palaces.[5] In this connection, it would be appropriate to mention that, whenever they could, his commanders wished to leave the hot plains of India and go back to Kabul or Kandahar, or even better, to their home place of Ferghana. This is in contrast to Mughal commanders in the time of Shah Jahan and Aurangazeb who hated to leave the (by then) luxuriously appointed dwellings in India for the difficult and cold country of Afghanistan.

Humayun was a poet who liked nothing better than either to read poetry or to write it. Akbar, although nearly illiterate, took pleasure in listening to the great musicians of the time, like Tansen, or to the reading to him of works of literature or philosophy or religion. His interest extended to discourses and learned disputations over religious matters, to painting, to science, to information on the history and culture of other countries, notably of Europe and so on.[6]

5. Gascoigne Bamber, *The Great Moghals* under "Babur". Also see Vincent A. Smith, *The Oxford History of India*, p.323.
6. Gascoigne Bamber, *The Great Moghals*. Also see Vincent A. Smith, *The Oxford History of India*, pp. 356, 357, 361.

Jahangir was a sophisticate who studied birds, flowers and the habits of animals. Long before William Audubon, Jahangir caused to be painted a great variety of birds, these paintings existing even today. He was himself no mean painter of birds, of flowers and of animals like elephants. But his main court painter was Mansur whose painting of a turkey and a falcon are well presented. Besides, Jahangir was a diarist as indefatigable and meticulous in observation and recording as his great-grandfather, Babur. His taste in building was also remarkable.[7]

Shah Jahan's place as a builder and architect in the world's history is a special one for creating one of the most beautiful buildings in the world, the Taj Mahal, which was his monument to the love he bore for his queen, Mumtaz Mahal. The ideas and decisions to use marble for the monument, the final approval of the proportions of the structure, the use of inlay work with semi-precious stones were all his very own. He also built many other famous buildings, for example, the marble structure on top of the Agra Fort, the Red Fort in Delhi and the Jama Masjid there.[8]

Aurangazeb was cast in a different mould. His scrupulous adherence to the teachings of the Quran led him into the area of fundamentalism and austerity. Yet it was he who was responsible for the building of the Pearl Mosque in the Red Fort at Delhi, which is considered a gem of sculpture in marble in bas-relief.

All these Great Mughals, as they are called in Indian history were, nevertheless, superb and confident commanders in the field. They were canny rulers who dominated the men around them and generally inspired their loyalty, except of course, Aurangazeb who was too suspicious and too much given to intrigue especially during the later half of his long reign. The

7. Ibid., p. 372.

8. Ibid., p. 398.

Great Mughals brought to their rule a more liberal outlook and tolerant attitude which helped them to establish and run the most successful and greatest empire in India since the time of the Mauryas and the Guptas, respectively nearly two millenniums and one millennium earlier.

The control of the territories of the empire was under 'mansabdars' or district officers responsible for certain specific areas, who were in turn responsible to the provincial governors.[9] Taxes were generally levied at one-sixth of the produce, but, in practice, because of additional levies based on the contingent requirements of the empire, taxes tended to amount to more. In fact, during certain periods of the rule of emperor Akbar, the taxes and impositions amounted to one-third of the produce. Over and above these payments which went directly to the treasury at Delhi or Agra or Lahore, the mansabdars and the governors had to obtain their own share for upkeep of the military contingents kept in readiness for the demands of the emperor, and for their own needs. But during the time of Akbar, some efforts were made to improve productivity of the land by the construction of canals for irrigation followed by somewhat feebler efforts by his successors. Law and order were maintained more effectively under the Mughals than under any other of the Muslim rulers of India.[10]

Other Muslim Rulers

The Bahmani sultans generally followed the pattern set by the sultans of Delhi and the Mughals. They were considerably dependent on Hindu officials especially in regard to their

9. But the Mughal empire, at its best, was still only "an assemblage of territories...held by naked military power". It was not an "organised empire" like that of the Ottomans or Persians or Romans. See *Clive of India* by Nirad C. Chaudhuri, p. 20.

10. Particularly under Akbar.

collections and accounting of revenue. The continuous internecine wars among the kingdoms gradually led to the impoverishment of the countryside.

Further south, towards the latter half of the 18th century, the state of Mysore with its capital at the old Vijayanagar kingdom's viceregal capital of Srirangapatna (Seringapatan) was taken over by the cavalry officer, Hyder Ali who.ruled in the raja's name from about 1765 to 1780. He was succeeded by his son Tipu Sultan. Hyder Ali, who rose from a humble military official in the lower ranks to the position of commander-in-chief of the state forces of the Hindu king, decided to take over as the head of the government although he continued to pay lip service to the Hindu king of the Wodeyar dynasty. Although he was illiterate in the tradition of two other great commanders, viz., Akbar and Shivaji, he was an effective ruler who extended his territories towards Salem and Madras in the east, towards Coorg in the south, and to Malabar in the west. He followed a policy of pragmatism treating Hindus and Muslims alike. His son and successor, Tipu, however took upon himself the task of spreading the religion of Islam along with his conquests. He converted thousands of captured Hindus to Islam from the territories he conquered. He also converted thousands of the peasantry of Mysore, especially from the most disadvantaged communities and increased the strength of his armies. Ultimately cornered in his capital Srirangapatna in the middle of the Kaveri river by Sir Arthur Wellesley, because of the treachery of his own Muslim commanders who were suborned with gold by the English, he sallied forth through the breach made by the English in the fortress walls and was killed fighting among his troops.[11]

Characteristics of Muslim Rule

Muslim rule, on the whole, was arbitrary, direct and despotic.

11. Vincent A. Smith, *The Oxford History of India*, p. 544.

The sultans and emperors kept control of their territories by proceeding on frequent expeditions with forces under their own direct command, or under commanders of proven loyalty and ability. While the earlier emperors were rather austere, the Mughals enjoyed great luxury during the times of Jahangir and Shah Jahan. When Jahangir decided to personally supervise the operations against the Deccan sultanate, his army followed by his baggage train and the inevitable camp followers was so large that the whole procession took twelve hours to pass any one particular place, according to the estimate of Edward Terry, the Chaplain who accompanied Sir Thomas Roe.[12] Jahangir himself was dressed in a gold brocade coat with sword and sword belt encrusted with diamonds and other precious stones. His turban with plumes had huge diamonds, rubies and emeralds tacked on. His sash was fitted with a chain strung with pearls, rubies and emeralds. Around his neck was a three ring chain of pearls, and on his arms were gold bands set with diamonds.[13] Around his wrists were bands of similar gold set with all kinds of precious stones. His hands had rings on every finger.

Most sultans, including the cultivated Mughals, often broke out into ungovernable rages when crossed,[14] and during those fits of temper could order the most cruel of punishments. Even lesser men like the successful commander, Mir Jumla, to whom four criminals had been brought for punishment on one occasion, ordered that one should have his feet and hands cut off and left in a field to bleed to death, one should be split open at the stomach and thrown into a drain, and that the two others should have their heads cut off; these sentences pronounced casually in-between other administrative work.

12. Gascoigne Bamber, *The Great Moghals*, under "Jahangir".
13. Ibid. Description by Sir Thomas Roe.
14. Gascoigne Bamber, *The Great Moghals* under "Akbar" and "Jahangir"; Also see Nirad C. Chaudhuri, *Clive of India*, p.21.

These ungovernable rages were the natural reaction of potentates as also individuals who enjoyed unquestioned authority without any opposition for long and hereditary periods. Even today in India, it is common to see such individuals burst out into fits of intense spluttering rage.

Congregational Worship

The individual characteristics of the monarchs were undoubtedly greatly influenced by religion, as were the characteristics of the supporting nobles, commanders and chieftains. The religion of Islam which enjoined on its followers worship five times every day, starting with dawn or early daybreak and ending at late dusk, and the strong recommendation that, unless impossible due to actualities of time and place, these ritual prayers should be conducted according to a particular procedure, altogether, in a congregation at a common place[15] of prayer, brought about a feeling of common interest and unity. The rigidity with which these systems were enforced brought about a habit of discipline practiced by large numbers together.[16]

The early Christian denominations whether Roman Catholic, Armenian, Greek Orthodox or Nestorian, similarly encouraged common worship, togetherness and respect for discipline. Congregational worship brought about a feeling of equality and oneness between the ruler and the ruled.

So also the practice of the Jews with their rigorous disciplines of worship in the synagogues, the compulsion to marry only Jews, and the basic belief that they were the chosen people.

On the other hand, the Hindus who could attain closeness to God by any of thousands of paths of their own choosing and

15. Sir Hamilton A.R. Gibbs, *Mohammedanism*, p. 55.
16. Sir Hamilton A.R. Gibbs, *Mohammedanism*, pp. 12, 13.

by following a rigorous system of self-discipline which glorified and stressed only individual effort, as opposed to common worship, suffered from a lack of collective discipline, and from an attitude of general tolerance. Hence, in the Hindu fold, logical and ethical arguments could be found to justify any action, whether moral or immoral, whether right or wrong. Hence, refraining from action which would entail fighting unfair powerful forces, could always be justified by seemingly impeccable arguments. Unity was difficult as self-interest supervened over the collective interest. So Hinduism generated hundreds and thousands of clever people who could not combine to safeguard the common interest. These characteristics prevented quick, disciplined and concerted action. The numerous factional commanders were jealous of surrendering their independence to an overall common commander, and teamwork in execution of plans was rare. Hindus always fought for the tribal interest or according to tribal or clan code. It was only the Mahrattas under Shivaji who combined to some extent through religious motivation, and that too because of the regular and continued debasement of their religion by the Muslims around them. Other strong motivation for the Mahrattas was gaining and occupying land, and the prospect of plunder.

The Buddhist religion had mainly to offer a path based on rationality, that is, the eight-fold path[17] of right action, right speech, right belief, right thought, and so on. A religion based on rationalism could never tap the roots of faith, that unfathomable, irrational and dynamic force that is the true companion of religion. Similarly, the Jain teaching of ahimsa or refraining from hurting anything living could not be expected to introduce a martial spirit in its followers.

Hence, the deadly purpose of destroying an infidel or pagan enemy could only arise with firm roots in the Christian and

17. A.L. Basham, *The Wonder That Was India*, p. 269.

Muslim religions where its followers were harangued every day by priests or Imams who passionately believed in their mission of either converting or destroying the unbelievers. At one time, it even helped the Jews during the times of Moses, later in the first four or five centuries of the Christian era, and later, during the 20th century, when the Jews at last regained their promised land by fighting against all comers, whether they were the Ottoman Turks, the British or the Arabs.

Religion, therefore, even in modern times, continues to be a formidable force in the groupings of people in contending among themselves. It is no surprise therefore that Islam carried all before it[18] until the intrusions of the Christians equally motivated by faith, but backed now by their mastery of science, technology and a cool rationalism.

Historians are apt to speak of the thousand years of the Muslim period in India, implying that the whole of India was ruled by the Muslims from the 11th to the 20th centuries. This is a misleading overstatement. Discounting the Arab invasion of Sind in 712 A.D. and the extension of Arab dominated territory upto Multan in southern Punjab, which remained confined there for over 300 years until ousted by Mahmud of Ghazni, actual Muslim occupation of India really commenced with the conquests of Muhammed Ghuri and the establishment of the slave dynasty by Qutubuddin Aibak in 1206. The Delhi sultanate had only a tenuous hold, and that over the lands of Punjab, Uttar Pradesh, parts of Bihar, Sind, Gujarat and northern Malwa. The rest of India continued to be ruled by the indigenous monarchs from the Vindhyas to Cape Comorin, until Hasan Gangu established the nucleus of the Bahmani kingdom in 1336 around the area of Bidar. Alla-ud-din Khilji's slave commander Malik Kafur made a spectacular raid down to

18. Through conquerors, Arabs, Turks, Afghans, from Arabia along the southern Mediterranean to Spain and France; through Arab traders and seafarers to Malaya, Indonesia and the Phillipines.

Madurai, but excepting for leaving weak and local governors in some areas, could not consolidate Muslim rule in the Deccan or in the peninsula. Strong kingdoms like the Chalukyas and the Hoysalas, like those of the Cheras and Pandyas, continued to exist independently. During the time of Muhammed-bin-Tughlaq, however, more lasting conquests on the Coromandel coast (Madras coast on the Bay of Bengal) and in Malabar were made, but these conquests became unviable once Tughlaq went back north to deal with rebellions in Gujarat, Sind and Bengal. Later, the Mughals and the Bahmanis ruled India effectively upto the Deccan. But throughout the period, Mewar was independent for all purposes; most of Malwa remained independent for most of the time upto about 1720 after the death of Aurangazeb in 1707. After 1720, the Rajput kings of Ajmer, Marwar and Malwa were independent; Bihar and Bengal were *de facto* independent countries. Karnataka and portions of Andhra south of the Krishna river remained under Hindu kings except for a short period of 40 years when Mysore was ruled by Hyder Ali and Tippu. Even in Uttar Pradesh, Bihar and Bundelkhand, Hindu chieftains and monarchs were in a state of frequent rebellion so that the Muslim writ was hardly law. Muslim domination of India effectively existed in North India for about 600 years and in the central Deccan between Narmada and Tapti for 450 years.[19] Hence, this concept of a thousand years of rule of India by the Muslims is a fallacy promoted by the tendency to compartmentalise the difficult and complicated history of India into the ancient, Muslim and British periods. This is good for historical division of the chronology but in actuality, these periods are only broad categorisations which are not fully true in detail.

As mentioned earlier, the riches and resources of India, together with the warm climate, rendered the Muslim rulers

19. An objective and detailed study of Indian history, from 1000 A.D. onwards, clearly establishes this.

indolent and luxury-loving. Their control of their empires depended to a great extent on a loose organisation of governors of provinces[20] on whom were imposed certain uncompromising demands, firstly on the amount of revenue they had to collect and send to the sultan or emperor, and secondly, on the number of troops they had to send to make up his armies for campaigns. These campaigns were frequent to chastise rebellious or independent-minded governors or to subdue Hindu kings and chieftains who were constantly rising against the emperors somewhere or other. Also, the sons of the sultan or emperor were always manouevring and positioning themselves for the succession to the throne, the conflicts being finally resolved only after costly, long and destructive fratricidal wars.[21] The luxuries of the court and of the provincial governors, and the costly wars denuded and impoverished the countryside so that large parts of hitherto fertile and productive parts of India became wastelands within 600 years of the coming of the Muslims.

A point of interest to be considered is the question of where the wealth of India has gone. The vast quantities of gold and precious stones and jewellery which were carried away by Mahmud of Ghazni and Muhammed Ghuri went to Afghanistan. The looted wealth carried away by Timur to Samarquand and Bukharo, by Nadir Shah to Persia and by Ahmed Shah Abdali to Afghanistan went to those countries. But from there on, where did the wealth go? Meanwhile, within India there probably existed many times the removed wealth in the vaults of the forts of the Mughals, their governors, the Rajput kings and the countless other kings and chieftains in the country from Kashmir to Cape Comorin, and

20. Nirad C. Chaudhuri, *Clive of India*, p. 20.

21. Vincent A. Smith, *The Oxford History of India*, refer the "Khiljis", the "Tughlaks", the "Lodis", "Akbar", "Jahangir", "Shah Jahan", and "Aurangazeb". Also refer the "Later Mughals". Also, other standard histories.

from Sind and Gujarat to Bihar and Bengal, not to speak of Assam. This wealth undoubtedly changed hands with the conquerors and vanquished within the country. Much gold and jewellery was obviously given away in lavish gifts to courtesans, dancers and concubines. Also, much lavish grants were made to the monasteries and religious establishments who perhaps spent it in paying the artisans, the craftsmen and labourers who built the temples and the mosques, the palaces, pavilions and gardens. But most of the money was spent in raising armies and financing military campaigns, in bribing soldiery in the succession wars, in acquiring weapons and horses[22] and in paying for food supplies which had to be obtained through traders. Later on, the British undoubtedly took away a lot of wealth both through their merchants and private individuals who were in positions of power. Much wealth of villagers and traders apparently lies buried underground as the earth was the safest place to hide wealth from raiders. The movement of the wealth down was apparently an inexorable process. Many princes of India, just before 1947, sent away their wealth, in boxes of gold and jewellery, by chartered aircraft to the bank vaults of the United Kingdom and Switzerland. But obviously, much wealth remains in the hands of old trading families and in the underground cellars of the 'havelis' or mansions of old zamindari families. Now it may have been gradually shifted outside the country.

Considering the long period of 600 years after the established rule of the Muslims, the continuous wars, the massacring of local population, considering the excessive taxation, it is indeed a miracle that the civilisation, the arts and crafts of the people and their creative capacity survived and

22. Gascoigne Bamber, *The Great Moghals* under "Babur". Babur in Kabul saw that, every year, 10,000 horses from Persia and Central Asia went to India in return for silks, precious stones, slaves, craftsmen, and so on.

endured. It is a mark of the genius of the Indian people, nurtured in humane values, in all religious denominations, that they survived with the minimum of resources of food, shelter and clothing, and that they continued to practice their arts and crafts. Weaving and dyeing, stonework or metalwork, building and sculpture, or casting metal and fashioning truly unique artistic images and figures, working in gold or silver or copper or iron or bronze, the unobtrusive creativity in the villages and the town mohallahs (streets with protection of barred gates and patrolling residents) never ceased. The village organisation, self-sufficient to itself, fulfilled its own needs and encouraged creative activity right from the women of the homes to the professional artisans of the village. The village organisation was, in fact, transferred to the mohallahs of the towns, and the people administered themselves. The knowledge of the people in all the fields of arts and craftsmanship was the result of profound experience and innovation gathered over generations and passed down from father to son, mother to daughter, and from master-artisan to apprentice. A long tradition of music, both folk and classical, continued to thrive, and a great synthesis of Hindu classical and Muslim stylised forms of poetical and musical expression gradually evolved to form today the core of North Indian classical and semi-classical music and culture. The vigour of the Muslims combined with the intense religious devotion of the Hindus to produce a truly distinctive and original art form of music. The ingenuity in creating a great variety of musical instruments with pumpkin shells and coconut shells, with finely drawn wire, with monkey skins and cane, with hollowed reeds and bamboo pipes, belongs to these peoples untutored in any formal academy, without benefits of air-conditioning or electricity or even financial support. The vidhwans and the ustads with their live-in disciples in the most modest of houses in the village, went ahead and kept alive a great tradition of art which was rooted in an intense culture of religious faith, relieved to some extent by the love of nature around them and the joy of living. They were also influenced by the sheer pleasure of their daily association with the familiar people around them.

Probably, this aspect of Indian life never changed throughout the ages whether in the Hindu period, the Buddhist period, the Muslim period or the British period. And so, control of the sub-continent gradually passed into the hands of a new kind of aliens, this time from beyond the seas.

7

The Decline of the Mughals and the Rise of the British

At the death of Aurangazeb in 1707, India presented a picture of turbulent governors, Hindu princes and chieftains jockeying to establish themselves with the greatest possible extent of autonomy over the largest possible extent of territory around their own centres of power.

Decline of the Mughal Empire

Kandahar and Kabul had been lost irrevocably to the Afghans during the previous rule of Shah Jahan. The newly martial Sikh people were emerging from their mountain refuges in the Kangra and Kumaon hills to reclaim parts of their homelands in Punjab from where they had fled to escape persecution and destruction by the forces of Aurangazeb.[1] The Muslim governors of Sind and Gujarat had become so self-reliant and independent that their support was being solicited by the sons and nephews of Aurangazeb in the inevitable fratricidal wars of succession. The Rajput states with their hill forts that dominated the countryside, were almost completely independent. Mewar which had never acknowledged the suzerainty of the Mughals took back control of its old territories. Marwar, Bikaner, Ajmer which had been friendly and supportive of the Mughals withdrew that support, thus

1. Vincent A. Smith, *The Oxford History of India*, p. 431.

demolishing one of the pillars of Mughal strength. The Afghans of Rohilkhand, the Muslim governors and Hindu princes of the Indo-Gangetic basin and the Muslim governor of Bihar and Bengal were independent in all but name. The old Hindu dynasties ruling in Malwa and Bundelkhand reasserted their control. The Mahrattas who, since Shivaji assumed their leadership in 1642 and cocked a snook at the overwhelming Mughal strength and had established a Hindu state from Surat to Satara in the teeth of Muslim opposition, were poised to expand their territorial extent and power.[2] The Nizam-ul-Mulk with his capital at Gulbarga became virtually independent although he remained, according to his own choice, a governor or feudatory of the emperor at Delhi for another one and a half centuries. In Mysore, the weak Wodeyar dynasty, originally governors to Vijayanagar, continued to reign. In the rest of the Carnatic, the Nawab established by the Mughals at Arcot became independent, but both in Mysore and the Carnatic, Paleygars or local chieftains (nayaks) held sway. Further south, the ancient Hindu kingdoms of the Pandyas, the Cheras, continued their existence in one form or another, almost completely insulated from the goings on in the Deccan and in north India. In east India, Assam, Manipur and Tripura remained independent powers except for a short encounter with the Mughals during the reign of Aurangazeb.

The British

A new element had introduced itself into India, namely, the British. At the death of Aurangazeb, they had already established their fledgling presidencies at Bombay (Mumbai), Madras (Chennai) and Calcutta (Kolkata).[3] The chief of the East India Company established at each of these places was called the president, or sometimes the governor. Hence, the name

2. Nirad C. Chaudhuri, *Clive of India*, p. 26.
3. Ibid., p.44.

Presidency to describe the establishment. Each Presidency was responsible directly to the Court of Directors of the Company in London,[4] and was responsible to develop its own trade with the surrounding countryside, mainly in spices but also in anything that could generate profits. The East India Company was interested only in trade and, at this stage, had no thought of territorial conquest.[5] However, as time passed, the Presidencies found that by dominating the countryside, or by forcing concessions from the local princes, they could increasingly monopolise the export trade in spices, indigo, and later, in raw cotton, precious and semi-precious gemstones, and so on. While initially they paid for their purchases in silver bullion brought from England, later on in response to the opposition in Britain to the drain of bullion, they could pay by barter of milled goods like cotton textiles from Britain. The British were shrewd enough to fortify their factories and the small areas given to them as concessions. Thus, when Shivaji attacked and sacked Surat in 1664, and again in 1670, he could not penetrate and destroy any part of the British factories or fortifications.

The Emperor Bahadur Shah I

Aurangazeb's eldest son, Prince Muazzam succeeded to the throne of Delhi after defeating and killing his younger brother Prince Azam, and assumed the title Bahadur Shah I in June 1707. The imperial treasure at Agra fell into his hands. He also defeated and killed another brother, Kambaksh, near Hyderabad in 1708. Bahadur Shah's reign was notable for the suppression of the Sikh rebellion under Banda who had defeated and revenged the Sikhs[6] on Wazir Khan of Sirhind for persecuting the Sikhs. For the time being, the Sikhs had to

4. Ibid., p. 45.
5. Ibid., p. 17.
6. Vincent A. Smith, *The Oxford History of India*, p. 432.

retreat once again into the hills. Their tenth guru, Gobind Singh had been murdered by an Afghan at Nanded in the Deccan in 1708. Bahadur Shah also defeated the Rajput prince, Ajit Singh of Mewar (Jodhpur), but worn out by the Sikh rebellion and the war against his brother, Kambaksh, he soon died at the age of sixty-nine in 1712.

The Later Mughals

A further period of instability followed with succession wars and the enthronement of the eldest son, Jahandar Shah, and later of his nephew, Farrukshiyar. The latter's reign has importance because of the grant of several trading concessions to the British at Calcutta in 1715.[7] Finally, Muhammed Shah ascended the throne in 1719, and although beset by much intrigue and faction fights (to which he himself was no mean contributor), continued to reign until his death in 1748. Muhammed Shah's reign saw the gradual break-up of the great Mughal empire, although the many independent powers that arose continued to acknowledge the Mughal emperor at Delhi as their sovereign albeit in name only. The Nizam-ul-Mulk became fully independent in 1724, as also Saadat Ali in Oudh at the same time. Alivardi Khan became sovereign in Bengal in 1740 and ruled till 1756, although he continued to remit taxes to Delhi from time to time. Bengal enjoyed great prosperity at this time due to the full development of riverine trade and export and import to the countries of the west which was facilitated by the British East India Company and, to some extent, by the French. In fact, although the Presidency of Calcutta was the last to be established (in 1692 by Job Charnock), during this period it became the most successful among the three Presidencies.

7. Nirad C. Chaudhuri, *Clive of India*, p.21.

The Mahrattas

Meanwhile, the Mahrattas had been having internal struggles of their own. After the death of Shivaji in 1680, his weak successors Sambhaji and later Shahu were overshadowed by the Peshwa (or minister) Balaji Vishwanath who exercised power from 1714 onwards, while the seat of the Raja continued to be Satara. He strengthened the office of Peshwa to such extent that, when he died in 1720, he was succeeded by his equally able son, Baji Rao who made the office of Peshwa a hereditary one. By 1720, the levy of 'chauth' or one-fourth of the revenue due to the Mughal emperor, by the Mahrattas was officially recognised and permitted by Muhammed Shah, with this right extending to the whole of the Deccan. Furthermore, an additional one-tenth of the revenue called 'sardeshmukhi' was allowed to be levied. However, the various Mahratta military chiefs forced the Peshwa to agree to their retaining these levies within their own spheres of authority, except for a small proportion paid into the central coffers for land rights in the home country. Baji Rao consolidated the system of the realisation of revenue through the military chiefs. At the same time, he was the first to exercise vision and see a far greater role for the Mahrattas in the wake of the weakening of the Mughal power. He reorganised the army and directed it towards the territories of north India. Asaf Jah, the Nizam-ul-Mulk occupying central Deccan with his capital at Hyderabad was becoming ambitious, but Baji Rao was successful in countering him and limiting his activities until 1731 when a treaty was signed between the two. The time of Baji Rao saw the rise and strengthening of the Mahratta chiefs of Baroda, Gwalior and Indore, who soon established their own houses and dynasties becoming known as the Gaekwad of Baroda, Scindia of Gwalior and Holkar of Indore. While the Gaekwad had been prominent, Scindia and Holkar were of humble origin and rose as officers of Baji Rao by dint of their own ability. The Mahrattas were well placed to fill the vacuum created by the weakness and disaffection in the Mughal court, and they did not hesitate to exploit the situation. They conquered Gujarat, Malwa, and Bundelkhand, and by 1737 had appeared at the gates of Delhi. However, they refrained from attacking Delhi while they turned their attention to the Deccan to curb Asaf Jah, the Nizam who was defeated and forced to cede territory.[8]

Nadir Shah

At this time, there occurred an intervention in the affairs of India that no one could foresee. Totally preoccupied with their own activities, neither the Mughal emperor, nor anyone else in the country had cast their eyes beyond the northern borders. In 1736, Nadir Shah had overthrown the Safavid dynasty of Persia and usurped the throne. The weakness of the Mughal power in Delhi had already attracted his attention. In 1739, he captured Ghazni and Kabul and invaded Punjab. He captured Lahore and advanced towards Delhi. Thus far, he had not encountered any opposition, but as he approached the Jumna, he met the imperial army barring his way at Karnal, 100 miles from Delhi and not far from Panipat. Within a short while, Nadir Shah had defeated and routed the Mughal army, killing more than 20,000 men in the process. Muhammed Shah felt further resistance to be futile and hastened to offer peace, attending personally on Nadir Shah at his camp. Nadir Shah treated him honourably and allowed him to accompany him to Delhi which they entered together. The city was subdued and orderly until a rumour spread that Nadir Shah was killed. The city rose as one man and slaughtered hundreds of Nadir Shah's troops. However, Nadir Shah quickly controlled the situation and left his imprint on the city by massacring thousands of people

8. Vincent A. Smith, *The Oxford History of India*, p. 436. Also see Nirad C. Chaudhuri, *Clive of India*, where the author cites contemporary writers like Robert Orme who say the Mahrattas of this period were rampant freebooters, p. 30.

irrespective of faith or status and stopped the killing only on Muhammed Shah praying him to desist. He then ordered the plunder of the city which was shorn of nearly all the wealth both of the court and the nobles as well as of the general population. His stay of 58 days in Delhi yielded enormous booty which he carried away unhindered to Persia. Along with all this treasure went the peacock throne of Shah Jahan which was never to return to India.[9] By a treaty concluded with Muhammed Shah in May 1739, he annexed the territory west of the Indus river. Punjab and Sind therefore were again the pawns between the power at Delhi and its rivals beyond the north-west Himalayan passes. The visitation of Nadir Shah can be said to be the real *coup-de-grace* to the effective rule of the Mughal emperor at Delhi.

Peshwa Balaji Rao

Baji Rao, the second Peshwa died in 1740. Of his three sons, the eldest, Balaji Rao succeeded him inspite of opposition from the other Mahratta chiefs who were now quite powerful men. In addition to the Gaekwad, Holkar and Scindia, the fourth chief, Raghoji Bhonsle had captured the Nagpur territories as also Orissa and was knocking at the doors of Bengal.[10] By 1750, Balaji Rao had consolidated his power, established his capital at Poona (Pune), and formed the famous Mahratta confederacy of which he became the head. Every major chief was entitled to land in the old Mahratta homelands of the western ghats (called 'swadeshi' lands), which they forfeited if they disobeyed the central power. The captured lands outside these traditional homelands, called 'moglai' lands could be taxed according to the system of 'chauth' and 'sardeshmukhi'. By 1758, the Mahratta hosts had occupied the whole of Punjab including

9. K.M. Panikkar, *A Survey of Indian History*, p. 235.
10. Vincent A. Smith, *The Oxford History of India*, pp. 438, 489.

MAHRATTA AND BRITISH CONTROLLED TERRITORIES, c. 1760 A.D.

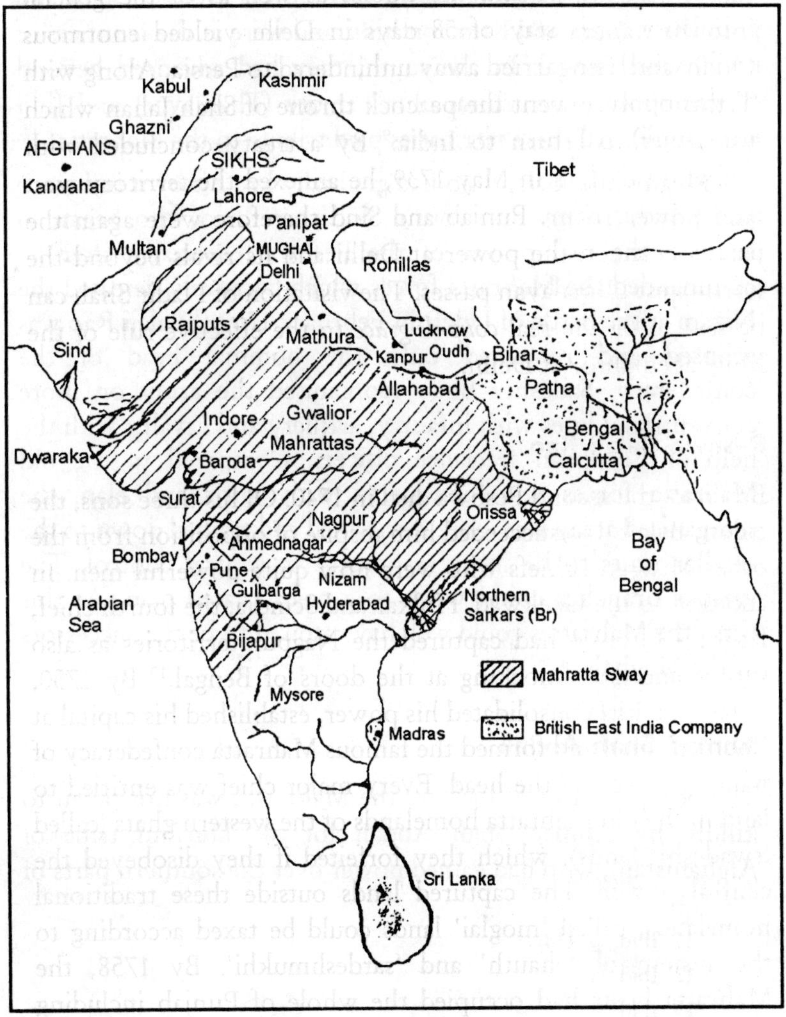

Lahore and spread out beyond Bundelkhand, posing a threat to the Nawab of Oudh (Avadh). At this time Mahratta power was at its height.[11] They had captured the north upto the Indus and the Himalayas, had established their forces around Delhi and into the Kangra and Kumaon hills, and were at the frontiers of Oudh and Bengal. In the south, they had advanced beyond Trichnopoly (Thiruchirapalli), Tanjore (Thanjavur) and Jinji (or Chinji). All these territories paid tribute to the Mahrattas.[12]

Meanwhile, Balaji Rao had gradually lost his own influence and power to his first cousin, Sadashiv Bhao who began to exercise the real power of the Peshwa, especially after he commanded the Mahratta forces which decisively defeated the Nizam at the battle of Udgir in February 1760.[13] Balaji Rao was eclipsed and remained only the nominal head of the confederacy. Sadashiv Bhao reorganised the army on more conventional lines with infantry, artillery and cavalry with the help of European freelance officers. Compared to the old Mahratta forces who conquered with spirit and elan, the reorganised army was more disciplined and trained down to the smaller units to be more responsive to central control. The various branches could work to a co-ordinated plan. At this time, the Mahrattas could well have aspired to be the successors of the Mughals.[14]

Ahmad Shah Abdali

The occupation of Punjab by the Mahrattas was not taken to kindly by Ahmad Shah Abdali (of the Durrani tribe of Afghanistan), who had gained power over the southern parts of

11. Ibid., p. 438.
12. Ibid.
13. Ibid.
14. For example, Raghoji Bhonsle of Nagpur fought Alivardi Khan of Bengal for 7 years and forced him to cede Orissa in 1781 and pay an annual sum of 17 lakhs of rupees. See Nirad C. Chaudhuri, *Clive of India*, p. 35.

Afghanistan including Ghazni and Kandahar. As a successor to Nadir Shah's eastern conquests, he regarded himself as the inheritor of Punjab. He invaded and reoccupied Punjab in 1759. In 1760, Sadashiv Bhao decided to reestablish the power of the Mahrattas and to drive out Ahmad Shah Abdali and his Afghans. The Mahratta army under the nominal command of Viswas Rao, the 17-year-old son of Balaji Rao, the Peshwa, but with Sadashiv Bhao in de-facto control, advanced to Delhi and occupied it. After the rainy season of 1760, Sadashiv Bhao advanced to Panipat and built up his defences there. Ahmad Shah who had encamped near Bulandshar during the rains, advanced across the Jumna and positioned himself, rather disadvantageously for him, about eight miles away, with his communications with the north rendered vulnerable to being cut by the Mahrattas. The Mahrattas did, infact, take advantage of the situation and harassed his communications to an extent where Ahmad Shah was sorely pressed for supplies and reinforcements, but with the boldness and sagacity of a brilliant commander he detached a force which attacked the Mahrattas sitting astride of, and dominating his supply lines, and opened up for himself the routes to his bases. But the Mahrattas themselves had enclosed their main force within, and in the environs of Panipat within a defence ditch all round, and themselves felt the pressures of lack of supplies. In addition to the army, there were over 2,00,000 population and camp followers within the enclosure who also had to be fed. Attempts at cessation of hostilities and a peace treaty offered by the Mahrattas were spurned by Ahmad Shah, so that there was no alternative except to fight.[15]

The Battle of Panipat between the Mahrattas and Ahmad Shah

In January 1761, the Mahrattas launched their forces in massive

15. Vincent A. Smith, *The Oxford History of India*, p. 4-39.

attacks on the Afghans, starting at dawn. Up to noon of the day of battle, the 13th of January, the Mahrattas were pressing the Afghans hard and gaining ground in one of the fiercest of battles. In this situation, Ahmad Shah launched a desperate counter attack with some reinforcement he had received. This unexpected counterattack surprised the Mahrattas who started to give ground. There was every chance of the Mahrattas rallying once they overcame their initial shock when, in the all too frequent such chances in the battles of the Hindus, Viswas Rao was wounded. It is difficult to exactly trace what happened then, but probably those nearest to Viswas Rao turned and fled, and within a few minutes the entire Mahratta forces turned and fled back. No determined generals or captains seemed to have materialised to stem the tide of this surge backwards. This happened about 3 o' clock in the afternoon. Ahmad Shah's forces pursued the Mahrattas relentlessly and are said to have killed more than 2,00,000 of the army, the camp followers and the population of Panipat. This decisive victory of the Afghans dealt a death blow to the Mahratta confederacy which never again regained the same cohesion and unity.[16] Although the Mahrattas continued to be the dominant power for a few more decades, their power no longer was the result of a united front but was more local in nature under the individual chieftains like the Gaekwad, Holkar, Scindia and Bhonsle. The Peshwa from Pune still was the acknowledged head of the Mahrattas, but increasingly only in name.

Ahmad Shah's army consisted of 41,800 cavalry and 38,000 infantry, that is, of nearly 80,000 regular troops and was supported by over 2,00,000 irregular troops and camp followers. The Mahratta army consisted of 55,000 cavalry and 15,000 infantry as regular, trained troops. In addition, they were supported by 15,000 Pindaris who were irregular horsemen accustomed to raiding and plundering in the Malwa

16. Ibid., p. 441.

and Bundelkhand regions, who had attached themselves to the advancing hordes of the Mahratta troops since the late 17th century. The fighting value of the Pindari freebooters in pitched battle was perhaps poor, but they were excellent for harassing the enemy's supply lines. In addition to these troops there were over 2,00,000 camp followers who, finally proved a crippling burden for the Mahratta commanders.[17]

Viswas Rao and Sadashiv Bhao were both killed in the battle, as were many of the best Mahratta commanders and troops. Scindia and Holkar escaped. The severely mauled and disorganised army abandoned their North Indian conquests and fell back to the Narbada river. Although the Mahrattas later regained most of the lost territories, that was under the leadership of the individual Mahratta chieftains.[18]

The Mughal emperor in Delhi was nothing more than a helpless spectator in the cataclysmic events described, which emphasised more than ever the weakness and decay of the once proud Mughal power. Henceforth the Mughal emperor, still nominally acknowledged as such by all the powers, was nothing but a pawn in the hands of whoever happened to dominate the area of Delhi and Agra.

Bengal and the British

While these events were unfolding Alivardi Khan had died in 1756, and his successor, the young and immature Siraj-ud-Daula had precipitated an adverse situation with the British in Bengal. From his capital at Murshidabad, he ventured forth to attack the British at Fort William in Calcutta. He probably did not even realise that his orders regarding the British prisoners were carried out in such a ham-handed and thoughtless way that over a hundred prisoners were said to have been imprisoned in a

17. Ibid., p. 440.
18. K.M. Panikkar, *A Survey of Indian History*, p. 238.

room less that 20 feet square, with a single small window and left there without food or water. The next day it was found that most of the prisoners had died in the room through suffocation, hunger and thirst. This room came to be known as the "Black Hole of Calcutta"[19] which inflamed British feeling not only in the Presidencies but also all over Britain. The incident set in motion a train of events and was probably the single event which suddenly changed the course of Indian history. Robert Clive, already famous as the hero of Arcot, was despatched to organise British forces in Calcutta with the help of a naval contingent from Madras, to confront and wreak vengeance on the Nawab Siraj-ud-Daula. The British forces met the Nawab's army on the field of Plassey (Palasi) in 1757 and inflicted a crushing defeat, helped greatly by the treachery of the Nawab's dewan Mir Jafar who at the last moment refrained from attacking the British.[20] According to the secret agreement, Mir Jafar was to be rewarded by the British with the Nawab's throne. Siraj-ud-Daula was defeated and killed, the British imposed their will on the whole of the rich province of Bengal, and the first involuntary step was taken for the ultimate conquest of India by Britain.

The British Progress

The Portuguese were the first to land in India in pursuit of the spice trade. Spices had become popular in Europe through Arab and European traders and were much sought after for the preservation of meat and for adding flavour to food.[21] Vasco da Gama landed at Calicut after a long voyage down the West Coast of Africa and after rounding the Cape of Good Hope. He

19. Geoffrey Moorhouse, *India Britannica*, pp. 45, 46.
20. Geoffrey Moorhouse, *India Britannica*, p. 46. Also see Vincent A. Smith, *The Oxford History of India*, p. 468.
21. Geoffrey Moorhouse, *India Britannica*, p. 27.

landed in 1498 and met the Zamorin ("Samoodhri" or "Lord of the seas") of Calicut and managed to obtain land for a trading post.[22] Whether by intention or accident, he had landed at the right spot, for Calicut had a huge hinterland where spices grew in natural profusion. Cardamom, pepper, cinnamon, clover and chillies were available. By 1510, the Portuguese with their superior naval power had fended off Arab traders and had captured a base for themselves in Goa from where they could have easy access to the bountiful Konkan and Malabar coasts.[23] Within a few years Alfonso de Albuquerque had established sea bases in Madagascar, Ormuz (entrance to the Gulf), Cochin (Kochi), Ceylon (Sri Lanka), Sumatra, Malacca and in Diego Garcia, controlling all from his base in Goa, and thus dominated the Indian Ocean, the Arabian Sea, and the entrance to the Bay of Bengal.[24] Under the protection of the navy, the Portuguese carried on a lucrative trade, making huge profits by the sale of their goods in Europe. However, their interest in trade was overshadowed by the desire of the powerful Roman Catholic clergy to spread their faith in what they called the "heathen lands".[25] Much of their efforts were pursued by the use of force and repression of the coastal peoples with whom they came in contact, and hence they were much feared and disliked. Yet, they established settlements further north along the coast at Bassein, Daman and Diu, and could send emissaries to the court of emperor Akbar at Agra, both for availing trading concessions and to familiarise the emperor with the Christian faith. They also established trading ports on the Hooghly in Bengal. However, although they monopolised the Indian trade, and trade with China and Japan, for a hundred

22. Ibid., p. 27.
23. Ibid., p. 28.
24. K.M. Panikkar, *A Survey of Indian History*, p. 223.
25. Geoffrey Moorhouse, *India Britannica*, p. 28.

years in the 16th century and even up to about 1610, events in Europe and their expanding empire in South America rendered their efficiency and their power in India increasingly weak.

They were soon eclipsed by the Dutch and the British who had gradually acquired greater sea-faring skills than before by ranging the Atlantic Ocean in the 16th century. In both these countries, companies were formed with monopoly granted to them by their governments for carrying on the so-called East Indian trade. Gradually, the trade in spices was supplemented by trade in cotton and piece-goods, in gold and ivory. The Dutch showed little interest in India with a major trading station only at Chinsura up the Hooghly river. They captured the trade in the spice islands later to be known as the Dutch East Indies, and later still, as Indonesia, Borneo, New Guinea. The Dutch fought off British efforts to get in there by a series of naval victories and by the action at Amboyna[26] (Ambon). The British were, however, able to win a major share of trade with India.

The British East India Company was granted a charter by Queen Elizabeth I in 1600. By 1612, they had obtained the settlement at Surat from emperor Jahangir, consequent on their demonstration of superior sea power by defeating the Portuguese off Surat.[27] By 1615, they had driven out the Portuguese from Ormuz at the mouth of the Persian Gulf and started expanding the port of Bandar Abbas at the mouth of the Red Sea. Henceforth, the Muslim pilgrim traffic between India and Arabia was freed from the attacks and exactions of the Portuguese navy and the Arab pirates, and was under the protection of the British navy. So also, sea-trade between India and Persia, Arabia and the east coast of Africa. In return for this benevolent protection, the British could win trading concessions, monopolies and settlements in India on payment of nominal taxes. The Madras (Chennai) settlement was started

26. Vincent A. Smith, *The Oxford History of India*, p. 332.

27. Geoffrey Moorhouse, *India Britannica*, p. 29.

in 1640 where later on Fort St George was built. In 1661, the island of Bombay (Mumbai) was given as part of the dowry of Catherine of Braganza on her marrying Charles II of England, and was given in 1665 as a settlement to the East India Company. In 1650 the emperor Shah Jahan allowed the British to set up a trading post in Bengal. By 1690, Job Charnock had established the settlement of Calcutta where he started constructing Fort William in 1696.[28] The fort was completed only in 1716. Calcutta proved the most fruitful centre for trade as the British could tap from there the trade of the very rich province of Bengal, as also of Bihar and Orissa which were added to the kingdom of Bengal by Murshid Quli Khan and his son Shuja-ud-Daula. These princes enjoyed complete independence except for the annual payment of Rs. 52 lakhs to the Mughal emperor at Delhi (Farrukhshiyar, 1713-1719). The trade was in cotton and silk textiles, sugar, yarn and saltpetre, of which last was greatly in demand for the wars in Europe.[29]

By 1700, the three Presidencies of Madras, Bombay and Bengal had been established by the British, the Presidencies so called because the chief of the settlement was called the President, or sometimes the Governor. Each Governor was responsible directly to the Court of Directors of the East India Company in London, he being responsible for the development of trade, for the administration of the factory (where goods were packed and kept ready for loading on to merchantmen or trading ship bound for England and where goods arriving from England were stored and distributed to Indian merchants), and for the development of profits and the rendering of accounts. Considering the propensity of local Indian rulers to attack and raid areas where they could plunder and obtain booty, the settlements developed their own defensive capability merely by ensuring that all British personnel were trained to fight, at least

28. Ibid., p. 32.
29. Vincent A. Smith, *The Oxford History of India*, p. 465.

defensively. The Company Directors allowed the trading settlements to fortify themselves. Thus, although Shivaji raided and sacked the rich port town of Surat, he was not successful in raiding and sacking the company factory there.[30] The factory establishment consisted of the President, senior merchants, junior merchants, factors and writers.[31] The writers were clerks responsible for account book entries, copying documents and so on, their salary being £5 per year. Managers of smaller factories were paid £40 or thereabouts per year like the manager of the factory at Dacca (Dhaka), now in Bangladesh.[32] However, these officials were allowed to engage in private trade to supplement their income, provided they did not trade in those goods which were reserved for the company by monopoly rights granted by the local potentates.

The government at London had no intentions of conquests in India at that time. They were fully occupied with European politics of the period, the war of the Austrian succession in 1743, and the Seven Years' War in 1746, and so on. But, as many important men of the ruling groups had invested in the East India Company which, in the initial 120 years or so, sold its goods in Europe at huge profits, sometimes as much as 2500 percent, the British navy protected the sea lanes and sometimes, the Army sent out some battalions and regiments to India to protect the Company properties. Furthermore, India was unlike other countries conquered at one time or other by the British, in that it was peopled by inhabitants steeped in old civilisations, Hindu, Muslim, Buddhist and Jain, and controlled by monarchies seemingly well-organised and dynasties which ruled for centuries. The country was vast, and any attempt to

30. Vincent A. Smith, *The Oxford History of India*, p. 415. The raid occurred in 1664.
31. Nirad C. Chaudhuri, *Clive of India*, p. 45.
32. Ibid. Also Vincent A. Smith, *The Oxford History of India*, p. 518.

conquer it would eat up vast resources. The time was not yet when the British had learnt to acquire territories in India by encouraging the Indians to fight themselves, and intervening at a suitable time with relatively fewer troops of high discipline and motivation.

The French

The French were late-comers to the India trade and arrived only in 1668. While the East India Company (henceforth referred to as the Company) had factories at Bombay with subsidiary ones at Surat and Malabar, at Madras with subsidiary ones at Vizagapatam (Vishakapatnam) and Cuddalore, and at Calcutta with subsidiary ones at Patna, Dacca and Kasimbazaar, the French only decided to enter India during the time of Henry IV in a tentative way. The French minister Colbert organised the Oriental Indies Company in 1664[33] and obtained the settlement of Pondicherry in 1674[34] on the Coromandel coast. However, France was embroiled in the wars in Europe of the Sun King Louis XIV and hence could not militarily support French ventures in India. Nevertheless, some trade was developed, and by 1740, Pondicherry had ben fortified and subsidiary trading posts had been set up at Chandernagore up the Hooghly, Masulipatam on the Coromandel coast, and in Malabar.[35] Some military and naval backing was available from Mauritius (Ile de France) and Reunion (Ile de Bourbon) islands in the Indian Ocean. French trade continued from these bases but did not pose any threat to the British Company just yet. Also British sea-power, always at the support of the Company, was superior to anything the French could produce in the region at the time. Hence co-existence was easy. But the French governor of Pondicherry, Dupleix, who had risen by formal

33. Vincent A. Smith, *The Oxford History of India*, p. 456.
34. Ibid.
35. Ibid.

services with the French Company saw the possibilities of an empire in South India controlled by the French. The feuding and succession wars among the Nawabs of the Carnatic, the instability of the Nizam's domains on the death of Nizam Asaf Jah in 1748,[36] were all fertile grounds for Dupleix's plans for capturing or dominating south India on behalf of France. The Nawab of the Carnatic, Dost Ali with his capital at Trichnopoly was getting ready to capture part of the Nizam's domains on the death of Nizam Asaf Jah who had grown very old, but the Mahrattas had other plans. They intervened in the Carnatic, killing Dost Ali and capturing Trichnopoly and capturing Tanjore together with its ruler Chanda Sahib, a son-in-law of Dost Ali. Safdar Ali succeeded Dost Ali but was murdered by his cousin Murtaza Ali in 1742. The old Nizam, however, reimposed his control by taking Trichnopoly and placing one of his own officers, Anwar-ud-din Khan, as the Nawab in 1743.[37]

Dupleix, appointed Governor of Pondicherry in 1742,[38] with the aid of Bourdonnais, the French naval commander located at Mauritius of which he was the Governor, defeated the British off Madras which was captured by the French[39] in 1746. Madras remained in French hands. Although the British with a fleet from the Hooghly besieged Pondicherry, they were not successful in taking the town. On the other hand, Dupleix besieged Fort St David south of Pondicherry but could not succeed in reducing it as a British fleet arrived to prevent him.[40] However, by the news of peace in Europe signed at Aix-la-Chapelle, Madras was returned to the British in exchange for Cape Breton island in north America returned to the

36. K.M. Panickkar, *A Survey of Indian History*, p. 239.

37. Vincent A. Smith, *The Oxford History of India*, p. 459.

38. K.M. Panickkar, *A Survey of Indian History*, p. 239.

39. Ibid.

40. Vincent A. Smith, *The Oxford History of India*, p. 459.

French. But Dupleix continued to interfere in the politics of the Deccan. A French force under Bussy was despatched to Hyderabad to weigh the scales in support of one contender or other, finally putting on the throne Salabat Jang who became Nizam in 1750. As a result of this intervention, the French received large grants of money. In the Carnatic, Dupleix had defeated in battle and killed Anwar-ud-din Khan, the viceroy of the old Nizam Asaf Jah in the Carnatic. His son Muhammad Ali then shut himself up in Trichnopoly where he was sustained by the British from Madras. Chanda Sahib of Tanjore had already been released and restored to his throne by the Mahrattas. Within a few years, Dupleix had advanced considerably towards realisation of his ambition of dominating south India starting from nothing.[41]

Robert Clive

Meanwhile, Robert Clive had arrived in England in 1744[42] as a writer of the Company, the lowest job available carrying an annual salary of £5 only. He was the son of an impoverished squire and faced the prospect of long years of service in the Company with little prospect of worthwhile advancement. A writer had to serve five years before he could be considered for the job of factor. A factor had to serve three years before he could aspire to be selected as a junior merchant. A junior merchant[43] had to serve three years before he became a senior merchant. A senior merchant had to serve at least ten years before he could hope to be selected for the powerful post of senior minister-in-council. Above that post was the president or governor, appointed directly by the Court of Directors. He could aspire and work for these posts all those years provided

41. Ibid., p. 461.
42. Nirad C. Chaudhuri, *Clive of India*, p. 44.
43. Ibid., p. 45.

he did not die by sickness and disease. Nearly 60 per cent of the staff of the Company died within a few years of service in India.[44] Clive was a stripling of eighteen years of age when he set out,[45] and he served in Fort St George in Madras. As one of the young men on the spot, he also underwent some military training as he had to participate in the defence of the Company properties. The French set out in 1751 to besiege Trichnopoly where Muhammed Ali, the ruler of the Carnatic had enclosed himself. The British sent a small force under Gingens to relieve the pressure on Muhammed Ali. However, Clive with 210 men persuaded his commander to allow him to capture Arcot, between Madras and Trichnopoly. Arcot was an important fort from where Dupleix's communication could be harassed. The French diverted part of their forces to invest Arcot where Clive held out for fifty days in September and October 1751.[46] The diversion of French forces allowed Muhammad Ali to win allies, namely, Mysore, Tanjore and the Mahratta chief Morari Rao. The threat of the French, and the momentum they had generated for either taking over south India, or at least, for exercising a predominant influence in the peninsula was permanently broken. Dupleix was recalled to France in 1754.

But Clive's career had been launched with Arcot. Learning all that he could of military science and art of the day from the old, experienced soldier, Stringer Lawrence at Madras, he had become a major military asset to the British at Fort St George.[47] He was allowed to resume a mercantile post he had been offered before the siege of Arcot, as a supplier of provisions for the Company troops at Madras in partnership with another Englishman, Robert Orme. Within two years, he could proceed

44. Geoffrey Moorhouse, *India Britannica*, p. 35.
45. Ibid., p. 44.
46. Vincent A. Smith, *The Oxford History of India*, p. 462.
47. Nirad C. Chaudhuri, *Clive of India*, p. 99.

to England on leave with his wife, having recently married, and a fortune of £40,000[48] as his share of the profits both in his business and the country trade, that is, the trade which Company servants were allowed to enter into with local businessmen without affecting the Company's regular business.

Having obtained an ensign's commission at Trichnopoly, before his capture and defence of Arcot, he returned to India from his English sojourn in 1755 as a Lieutenant Colonel posted as second-in-command of the company forces in South India.[49] Meanwhile, in England, he had also been able to become a member of Parliament for one of the boroughs, winning the election by 5 votes in a total voting electorate of 55. Rumours were rife that most of his votes were bought.[50] After his return he showed a talent for political matters by arranging an alliance with the Mahrattas to destroy a pirate stronghold from where both Company and Mahratta shipping were being attacked and plundered.[51]

Clive and Bengal

Then in June 1756 happened the "Black Hole of Calcutta". Nawab Siraj-ud-Daula, but recently succeeded to the seat of Alivardi Khan, held the imperial 'firman' for the control of Bengal, Bihar and Orissa, the last two states added by Alivardi Khan. Provided he paid Rs. 52 lakhs every year to the Mughal emperor at Delhi (who during the period hardly had the strength to enforce his firmans), he could generally do whatever he liked. According to old practice, the British were to pay customs dues and taxes on their traded goods. Due to disputes on the payments, Siraj-ud-Daula marched on Fort William with

48. Geoffrey Moorhouse, *India Britannica*, p. 45.
49. Ibid.
50. Ibid.
51. Ibid.

a force of 30,000 infantry, 20,000 cavalry and 400 elephants along with 80 cannon. The British who had no resources to resist him fled, but a handful were captured. The Nawab merely ordered that the prisoners who were 64 in number should be locked up for the night. Unfortunately, the subordinate who carried out the order, locked them up in a small room which he could find, and which, it turned out, had always been called the Black Hole as it had only one small window.[52] The date was June 20th, 1756, an oppressively hot day. The next day, when the room was unlocked, it was found that out of 64 persons locked up, 43 had died due to suffocation, hunger and thirst. However, John Zephaniah Holwel, a council member and survivor propagated the story that 146 people had been locked up inside and only 23 had survived, the rest including some women having died. This story called "The Black Hole of Calcutta" spread rapidly to all the British presidencies, but most important back to England and so inflamed the passions of the British against the inhuman treatment by the Nawab that all parties were universally of opinion that vengeance should be wreaked on the Nawab at the earliest. Clive was sent with a naval force and marines. He recaptured Fort William without difficulty, and further, sailed up the Hooghly towards Murshidabad, the Nawab's rich capital.

The Battle of Plassey

Within a year, in 1757, he confronted the Nawab's forces on the field of Plassey, but not before taking some characteristic precautions. He subverted the Nawab's principal minister, Mir

52. "In India, and oriental countries, generally, more cruelty is perpetrated and suffering inflicted through negligence, indifference and inefficiency than through deliberate brutality." See Nirad C. Chaudhuri, *Clive of India*, p. 189.

Jafar who desired to himself become the Nawab, and arranged that after the defeat of the Nawab, Mir Jafar would be installed as Nawab. This was conditional to Mir Jafar ensuring that his own forces backed out of attacking the British in the battle. The two forces met at Plassey. Clive had 800 Europeans and 2200 Indians while the Nawab had assembled a force of 50,000 ill-coordinated troops.[53] After a prolonged cannonade Major Kilpatrick advanced on his own initiative.[54] Somehow, this unexpected move after the cannonade seemed to have frightened Siraj-ud-Daula or his commanders. The Nawab, a vain and arrogant stripling of 20 years age, fled the field of battle. Mir Jafar, who had kept aloof according to the plan hatched with Clive, arrived next day, to be installed on the 28th of June as Nawab at Murshidabad. Siraj-ud-Daula, who had fled to Bihar, was captured by Mir Jafar's son and executed forthwith.

The Domination of Bengal by the Company

This battle, or non-battle, of Plassey simply transformed the British into the most powerful force in Bengal, Bihar and Orissa. The new Nawab, Mir Jafar, owing his throne to Clive, could not refuse him anything. There ensued for the next several years the most systematic plundering of Bengal by the British. As reward for the Britishers, starting with Clive, Mir Jafar bestowed huge sums of money on all the important officers, military and civil, freed the Company from the requirement of paying customs duties and taxes (which Indian and other merchants were required to pay), and allowed the Company officers additional concessions for Company trade as also for private trade. In fact, although the exemption of duties and taxes was granted only for the Company, its officers

53. Vincent A. Smith, *The Oxford History of India*, p. 468. Also see Nirad C. Chaudhuri, *Clive of India*, p. 269.

54. Ibid.

appropriated the same exemptions for their own trade. For the battle where only a little over 3000 company troops were involved, the compensation that Mir Jafar had to pay amounted to £1,87,000 to the Company; £2,75,000 to the Army; £2,11,500 to Clive; and about £3,89,000 to the various officers of the Company, to each a share in accordance with the importance of his role both in the battle and in the events leading up to the battle, as also according to the pressure and influence the individual officer could exercise on his superiors. In addition, Clive was given a lifetime payment of £27,000 per year which he drew even in England until his death. The presents to the British in 1757 alone amounted to £12,39,000 and between 1757 and 1781 they totalled £47,50,000.[55] This was at a time when the chief of the British factory at Dacca was paid £40 per annum, and a writer's pay was only £5 per annum as salary.

The Company itself gained little or nothing except through the normal trade, as mentioned already, in cotton and silk goods, in sugar, spices and in saltpetre for all of which it held a monopoly, and which was paid for in bullion brought from England. Neither the Company nor the British Government viewed these events with any enthusiasm. The Company saw a large share of its trade being diverted to private or individual hands. The Government was placed in the position of supporting these exploits with ships and trained troops at a time when it had just coped with the war of the Austrian succession and the Seven Years' War.[56] Also it was facing severe discord with the American colonies which declared their independence in 1776, and was soon to be confronted with the French revolution and its fallout. Conquests in India were discouraged. Also, there was considerable envy of, and opposition to the new-rich Company officers who built or acquired palatial mansions and bought up extensive and

55. Geoffrey Moorhouse, *India Britannica*, p. 48. Also see Nirad C. Chaudhuri, *Clive of India*, p. 284.

56. Vincent A. Smith, *The Oxford History of India*, p. 474.

valuable properties in Britain. They had acquired the appellation of "the Nabobs".[57] The Court of Directors of the Company as well as the Government felt that something had to be done to restrain the Company officers in India and to restore the company to its chartered duties instead of interfering in the politics of India.

Although Clive, who had become Governor of Bengal and later returned to Britain due to ill-health, was sent out again with clear instructions to control the situation, he could not do much. He passed a law that Company officers would be committing an offence if they accepted any more presents, but officers found ways and means to avoid compliance. Also the Nawab of Oudh, desiring protection from the Rohilla Afghans who had occupied some of the areas north of the Ganges, entered into a treaty with Clive whereby Company troops were located with Oudh to discourage attack on the province from outside, the cost of the troops and their maintenance being borne by the Nawab.[58] This was the forerunner of the subsidiary treaties which were so successfully concluded by the Marquis of Wellesley a few decades later. Clive also placed Najim-ud-Daula, the son of Mir Jafar, as the Nawab consequent on the defeat of Mir Kasim at the decisive battle of Buxar near Patna and apart from providing protection to Shuja-ud-Daula of Oudh, managed to reinstate the refugee Mughal emperor Shah Alam on the seat of Delhi.[59] The result was the appointment of the Company to the Diwani of Bengal, thus eventually rendering Najim-ud-Daula totally ineffective. However, Clive ensured that the Company confined its territorial domain to Bihar and Bengal, and created a buffer state in Oudh which was designed to insulate the two provinces from the Mahrattas and the Afghans of Rohilkhand. Instead of

57. Geoffrey Moorhouse, *India Britannica*, p. 49.

58. Vincent A. Smith, *The Oxford History of India*, p. 476.

59. Ibid.

reducing territorial responsibilities, he increased them. Although he won concessions from the Mughal emperor and established a virtual monopoly for Company trade in Bihar and Bengal, he could not completely do away with the private trade or the 'country trade' of the Company officials. In spite of vigorously restricting private trade, of forcing erring officials to either resign or comply with his measures, in spite of reducing expenses of the Company on allowances to officers and of enforcing a firmer rule, the acceptance of presents in return for favours done and the country trade continued,[60] although more covertly and less rampantly. In spite of all his efforts, the Company faced near-bankruptcy when Clive returned to Britain finally in 1767.

But his vision and forceful, energetic personality had established Company rule over two of the richest provinces of India with the advantage of riverine communications for their full exploitation by trade. He was the first empire builder in India, bold and buccaneering by nature, who showed the way to his successors as to how Indian kings and princes, controlling quite powerful kingdoms consisting of people sophisticated in politics, martial arts, trade, religion and literature, could be manipulated and exploited for the advantage of the British in acquiring land, dominating trade, and deriving heavy profits. However, in spite of his considerable successes, he had to face inquiry proceedings in his own country.[61] Although, he emerged officially unscathed he appears to have suffered from the bitter fight against his tormentors, notably Colonel Burgoyne, the chairman of the Select Committee of Parliament inquiring into the charges against Clive. Also, although a famous and rich man, admired for his achievements, he does not seem to have been able to enter the more aristocratic levels of British society where he did not belong. He had after all, been granted an Irish peerage considered inferior to an English

60. Ibid., p. 477.

61. Ibid., p. 478.

one.[62] These disappointments, along with an increasing addiction to opium, ostensibly in order to relieve his rheumatic and arthritic pains, seem to have driven him to commit suicide, the ultimate contradiction in the nature of a man of action which he had undoubtedly proved himself to be.

The Struggle for Supremacy Among the Indian Powers

From about 1750 to about 1810, northern India witnessed the struggle for supremacy between the Afghans, the Mughals and the Mahrattas. While the Afghans retained control over Punjab and Sind which they reckoned as their own, they also raided Delhi under Ahmad Shah Abdali. Also the Rohilla Afghans north of the Ganges river raided frequently into Oudh and interfered in the Delhi area from time to time.[63] The Mughal emperor Najib-ud-Daula as also his successors notably Shah Alam were largely only nominally in control except for short periods.

The Mahratta hosts advanced rampantly into Rajasthan, Punjab, Oudh and Bihar and even upto the borders of Bengal. In spite of the serious setback they received at the hands of Ahmad Shah Abdali (Durrani) in 1761 at the battle of Panipat, they continued to dominate these areas although in a less cohesive manner. This was because, after the battle of Panipat, the central control of the Peshwas over the Mahratta chieftains weakened dramatically. The great Mahratta chiefs, Gaekwad of Baroda, Holkar of Indore, Scindia of Gwalior and Bhonsle of Nagpur became virtually independent, levying taxes as they desired, establishing their own dynastic succession, and following their own individual policies. Occasionally they combined together as when they defeated the Nizam-ul-Mulk, Asaf Jah at the battle of Kharda in 1795, but their confederacy fell apart immediately thereafter as a result of their endless

62. Nirad C. Chaudhuri, *Clive of India*, p. 326.

63. Vincent A. Smith, *The Oxford History of India*, p. 487.

disputes and dissensions.[64]

The Mughal power could not re-establish control over the empire which broke up. The Rohillas became virtually independent. The Nawab, Saadat Khan, of Oudh was another to become independent although he continued to regard the Mughal emperor as his overlord in name. Alivardi Khan of Bengal also became independent in spite of irregularly transmitting to the emperor his tribute every year. The Nizam at Hyderabad, who like all his successors until 1926, regarded himself as only a governor of the Mughal emperor, was independent for all practical purposes. The emperor had no control over the Rajput states of Jaipur, Jodhpur, Udaipur or Mewar. These states and innumerable others remained independent although in a condition of decline and decay, and although frequently harassed and preyed upon by the Mahrattas. The Sikhs had come down from their mountain refuges in the Kumaon and Garhwal areas and established their own principalities and kingdoms in Punjab, like Lahore in 1764 and Patiala in 1767. The Amirs of Sind still were under fealty to the Afghans and paid taxes annually to the Afghan king at Kabul. Apart from the Delhi and Agra areas, the Mughal emperor had no control over any other area. However, it suited everyone, including the Mahrattas and the British who had assumed the Diwani of Bengal, after 1757, to acknowledge the emperor at Delhi as the ultimate temporal authority on whose behalf they acted.[65] The Bahmani kingdoms had been defeated one by one and obliterated firstly by Aurangazeb, then by the Nizam and the Mahrattas. From the period of about 1780, the Mughal emperors continued at Delhi in a titular role until the last was pensioned off and exiled after the end of the Mutiny in 1858.

64. Ibid., p. 487.

65. Ibid., p. 484.

The Rise of the British

On the other hand, the British gradually exercised greater influence in all the three Presidencies of Bengal, Bombay and Madras. The East India Company and its officers exercised greater powers in the captured territories of Bengal and Bihar. They maintained small but disciplined, well equipped armies in Bombay and Madras breaking Portuguese and French armies and navies. They could dominate the hinterland of the ports and imposed unfavourable terms of trade on the local merchants, and monopolised commerce in salt, cotton, spices, saltpetre, indigo and so on. British sea-power commanded exits and entrance into the Arabian Sea, the Bay of Bengal and the northern areas of the Indian Ocean. The French bases at Ile de France (old Dutch island of Mauritius) and the Ile de Bourbon (old Portuguese island of Reunion) had been captured and the French navies destroyed. The period between 1750 and 1810 saw the French threat under Dupleix and Admiral de Bussy finally laid to rest with Wellesley's bringing the Nizam under the subsidiary treaty system and getting the French troops and officers helping the Nizam disbanded.

Warren Hastings

Although the East India Company continued to enjoy monopoly trade, keeping out not only companies of other European countries but also other interested companies of Great Britain, the private trade indulged in by the Company officers and the acceptance of gifts by them were drastically curbed by Warren Hastings.[66] Warren Hastings who had risen through the ranks of the Company became Governor of Bengal in 1772. A bright administrator and diplomat, he persuaded the Court of Directors of the company and Pitt the younger, Prime Minister of Britain, to pass the Regulating Act of 1773 which

66. Geoffrey Moorhouse, *India Britannica*, p. 56.

was to apply for the next twenty years and the (Pitt's) India Act of 1784. By this Act of Parliament, the political and commercial activities of the Company were separated by bringing the political arena under the control of a Board of Governors whose members were appointed by Parliament.[67] The court of directors of the Company continued to dictate policy to the Company in financial and commercial matters. This was the time when the war of the Austrian succession in Europe as well as the Seven Years' War there had just been tided over. A major problem had manifested itself in the American colonies of Britain in the form of the war for American independence, and Pitt had his hands full. Military adventurism in India was not to be encouraged, especially as it had hitherto been seen as a means by which the Company officers could indulge in trade over wider areas principally for their own individual benefit[68] for which troops and ships were sucked in from Britain. Warren Hastings was given the brief to refrain from military actions with neighbouring Indian powers unless it was to safeguard the material possessions of the Company and the well-being of its personnel. His powers were widened by making him Governor General in 1774 with a council of three appointed members to advise him and approve his orders. This council of four, including the Governor General and presided over by him, deliberated all measures before passing them for executive action. Any orders passed by the Governor General, or any action taken by him under exigent circumstances, had to be ratified by the council by majority vote.[69]

Warren Hastings is regarded as the second great empire builder in India. What Clive achieved by bold military action,

67. Bisheshwar Prasad, *Bondage and Freedom 1707 to 1947*, Vol. I, "Bondage, 1707-1858", pp. 372, 373.

68. Ibid., p. 368.

69. Vincent A. Smith, *The Oxford History of India*, pp. 504, 505.

Hastings achieved by shrewd diplomatic moves. He consolidated the Diwani of the Company over Bengal and Bihar by which it was empowered to collect revenue from these states by the Mughal emperor in return for a payment of Rs. 52 lakhs per annum. By continuing the old tradition in collection of revenue, by imposing the salt tax, at a reduced rate, on all merchants both Indian and European equally, by reducing the revenue and customs collection centres to five, that is, Calcutta, Patna, Dhaka, Hooghly and Murshidabad and stimulating commerce, by reducing pension payments to the Nawab at Murshidabad from 32 lakhs to 15 lakhs, and by greatly reducing private trade and the acceptance and canvassing of private gifts, he enhanced the profits of the Company from a negative amount of £1.5 million in 1772 to £13.5 million by 1785 when he left for England on retirement.[70]

However, Hastings could not fully avoid military involvement with Indian powers. Before he arrived, the then independent presidencies of Bombay and Madras had already got involved in wars with the Mahrattas, and with the Nizam and Hyder Ali respectively. Oudh already had a Company force located within it in continuing the policy of Clive when the latter was Governor of Bengal in 1765. Oudh was maintained by Clive's and later by Hastings policy, as a buffer state against the restive Afghans and the Mahrattas. The Mahrattas had recovered from their defeat by Ahmad Shah Abdali in 1761, and in 1769 they forayed north across the Narmada and threatened Oudh. But the presence of a British brigade made them pause. However, they persuaded Shah Alam, a claimant to the Mughal throne who was in refuge at Allahabad, to return to Delhi under their protection and occupy the throne rendered vacant by the death of Najib-ud-Daula. The *quid pro quo* was the ceding of Kora and Allahabad, both within Oudh, to the Mahrattas. Hastings averted war but helped Oudh prevent the transfer of these two

70. Ibid., p. 503. Also see Geoffrey Moorhouse, *India Britannica*, p. 60.

important towns to the Mahrattas. At the same time, the Rohilla Afghans who were protected from the Mahrattas by the forces of Oudh under Shuja-ud-Daula and the Company refused to pay Rs. 40 lakhs which they had agreed to pay for the services rendered. War was declared against the Rohillas who were defeated at the battle of Miranpur Katra in 1774, and Rohilkhand was absorbed in Oudh. Hastings had succeeded in augmenting and empowering Oudh so that it continued to remain an effective buffer state for the defence of Bihar and Bengal.

Also, Benares was annexed to the Company's territories. The Regulating Act of 1773 had empowered the Governor General to supervise and direct the affairs of Bombay and Madras Presidencies in addition to that of Bengal.[71] Hastings proceeded to extricate them both from their involvement with the neighbouring powers. In the Mahratta succession disputes in the court of the Peshwa at Pune, one of the parties appealed to the Company at Bombay to intervene on his behalf. The price the Company at Bombay demanded was the grant of the Salsette island and of Bassein which were coveted by the Portuguese at Goa. In spite of refusal by Raghunath, the supplicant, the Bombay authority seized Salsette. In March 1775, the Bombay council concluded a treaty with Raghunath at Surat by which they promised 2500 English troops to restore Raghunath to the Peshwaship at Pune in return for Salsette and Bassein and additional compensation in cash, and promises to check the Mahrattas from raiding Bengal and the Carnatic. While Hastings backed up by the council intervened to repudiate the Treaty of Surat, the Directors from London ordered that the Treaty should be revived and Raghunath supported. This led to four years of an inconclusive war with the Mahrattas during which Company forces suffered some

71. Bisheshwar Prasad, *Bondage and Freedom 1707 to 1947*, Vol. I, "Bondage, 1707-1858", p. 368.

reverses. However, Hastings extricated the Company from the fruitless campaign by the Treaty of Salbai in 1782[72] by which Raghunath was pensioned off by the Peshwa, the lands taken by the Company from the Gaekwad of Baroda and Scindia of Gwalior were restored, but by which Salsette was retained by the Company. Thus the Mahratta confederacy was neutralised and prevented from interfering with the Company activities, especially in relation to the matters relating to the Madras Presidency as mentioned below.

The Madras council had got itself into difficulties in 1779-80 as the major three powers of the Deccan, namely the Nizam of Hyderabad, the Mahratta confederacy and Hyder Ali of Mysore had formed a loose coalition to subdue the British at Madras. Although the three powers were mutually suspicious of one other, and could not effectively coordinate their actions, there still was a real danger that they would combine to drastically limit the activities of the British. Meanwhile, the grip of the council on dependent rulers like the Nawab of Carnatic and the Raja of Tanjore weakened. Hyder Ali saw his opportunity and raided the Carnatic. Colonel Baillie's brigade was defeated and destroyed. Thomas Munro's force was also beaten and forced to withdraw with losses. In this situation, Hastings despatched Sir Eyre Coote, the commander-in-chief at Bengal, by sea with a formidable force, and another force over land along the coast under Pearce, to regain control of the Carnatic in which Arcot had been captured and which had been laid waste. Coote met with Hyder Ali's forces and defeated them at Porto Novo in July 1781.[73] Hastings had been able to prevent the Raja of Berar and the Nizam from interfering, while he kept the Mahrattas diverted and engaged in the west and north. Coote joined up with Pearce and

72. Bisheshwar Prasad, *Bondage and Freedom 1707 to 1947*, Vol. I, "Bondage, 1707-1858", pp. 102, 113.

73. Vincent A. Smith, *The Oxford History of India*, p. 512.

defeated Hyder Ali at the two battles of Pollilore and Solingur.[74] Although Hyder Ali teamed up with French forces and took Cuddalore, his further five battles against the British were inconclusive. Hastings, by his timely measures had weathered the storm, and after Hyder Ali died, the immediate threat to Madras had passed. Hyder's successor, Tipu had deemed fit to march on Mangalore. By early 1783, Lord Macartney had taken over as Governor of Madras and was able to stabilise and strengthen the Company's position. A peace was concluded with Mysore by the Treaty of Mangalore in 1784.

At a time when Britain was deeply engaged with the war of American independence across the Atlantic, and with the Seven Years' War in Europe, Hastings was able to maintain and strengthen the Company's power in India by a combination of force and skillful diplomacy. From 1784 on, the Company could be said to be the strongest power on the sub-continent. At the same time, he had increased the Company's profit, introduced considerable discipline in the ranks of the Company officers, created an independent new judiciary, and had taken the first steps in reviving the culture and in exhuming the history of India. The countryside of Bengal was again becoming productive. The process of consolidation of Britain's hold on India had been started. The Regulating Act of 1773 enabled Parliament to exercise control over the Company in matters of administration of the people in the territories controlled by the Company through appointment of the Governor General and his three council members. A supreme court was established. By Pitt's India Act of 1784,[75] the Governor General was made supreme by empowering him with the casting vote when introduction of new measures reached an impasse in the council. While the Court of Directors of the Company were

74. Ibid., p. 512.

75. Bisheshwar Prasad, *Bondage and Freedom 1707 to 1947*, Vol. I, "Bondage, 1707-1858", p. 378.

left free to regulate the commercial operations, the Board of Control appointed by Parliament oversaw the conduct of political and administrative affairs by laying down policy. For example, the Governor General and council were forbidden to engage in war or aggression without the prior permission of the Board. The collection of revenue and the systems for the same were to be approved by the Board. While the Governor General was free to act, he had to do so within the parameters and general policies laid down by the Board of Control from time to time. Warren Hastings' contribution to the enactment of these legislative measures was indeed considerable.[76] His place among the empire builders of British India remains high. It is another matter that, on his return to England, he was impeached by Parliament. This was perhaps more due to the efforts of his enemies rather than his exceeding the brief he had from Government regarding non-interference. However, he was eventually acquitted of all charges although he was debarred from any future employment by Government.

Lord Cornwallis

Lord Cornwallis succeeded Warren Hastings as Governor General coming to India in 1786, after a short interregnum of eighteen months. He accepted the post on condition that the Governor General would also be the commander-in-chief of the Company forces. He demanded that the Governor General should be empowered to supersede the advice of his council which was reduced to two members other than himself. Thus, the Governor General's position became supreme in the Company in India, and he automatically superseded the Governor of Bombay or Madras Presidencies. Armed with these powers, and with his own social standing among the aristocracy in England and with the political support he enjoyed, Cornwallis set out to reform the

76. Vincent A. Smith, *The Oxford History of India*, p. 522.

administration.[77] He was himself a successful general and administrator (except for his surrender to the American forces in Yorktown) and a person of benign but firm character. He finally and fully separated the commercial and revenue branches of Company activities. While civil justice and collection of revenue were the duties of collectors, criminal justice was administered by courts of circuit which toured the districts twice a year. The collection of revenue was hitherto on the basis of one-third of the produce and had been collected by zaminders who however had no rights over the land. Cornwallis introduced the system whereby the revenue was assessed and fixed (whatever be the produce), and the zamindars were responsible to give the Company the assessed revenue even if it meant alienating the peasant from the land. Thus zamindars became virtual owners of the land, brought increasing areas under cultivation, but continued to pay the fixed revenue. This system became known as the Permanent Settlement[78] which, while it ensured the desired revenue accruing to the company, destroyed the organic relationship between peasant and zamindar which had existed earlier. From now on the peasant merely became a tenant farmer whereas, earlier, he owned the land. This was his principal act in the field of revenue collection.

By his introduction of the system of revenue collection and judicial officers, he set in place the system which became the forerunner of the civil service. During his period private trade by company officers was completely abolished, whatever vestiges of it remained. Cornwallis was ruthless in eradicating corruption, and set the standards for a civil service which gradually became known for integrity and efficiency.[79] In a

77. K.M. Panikkar, *A Survey of Indian History*, pp. 250, 251.
78. Bisheshwar Prasad, *Bondage and Freedom 1707 to 1947*, Vol. I, "Bondage, 1707-1858", pp. 308, 311.
79. Vincent A. Smith, *The Oxford History of India*, p. 533.

short period of seven years he had restored tranquillity to the countryside. The Permanent Settlement caused disruption in the old system of collection of revenue and was modified from time to time in later administrations, but the basic structure, which was a departure from the Mughal system, was laid and evolved.

The Third Mysore War - Tipu

Cornwallis could not entirely avoid getting involved in wars with Indian powers. The Madras council had injudiciously become embroiled in local politics with the Nizam, the Nawab of Carnatic, the raja of Tanjore, the Mahrattas, and above all Tipu Sultan. The Nizam's dominions were a protectorate, in effect, of the British as he counted on them to help him whenever the Mahrattas were aggressive. The Nawab of Carnatic, the Nawab Wallajah was deeply in debt to the Company as such and also to its officers by way of private trade, and he was an enemy of Mahratta supported Raja of Tanjore, Tanjore being included in his kingdom. The Mahrattas were interested in Tanjore and also sought to expand their territory beyond the north-west boundaries of Mysore. From 1761 onwards, Mysore under Hyder Ali had expanded its conquests towards Malabar on the west, Cuddalore in the south-east, Chitradurga and Bellary on the north-east (this last at the expense of the Nizam), and towards Coorg on the south-west.[80] After Hyder Ali died in 1783, Tipu anointed himself 'Badshah' while the Hindu dynastic heir was still alive, and embarked on a programme of conquest towards Mangalore and Travancore in the south-west, Dharwar and Hubli in the north-west and towards the Carnatic on the east.[81] His aims

80. Bisheshwar Prasad, *Bondage and Freedom 1707 to 1947*, Vol. I, "Bondage, 1707-1858", p. 109.

81. Ibid., pp. 118, 119.

were merely conquest and the extraction of money and goods from the princedoms and fiefdoms he conquered. Like his father before him, he had not thought of governing the lands he conquered but of merely subjugating them. He was rabidly preoccupied with these aims and with the aim of throwing out the British from India.[82] He had wild ideas of enlisting the help of the sultan of Turkey and that of Napoleon Bonaparte, then still the first consul of the revolutionary regime in France and fully engaged on his Italian and German campaigns. Enjoying considerable personal force and energy, and having some knowledge of military tactics, he pursued his campaigns in a manner that made him a troublesome nuisance to all the three other powers of the Deccan, that is the Mahrattas, the Nizam and the British.[83] Although he gained a few victories against outlying forts of the southern Mahratta dominions and against the British, he could not expand his territories far beyond what they were at the time of Hyder Ali.[84] Before long, Cornwallis allied himself with the Nizam and Mahrattas and came south to command the operation himself. He took the fortress of Bangalore in 1791 and forced Tipu back into the fortress of Seringapatan. He dictated a peace treaty with Tipu in 1792 by which half the lands of Mysore were annexed and distributed between the British, the Mahrattas and the Nizam. Tipu had to further pay the Company an indemnity of Rs. 330 lakhs and had to give his two sons hostage to the Company as an insurance for his further good behaviour.[85] At the time, there could not have been a more humiliating treaty for Tipu who had declared his pretensions to be able to throw the British out of India. Tipu's conquests in Malabar and Wynad, in

82. Ibid., p. 118.

83. Ibid., pp. 118, 121.

84. Ibid., p. 119.

85. Vincent A. Smith, *The Oxford History of India*, p. 542.

Coimbatore and Tanjore were annexed by the Company and became Company administered territories. The areas of Raichur, Dharwad were given back to the Mahrattas, Bellary and Gooty were handed to the Nizam, and Tipu was left with the old Mysore state. The peace that resulted in the south endured for five years except for the short, sharp campaign between the Mahrattas and the Nizam which resulted in the crushing defeat of the Nizam at Kharda in 1795.[86]

In expanding his territories, Tipu fought against minor chieftains and rajas like the Raja of Wynad, the Zamorin (Samoodhri) of Calicut and the Raja of Travancore on the west. In the east he fought the troops of the Nawab Wallajah of the Carnatic and the Raja of Tanjore. In the north, he captured outlying forts of the Mahrattas at Kittur and Dharwar and local Palegars (Palegars or chieftains or Nayakas of forts who exacted tribute from the surrounding agricultural lands and merchants). All these powers were basically weak powers that were sunk in indolence, and in living on the exaction of taxes from a battered peasantry.[87] In Coorg, his columns to relieve the forts of Madikeri and Beppunad were severely mauled and thrown back.[88] When fighting alliances of the Mahrattas the Nizam and the British, the Nizam was non-effective, the Mahrattas distant and enigmatic, and the British slow-moving with their Indian sepoys and artillery trains. While he had a few minor successes, when confronted with systematic and good generalship he could not defeat the enemy. He had problems keeping his own commanders in line.

The short period that Hyder Ali and Tipu Sultan ruled Mysore, from 1760 to 1799, that is thirty nine years, did not see any effort on the part of the two rulers either to reform

86. Ibid., p. 543.

87. Ibid., pp. 541, 542.

88. N. Chinnappa, *Pattole Palame*, 1910, Reprint by K. Kodava, Sahitya Academy, 1996 (in Kannada Script).

anachronistic laws, or to improve the living of the people. Because of the great demands for money and goods on the common people to finance their military campaigns, the countryside was devastated and the people impoverished. They were no different than a long line of such local rulers both Hindu and Muslim, like the Palegars and chieftains before them. Their control on the areas they conquered was broken no sooner their back was turned. Their net effect was to merely leave behind large numbers of Muslims converted by force from the lower orders and the depressed segments of the population.[89]

Their importance in Indian history is because the British sent glowing reports home of the defeats they inflicted, in order to enhance their own reputation and to justify their interference and wars with Indian states, which was against the policy imposed by the Board of Control and of the Directors of the Company to avoid involvement in wars with Indian powers unless their own settlements were directly threatened. The British themselves were only at the initial phase of their military exploits.

When Cornwallis went home to England in 1793, he could look back on a period of achievement during which the order restored by Hastings was further well strengthened. Except for the campaign against Tipu, the Company had largely stuck to the British government policy of non-intervention in the affairs of Indian states, even to the extent of tacitly repudiating treaties with the Nizam whereby the Company was to go to his help if he was threatened. Large areas of the Carnatic and Malabar had been annexed to the Company by which greater control was

89. Hyder Ali followed local laws with an attitude of pragmatic commonsense and administered his territories reasonably, but Tipu's attitude was somewhat affected by his desire for conversion of Hindus and Christians into Muslims. Also see Bisheshwar Prasad, *Bondage and Freedom 1707 to 1947*, Vol. I, "Bondage, 1707-1858", p. 130.

established over the hinterlands which were agriculturally very productive, like the Kaveri river valley and the rich spicelands of Malabar which produced the best spices in the world. Bengal, Bihar and Oudh were stabilised. In Bombay, reasonably good relations prevailed with the Peshwa. Although exploitation of the countryside for trade continued and that, in a more systematic manner, the rudiments of enlightened administration were introduced in the Company territories, enabling greater productivity under conditions of peaceful order. The legal system of both civil and criminal justice was strengthened largely in accordance with Hindu, Muslim and customary law wherever appropriately applicable.[90]

Lord Wellesley

The arrival of Lord Wellesley in 1795 was preceded by the Governor Generalship of Sir John Shore, a Company man who filled the job until the selected person could come out from England. It was a relatively uneventful period when the policy of non-interference was followed strictly. When the Nizam was attacked by the Mahrattas in 1795, Sir John Shore refrained from interfering although treaty obligations required the Company to come to the assistance of the Nizam. The Mahrattas had combined together, and any embroilment of the Company could have resulted in prolonged and infructuous warfare. After Wellesley arrived, the whole scene changed. Determined to see that French influence had no chance to spread in India with the successes of Napoleon Bonaparte in Europe, he regarded every development with those tinted glasses, at least in the initial few years of administration.[91] He was, furthermore, of aggressive intent, frankly desirous of distinguishing himself as a conqueror who could impose his will on those around him. Britair was totally preoccupied in

90. Vincent A. Smith, *The Oxford History of India*, pp. 537, 542.

91. Ibid., p. 543.

coming to grips with the new phenomenon of Napoleon in the aftermath of the French revolution, and paid little attention to the goings on in India.

Defeat of Tipu

To start with, Wellesley was seriously disturbed by Tipu's efforts to obtain French support which he tried to win by sending a mission to the governor of the French island of Mauritius. The governor promised support and sent a contingent of officers who landed on the Malabar coast. Tipu's intentions were clearly to train an army with French officers with the aim of recovering the territories he lost by the Treaty of Seringapatam in 1792. His thoughts were also dominated by the desire to form a grand alliance of the southern powers to oust the British from the peninsula. Wellesley himself moved down to Madras and made preparations for attacking Tipu. He first ensured the Nizam's neutrality and support by imposing on him his subsidiary alliance, by which the Nizam was protected against his external enemies by the presence of a substantial British force, the cost of which was borne by the Nizam himself. Wellesley, according to the terms of the Alliance was to refrain from interfering in the internal affairs of the Nizam's dominions. The Nizam, in fact became the first Indian ruler to come under the scheme of the system of subsidiary alliance in 1798.[92] The idea which originated with Clive in relation to Oudh was expanded for application to as many of the powers of India as possible. Oudh, Benares, Bihar, Orissa and later the Mahratta Peshwa were all brought in. Four battalions of British troops were stationed in the state at a cost to the Nizam of Rs. 2 lakhs a month. The Nizam's foreign relations were taken over by the Company. Although the Peshwa did not agree to come under the subsidiary alliance

92. Vincent A. Smith, *The Oxford History of India*, pp. 552, 553.

treaty scheme, he remained aloof giving a free hand to Wellesley.

After Tipu had replied disdainfully to Wellesley's demand for an explanation of Tipu's Mauritius activities, Wellesley launched a two-pronged attack on Mysore from Madras and Bombay. After two months' campaigning, Wellesley was able to force Tipu into Seringapatam and lay siege to him there. Tipu was asked to agree to surrender half his territories and to pay an indemnity of £2 million (Rs. 20 lakhs) which he refused to do. Seringapatam was stormed on 6th May 1799, a breach having been made in the walls on the north-eastern side. Tipu died fighting and was found lying in the breach with his sword in his hand. It is apparent that Wellesley secured Tipu's defeat by guile as much as by military action, as he is known to have subverted some of Tipu's commanders with money. The old Mysore state was restored to an heir of the Hindu rajas displaced by Hyder and later by Tipu. The state was brought under the subsidiary alliance with a Resident being stationed in Bangalore with an adequate force of the Company.[93]

Wellesley and the Mahrattas

Later, Wellesley dealt with the two major Mahratta powers of Bhonsle and Scindia. He first defeated Bhonsle in the two battles of Assaye[94] and Aramgaon by which he gained Cuttack in 1803. He next defeated Scindia's troops commanded by General Perron at Aligarh. General Lake next defeated General Perron at Delhi and captured Delhi. The British again defeated General Perron at a third battle at Laswari[95] and Scindia was forced to conclude a peace. Both Bhonsle and Scindia agreed to

93. Bisheshwar Prasad, *Bondage and Freedom 1707 to 1947*, Vol. I, "Bondage, 1707-1858", pp. 125, 126.
94. K.M. Panikkar, *A Survey of Indian History*, p. 250. Bhonsle was defeated and brought under the Alliance.
95. Ibid.

the subsidiary treaty but refused to agree to British troops being stationed within their territories. Holkar remained to be dealt with, but proved a hard nut to crack. War broke out in April 1804 between Jaswant Rao Holkar and the British. The British forces under General Monson were soundly defeated near Kotah and had to fall back on Agra, and further to retreat to Delhi. Holkar pursued the British and laid siege to Delhi. A second British force under General Lake was unable to dislodge the Mahrattas from Bharatpur on the approaches to Delhi.[96] This series of reverses to the hitherto unvanquished troops of Wellesley alarmed the British Government in London. They suddenly had visions of Indian states combining under the leadership of the Mahrattas and ousting the British from India. All the hard won conquests of fifty years were obviously in dreadful jeopardy, all because of the adventurism of a Governor General who had consciously flouted the Government policy of non-interference. Wellesley was recalled to England in 1805, thus ending one of the most expansionist phases of British conquest in India.[97]

Although the magic of Wellesley's invincibility was dispelled in one year, his sojourn in India resulted in the acquisition of large areas of territories in the south and above all, British domination of states like that of Mysore, Hyderabad, of the territories of Peshwa, Scindia and Bhonsle, not to speak of the smaller states like Cochin and Tranvancore. In fact, the whole of the Deccan and peninsular India came under the effective control of the British. Along with Clive and Warren Hastings, Wellesley can be classed as a true empire-builder. His political sagacity and bold military strategy enabled him to acquire territory and dominate India from Delhi and Agra in the north to Mysore in south, and from

96. Vincent A. Smith, *The Oxford History of India*, p. 556. The campaign of 1804.

97. Ibid.

Bombay in the west to Bengal in the east.

British historians seem to have glossed over the magnitude and psychological effect of the defeats sustained by Wellesley's forces at the hands of Jaswant Rao Holkar. These defeats seriously troubled not only the British Government but also the Company's officers and troops, and brought home to the latter their vulnerability in a strange, far-off land at the mercy of a great unpredictable people whom they had held mesmerised for long. Until Lord Hastings took over, there was a palpable atmosphere of gloom among the Company's personnel.[98]

Lord Minto

Wellesley was succeeded by Lord Minto in 1806 after a brief stint by the man in place, Sir John Barlow. Minto came at a time when Russia had been exploring a way by which it could gain access to an all-weather port, and the most practicable routes lay through Persia on the one side and through Afghanistan and India on the other. Minto sought to safeguard the north-western approaches to India by obtaining the co-operation of Persia and by maintaining Company and Company-friendly forces in Afghanistan.[99] Also by securing Delhi and Punjab east of Sutlej, and by signing the Treaty of Amritsar, negotiated by Charles Metcalfe, with Maharaja Ranjit Singh of the first Sikh kingdom in 1809, Minto largely achieved his aims.[100] The treaty lasted till 1845. The Napoleonic wars were in full swing in Europe and Russia and France had concluded the Treaty of Tilsit in Poland in 1807, which enabled Russia to spare the effort to look for an all-weather port. Minto meanwhile could neutralise the French influence in India.

98. Vincent A. Smith, *The Oxford History of India*, p. 556.
99. Bisheshwar Prasad, *Bondage and Freedom 1707 to 1947*, Vol. I, "Bondage, 1707-1858", p. 251.
100. Vincent A. Smith, *The Oxford History of India*, p. 560.

When Napoleon seized Portugal, Minto occupied the Portuguese enclave in Goa. He also sent naval expeditions to capture Mauritius in the south-west of India, and to capture Macao (1809), Amboyna and Maluccas in the Dutch East Indies (1810), and Java (1811). As Holland, captured by Napoleon, was fighting on the side of the French, Minto felt justified in conquering Amboyna and Maluccas and Java. Minto left Java in command of Stamford Raffles who later became famous as the founder of Singapore. Minto had thus opened avenues for new British expansion in the east.[101]

During Barlow's time, treaties had been concluded with Scindia of Gwalior and Holkar of Indore, specifying the river Chambal as the northern border for both. However, they had not been prevented from exploiting the various states of Rajputana. These states had become weak through the lethargy, self-indulgence and corruption of the rulers, and were easy prey for the Mahrattas[102] who found extracting revenue from their own territories was proving more difficult because of the devastation and waste caused by endless conflicts and wars. Raghoji Bhonsle of Nagpur did not display any energy but remained immobile and quiet in Nagpur. The Gaekwad of Baroda had agreed to a subsidiary treaty and had admitted Company forces into his kingdom. With Britain preoccupied in Europe, no resources could be spared for any campaigns in India, even though the Pindaris who were marauding bands of unattached fighting men, were plundering the countryside and harassing the peasantry without regard to borders of kingdoms. The Peshwa's authority was largely in name and his role was confined to intriguing with the other Mahratta powers with a Company force established in Pune.

The British Government realised that no major disciplined

101. Ibid., p. 561.

102. K.M. Panickkar, *A Survey of Indian History*, Mahadji Scindia had trained his army with help of the Frenchman, Comte de Boigne, pp. 248, 249.

power existed in India except the Sikhs who adhered to their treaty and limited their activities to Punjab west of the Sutlej, to Sind, to Kashmir, and to protection of their north-western approaches. India as a whole lay almost prostrate with the whole country ravaged by 150 years of war from the time of the emperor Aurangazeb. The British regarded themselves as the right power to fill the vacuum, but did not dare to do so as they could not command the resources for the task. Any venture on their part at this stage could perhaps provoke unpredictable and unfavourable developments like for example, a coalition of Indian powers against them.[103]

Lord Hastings

Lord Hastings assumed charge in 1813 and felt that there were many situations that needed to be solved by a resort to arms. The major problems seemed to be caused by the continued restiveness of the Mahratta chieftains and connected with them, by the marauding bands of the Pindaris who were laying waste the countryside. However, he was unexpectedly confronted by the aggressiveness of the Gurkhas of Nepal. While the Gurkhas had been steadily expanding eastward and westward from their original kingdom in the Khatmandu valley (which is still called Nepal by the population, whereas the other districts of Nepal even today are called by other names, like Pokhra or Navakot), they had not come in conflict with the British. In 1814 they felt strong enough to lay claim to the densely forested strip of plains between the foothills and the Gangetic plains, called the 'terai'. They spread out their boundaries to the south to include this highly malarious strip of jungle full of forests and wild animals. Meanwhile, the British had progressively advanced their territories after conquering Bihar, Oudh, Rohilkhand and towards Almora and Kumaon over fifty years of conquest. The Gurkhas collided head on with the British power.

103. Vincent A. Smith, *The Oxford History of India*, pp. 577, 578. "They believed they were sitting on a social and religious volcano..."

The Two Gurkha Wars

Hastings immediately created the forces necessary to attack the Gurkhas. He sent three columns towards Khatmandu and one column (under General Ochterlony) on the western side towards Kumaon and Almora which were Nepal's most recent conquests and where they had been stopped by the existence of the strong Sikh state of Ranjit Singh. To the surprise of the British, the three central columns were beaten back by the Gurkhas causing heavy losses in men and material.[104] The western column enjoyed sufficient success as it penetrated deep into the Kumaon and Garhwal hills. Although Hastings had taken the precaution of maintaining sufficiently strong forces in the plains before sending up his columns into Nepal, the news of the setback caused the Mahrattas to speculate on the possibility of attacking Company forces in this new situation. But Hastings remained cool, and without weakening his guard against the Mahrattas or the Sikhs, he recreated sufficient forces against Nepal, and again attacked Nepal, this time all the columns being under the overall command of General Ochterlony. This determined advance made sufficient progress between January and March 1816 to force the Gurkhas to sue for peace. At the Treaty of Sagauli (in North Bihar or Mithila) in March 1816, the Gurkhas agreed to give up Kumaon, Almora and the Shimla hills, to give up their claims to the 'terai' and to allow the company to post a Resident at Khatmandu. This treaty was never violated by either party until the British left India in 1947.

The Pindaris

After these two Gurkha wars, Hastings turned his attention to eradication of the Pindaris. These Pindaris consisting of unemployed soldiers and freebooters on horseback had

104. Vincent A. Smith, *The Oxford History of India*, p. 566. Also see Netra B. Thapa, *A Short History of Nepal*, pp. 121, 122.

organised themselves in bands and had attached themselves to the Mahratta armies, variously functioning as scouts and auxiliaries. They had been in existence for two or more centuries, having their bases at Nemawar on the Narmada river and other inaccessible hideouts in the Malwa area.[105] They lived by raiding and plundering the villages, but found their most lucrative adventures as unofficial auxiliaries of the Mahratta armies. Before the battle of Panipat in January 1761 between the Mahrattas and Ahmad Shah Abdali, the Pindaris were most effective in cutting the rear lines of communications of Ahmad Shah's army and could have caused his defeat. It was only by detaching a strong force of cavalry and hunting and killing Pindaris that Ahmad Shah could protect his communications. Likewise, the Pindaris had participated in the forays of Holkar and Scindia towards the Jumna and Rajput states, and of Raghoji Bhonsle towards Orissa and Bengal, with much profit to themselves. Under the prevailing unsettled conditions during Hastings' period in central India and the Deccan, these hordes had become quite numerous. They would concentrate themselves to attack and pillage and could disperse and disappear into their hideouts with considerable skill. In 1814, they plundered the Nizam's dominions and dispersed with booty estimated at over a hundred lakh rupees. It was this menace that preyed on the countryside that Hastings set out to obliterate.

He organised three armies from the Ganga-Jumna Doab towards Bundelkhand and Malwa and one army from the south, he himself taking the field with the northern armies.[106] The systematic encirclement of the Pindaris and the hunting of their groups began to bear fruit. By 1816-17, they had been harried, pursued and killed until the remnants hurried back to their hideouts. The Pindaris having raided the northern parts of

105. Vincent A. Smith, *The Oxford History of India*, p. 567.

106. Ibid., p. 569.

the Madras Presidency in 1815, impelled Britain to support Hastings' plans for their final elimination. The subsidiary treaty entered into by the Bhonsles enabled the British to station a military force in Nagpur which helped in sealing off one of the directions of movement of the Pindaris. Also, a Mahratta force was trained and organised at Nagpur. Smaller forces were stationed in Gujarat and in Adoni (in Andhra) to cut off escaping bands. The net was gradually closed and the Pindaris were disarmed and dispersed. The widespread menace was finally removed. Over 1,00,000 troops were involved in the whole operation which lasted nearly two years.

While the campaign against the Pindaris was taking place much turnoil occurred among the Mahrattas, unconnected with the Pindaris. The Peshwa Baji Rao attempted to raise troops by proxy through the escaped Trimbakji, but the British at Pune confronted the Peshwa with the threat of force and prevailed upon him to sign the Treaty of Pune in 1817 by which all foreign agents were expelled from the court, and by which the Peshwa formally renounced his leadership of the Mahratta confederacy.[107] Both his title and the confederacy existed only in name since many years, and the renouncement was only a recognition of the *de facto* situation. Appa Sahib Bhonsle who tried to attack the subsidiary force was himself defeated. Tulsi Bai who was the Regent at Holkar was murdered by one of the factions in Indore, and the army of Holkar fought the British at Mahidpur in December 1817 but was defeated. The Peshwa who again attempted to fight and dislodge the British was defeated in June 1818. The Mahratta confederacy was broken up completely. The Peshwaship was abolished and the Peshwa pensioned and exiled to Bithur on the Ganges.[108] The Peshwa's dominions were annexed to the

107. Bisheshwar Prasad, *Bondage and Freedom 1707 to 1947*, Vol. I, "Bondage, 1707-1858", p. 178.

108. Ibid.

Company as part of Bombay Presidency. The Bhonsle territories were broken up and distributed between the Nizam and Madras, some portions remaining separate as territories under the British. Amirs of Sind remained independent. Hastings had progressed the hegemony of the Company far beyond what he himself would have thought possible when he set out for India. He was helped in his task by a group of brilliant assistants, chief of whom were Elphinstone at Pune, Jenkins at Nagpur and Metcalfe at Delhi. Munro, although further removed at Madras contributed his share.

During his travels and tours, Hastings had seen the utter devastation of the countryside and realised something had to be done to revive confidence in the people and to promote agriculture and commerce.[109] Thus far, the ordinary denizens of the villages and small towns saw in the rise of the British power only another power in the long line of powers that had exploited them and rode roughshod over them for centuries. It was the chieftains and the nawabs, the rajas and the Sultans who hated the British for dominating them and for restricting their untrammelled exploitation of the people. The British on the other hand saw that, unless the land was made more productive and confidence restored among the people, anarchic conditions would continue to prevail, thus making it that much harder for the British to exercise control over their extensive acquisitions.

Hastings ordered the repair and restoration of the old Mughal irrigation canal, to start with.[110] Next, he set the process for repair and restoration of the roads. The elimination of the Pindaris, the restriction of levying taxes and ad hoc imposts from the people, and the general restoration of law and order, combined with the development works initiated, slowly saw the regeneration of the countryside, at least within the

109. Vincent A. Smith, *The Oxford History of India*, p. 585.

110. Ibid.

Company territories. The long operating enclaves of sea pirates on the Konkan coast were dismantled so that coastal commerce became safe. Small revolts and uprisings in the states were put down with a firm hand, though with an understanding approach to relieve the pressures which caused those uprisings. Hastings' period although eventful, was highly productive. For India too, there was a glimmer of hope of better conditions to come.

Lord Amherst

Lord Amherst came out after Hastings returned to England, arriving in August 1823. Soon he was embroiled in the Burman war which went on till 1826. Indian troops who were ordered to proceed by sea to attack the west coast of Burma mutinied in 1824[111] at Barrackpore, as their castes considered travelling by sea (kala pani or black water) as a personal pollution entailing excommunication. Although the Burman war was won, it was at considerable loss, the situation being somewhat retrieved by the Treaty of Yandaboo by which some Burmese territories had to be ceded to the British.

Lord William Bentinck and His Successors

Amherst left in March 1828, and was succeeded by Lord William Bentinck. Bentinck was a full General who had also distinguished himself in irrigation works in England and in reclaiming the marshy lands on England's west coast. His stint as Governor of Madras came to an adverse end due to the mutiny of the Company's Indian troops at Vellore in 1806.[112] Bentinck was recalled to England although he protested that the mutiny was a freak because of the sudden orders of the

111. Kushalilal Srivastava, *The Revolt of 1857 in Central India---- Malwa*, pp. 80, 82.

112. Vincent A. Smith, *The Oxford History of India*, p. 586.

English officers of the troops to the men to cut their hair, to shave off their beards and to stop using caste marks on their faces. The officers of the time were not the old officers of the Stringer Lawrence school but newly brought in over the last few years, who neither understood the psychology of the men nor attempted to understand them. It was after twenty years, and due to shifts in the political climate of England that Bentinck won his case for rehabilitation, and that, as Governor General. As the son of a former Prime Minister of Britain, Lord Portland, he had the necessary access to the political circles which mattered.

Bentinck came out with a solid reputation as a true liberal. The mood of British ruling and intellectual circles was also in tune, as great debates raged since the time of Pitt in the period 1770 to 1795 as to how to administer India for the good of her people. This may sound quite strange to the modern generation in India which was taught to believe that the British were mere exploiters who 'enslaved' this country and did nothing good. Nevertheless, the existence of that mood of good government for the people was very real. While this aspect will be dealt with a little later in this book, suffice it to say here that Bentinck's liberalism found wide support in Britain which was a great help to him.

Initially, he re-examined the systems of revenue collection[113] and administration of justice. He modified the permanent settlement system of Cornwallis by combining it with the 'Ryotwari' system introduced in Madras by Thomas Munro during the time of Lord Hastings. The 'Ryotwari' system eliminated the middlemen or zamindars or owners. For every area of land, the revenue was assessed and fixed based upon its productivity, and this fixed revenue was collected direct from the peasants or ryots by officials directly employed

113. Bisheshwar Prasad, *Bondage and Freedom 1707 to 1947*, Vol. I, "Bondage, 1707-1858", p. 327.

by the Company for the purpose.[114] There was little or no room for exploitation of the peasant farmer. Bentinck in his tour of the north-western areas of the Ganga-Jumna Doab got the land assessed for revenue and confirmed the system for thirty years, recognising at the same time the existing rights of landholders, village communities and individual cultivators. This enabled all these producers to be confident that their land would not be alienated for a minimum of thirty years, and hence they could exert themselves to make improvements on their land and increase production. This 'Mahilwari' or "semi-permanent settlement" was a great improvement on the earlier system as the fixed revenue would be paid by the cultivator direct to government, and as greater productivity due to the exertions of the cultivator accrued to himself.[115] In judicial reform, Bentinck abolished the courts of circuit because of which there was a large accumulation of undecided cases. He organised courts from the district upwards, including courts of appeal. He made the local language the language of the lower courts instead of Persian, and made English the language of the higher courts. He appointed many Indian judges, thus reducing expenditure on the judiciary while at the same time utilising the abilities of Indians.[116]

He streamlined the management of the Company commerce and administration, reducing or eliminating much abused allowances, and increasing the profitability of the Company. He systematised inland steam water transport so that goods could move up and down the Ganges at much reduced cost. By planning a network of new roads and by improving and repairing existing roads, he improved commerce and ultimately the profits of the Company, and the well-being

114. Ibid., pp. 327-329.

115. Ibid., p. 329. Also see Vincent A. Smith, *The Oxford History of India*, p. 588.

116. Ibid., p. 588.

of the people. He started work on the Grand Trunk road between Calcutta and Delhi. He planned irrigation dams and canals. He started coffee and tea cultivation, as also coal and iron production. In 1831, he opened up the Indus river for steam transport from the port of Tatta.

He put an end to 'sati' or widow-burning and greatly reduced female infanticide in the teeth of opposition by religious and social groups. His justification for interfering in these customs of the people was that the universal moral law of humanity superseded all other laws including those which had religious backing and sanction. Through the indefatigable efforts of Colonel Sleeman, he put an end to "Thuggee". The 'thugs' were votaries of the goddess Kali (both Hindu and Muslim Thugs were devotees) and they believed they killed people in praise of the Goddess. They operated in bands on the pilgrim and business routes, falling in with wayfarers, pretending to be pilgrims or business people themselves, and killing them at lonely locations and burying them. They killed by strangulation by a kerchief or cloth which had a knot in the centre or a coin knotted into it. They fell in behind the wayfarer, throwing the kerchief over the head, tightened it round the neck with a twist of their fists at the back of the neck. Strangulation and loss of life was almost instantaneous. They appropriated to themselves the money and goods of the wayfarer. Three thousands thugs were caught, tried and sentenced to death by hanging and their bands were exterminated.[117] They had been killing about 30,000 people annually. Their methods and their adventures are immortalised in the book, *Confessions of Amir Ali, the Thug* written by a British officer by questioning one of the more famous thugs, Amir Ali, when he had been sentenced to death and was awaiting execution in prison.

It was Bentinck who set the course of official Indian

117. Geoffrey Moorhouse, *India Britannica*, p. 93.

education. He decreed that the content of education of Indians should be western and the language of education should be English.[118] Science, mathematics, philosophy and English literature should be the main subjects as taught in the west, while Indian languages and history should form subsidiary but important components. He wrote to Charles Metcalfe, one of the Residents, that "general education is my panacea for the regeneration of India".[119] In his plans and implementation of education policy, he was greatly helped by Thomas Babington Macaulay who joined Bentinck's council as a fourth member in 1834. In Macaulay's famous *Minute on Education* he stated that Indians were a great people sunk in superstition who needed to be educated in British culture and values, in western science and laws. He opined that Indians should be made to respect reason over what he called "barbarism" and introduced to the eternal treasure house of British morals and laws. In his *Minute*, Macaulay expressed his very poor opinion of the literature of Sanskrit and the vernacular languages. Perhaps being still a young man, although well learned in Indian literature, and brought up in an age in Europe when reason was almost God, he did not understand the deep cultural attachment and pride of Indians in their epics. He spoke disparagingly of Hindu history "abounding in kings 30 feet high and eons 30,000 years long, and geography made up of seas of treacle and rivers of butter".[120] Bentinck's own independent views before Macaulay arrived were merely confirmed by Macaulay's *Minute on Education*. Bentinck made Macaulay the legislative member of his council enjoining him not only to make a framework for the implementation of the education policy but also to create a code for criminal justice.

Forty seminaries were started in Bengal alone to implement

118. Vincent A. Smith, *The Oxford History of India*, p. 588.

119. Ibid., p. 589.

120. Geoffrey Moorhouse, *India Britannica*, p. 99.

the education policy where English teaching and western science were imported. The induction of Indian judges by Bentinck, and his inclusion of Indians in various study committees were an added inducement for Indians to adopt the new education. In Bengal especially, there was a great rush to enter the new colleges where caste was no bar for entry of students. In even less than three years, the Calcutta Book Society sold over 30,000 English texts and 1100 students were admitted to the English faculty alone in the new Hooghly College.[121] Even Macaulay became perturbed that a new class of intelligentsia would develop, separated from the old society, and felt constrained to remind the administration that the newly educated youths were meant to be "conductors of knowledge to the people, and it is of no use to fill the conductors with knowledge at one end, if you separate them from the people at the other." However, English education continued apace, creating in time a great new force that would usher India into easy interaction with a hundred different countries in the world.

Bentinck's entrusting the work of framing a legal code for criminal justice to Macaulay also proved to be of signal benefit for India. Macaulay took just two years to draft the whole criminal code, drawing heavily upon the Code Napoleone which had taken nine years to complete and the Louisiana Code which had taken four and a half years.[122] He covered all the five systems of law then prevailing in the British territories.[123] Although he had displayed arrogance in his *Minute* in regard to Indian history and Sanskrit works, in drafting his code of criminal justice he showed compassion and understanding and total respect for Indian customs like the importance of purdah among Muslims and the absolute

121. Ibid., p. 99.
122. Ibid., pp. 100, 101.
123. Vincent A. Smith, *The Oxford History of India*, p. 526.

adherence to caste among Hindus. After the Company's judges and administration had expressed support for Macaulay's code with a few modifications, it was sent to Britain for approval which took considerably longer. It was only in 1860, after the Mutiny, that his code was adopted with scarcely any change as the Indian Penal Code and the Code of Criminal Procedure.[124] Every possible offence was foreseen, described and justice provided for, with elucidation being provided by illustrative case studies. This forms the basis for the Indian legal system. The team of Bentinck and Macaulay had delivered the goods and put in place a system which has wide acceptance even today.

Overall, the liberal and enlightened stewardship of the Governor General's post by Bentinck has influenced the social and cultural life of India for over a hundred and fifty years.

In the political field Bentinck brought under Company administration, the principalities of Coorg (Kodagu) and Cachar, both with the express consent of the people who had suffered cruel misrule for decades. Due to the total deterioration of administration of the Maharaja of Mysore, Bentinck took over the rule of the state for which due provision existed in the subsidiary alliance treaty. As mentioned already, the Indus was opened to steam transport, supported by a commercial treaty made with Ranjit Singh at Lahore. A watchful eye was maintained on the north-west for signs of Russian efforts to reach the sea through Afghanistan and India. He left for England in 1835.

Lord Auckland took over in India in 1836, and continued Bentinck's policies in education and irrigation, the upkeep of roads and so on. He dealt with the famine of 1838 with resolution, spending Rs. 40 lakhs on relief measures. Yet, the severity of the famine took 8,00,000 lives,[125] in spite of

124. Ibid., p. 526.

125. Vincent A. Smith, *The Oxford History of India*, p. 590.

foodgrains being shifted expeditiously. He faithfully implemented the directions from England to abolish the pilgrim tax and to sever all official involvement with temples or religious societies. Henceforth, the neutrality of the Government towards religion, including Christianity, became a pillar of British policy right through until 1947. The raja of Satara was deposed in favour of his brother for intrigue against the Company, and the raja of Karnal was deposed altogether for fomenting uprisings against the Company. Auckland also forced a treaty on the king of Oudh in 1837 in spite of the advice of the Directors from England to the contrary.

This was the period of Prime Ministership of Lord Palmerston, who was worried about Russian attempts to influence Iran and Afghanistan towards granting access through their territories to the Indian Ocean. He had therefore been engaged in diplomatic manoeuvres to keep out Russia and have a ruler in Afghanistan who would fully support Britain. British troops were deployed in Kabul, Kandahar and Jalalabad. Intricate political forces were at play among the Barkezai brothers, the Durrani (Abdali) clan and sundry other parties. British interference resulted in the first Afghan war in which Ghazni was occupied by the forces of Dost Mohammed and Kabul was besieged. Although the besiegers agreed to let the British give up Kabul with the condition that they would have safe passage, when British and Indian troops and their dependents and followers, in all amounting to 16,000 persons, left Kabul in column for Jalalabad, they were harassed en route and all killed except for a British doctor, Dr. Brydon.[126] This was one of the worst defeats and calamities suffered by the British. Generals Potts and Nott at Kandahar and Jalalabad however defeated the Afghans and recaptured Kabul.[127] For the rest, there was peace in India up to 1839 and education and

126. Ibid., p. 605.

127. Ibid., p. 606.

development went hand-in-hand. According to Professor Vincent Smith, the stability of India was being assured and the first step had been taken to promote the Indo-British cultural synthesis which contributed to the inner force of the Indian independence movement.

Lord Ellenborough replaced Auckland in 1842, as the Afghan war was in progress. Trained under Wellington, he was eager for conquest but his impulsiveness and erratic behaviour was not conducive to high distinction. He flouted the policy of non-interference by forcing out the Amirs of Sind at the battle of Meanee and attaching Sind to the Company territories. The executor of his policies, Sir Charles Napier was himself a fire-eating conquistador who probably went even further than his master intended. Ellenborough's defeat of Scindia's army in 1843 helped guard his rear areas in the event that the Sikhs attacked British territories. After Ranjit Singh's death in 1839, the Sikhs were showing signs of internal disturbance and discontent. However, Ellenborough did not precipitate a war with the Sikhs. His tendency to exceed his directives and the display of an aggressive attitude towards Indian states impelled the Directors to recall him in December 1843. His activities were once again prejudicing the profitability of the Company which had lost its monopoly of the Indian trade by the Parliamentary Charter Act of 1813. These conflicts and wars when deliberately precipitated as in the case of Sind, proved costly and avoidable.

Sir Henry Hardinge arrived in 1844 with the distinguished record of having fought under Wellington at Waterloo, of having held high civil offices of Secretary-at-War and of Chief Secretary for Ireland. He worked on and developed the great irrigation system of the Ganges, and made the first plans for an Indian railway system.[128] He continued to detect and suppress

128. Ibid., p. 593.

the remnants of the practice of sati and of infanticide and waged an all-out campaign for the eradication of human sacrifice, especially in the hill tracts of Orissa, which was finally put an end to with the efforts of John Campbell between 1847 and 1854.

However, by December 1845, Hardinge had to confront the Sikhs who crossed the Sutlej, thus violating the treaty concluded with Maharaja Ranjit Singh in 1809. They attacked eastern Punjab but were beaten and thrown back at the two battles of Mudki and Ferozshah. Their thrust towards Ludhiana was stopped at the battle of Aliwal and they were finally beaten and the Sikh army broken up at the battle of Sobraon in February 1846.[129] This was the end of the first Sikh war. By the Treaty of Lahore in March 1846, the Sikh army was limited to 20,000 infantry and 12,000 cavalry. The Jalandar Doab and Kashmir were annexed to the Company territories.

Lord Dalhousie

This Scottish peer landed in India in January 1848 when he was only 36 years old. An arrogant man, he had to his credit a distinguished record of work in Britain where he had been a member of Sir Robert Peel's cabinet as President of the Board of Trade, and where he had directed and coped successfully with the railway boom in Britain in the 1840s. Knowing little of India, and that by long range in Britain through official reports, he came with the surety of the ignorant, determined to "civilise" India through imparting western knowledge and through the imposition of western value systems and western methods of administration. His activism rode roughshod over local feelings of pride, religious sentiment and tradition. He arrived at a time when all major powers, Hindu, Muslim and Sikh, had exhausted themselves through fratricidal wars, religious antagonism and discord, through indolence and great

129. Ibid., p. 617.

self-indulgence because of the success they had in exercising tyrannic power. The Mahrattas had split up and rendered themselves ineffective through their own lack of wisdom in being continually involved in intrigue and internecine quarrels, although their dominions still extended far and wide, from Gujarat in the west to Cuttack in the east, from Gwalior in the north to Satara in the south. The Mughal emperor was little more than a figurehead being made use of by everyone needing to invest their actions with a kind of legitimacy by securing his approval. The strong Sikh state of Maharaja Ranjit Singh which had conquered and held Lahore in 1801, Amritsar in 1802, Ludhiana in 1806, Multan in 1818-19 and Kashmir in 1833, Ladakh in 1834, and which had successfully held Peshawar against Dost Muhammad Khan from Ghazni in 1837, was affected by serious discord after Ranjit Singh's death in 1839 at the age of 59 years. In the succession struggles to the throne, three sons of Ranjit Singh were murdered between 1839 and 1842. A regent, Rani Jindan, for a fourth son, Dalip Singh, ruled in Lahore. The Rajput states, although not full-fledged members of the subsidiary alliance system as they did not have company troops in their kingdoms, were yet very weak, with their rulers giving themselves up to willful and vicious self-indulgence, and did not have the energy even to fight among themselves. They were sunk in decay. Mysore, Cochin and Travancore were passive states. The Nizam, confident in the security of the area he had carved out for himself since 1720, remained inert and satisfied. As one of the first signatories of Wellesley's subsidiary alliance treaty he had British troops within his territories for his safety from 1798. Oudh was only a protectorate of the British and exercised little or no administration with the writ of the Company running large within the state.

Had he arrived at the height of either the Mughal power, or during the heyday of the Mahratta confederacy, it is difficult to say how successful he would have been, with his in-built prejudices. Had he remained as Governor General for five more years, it is interesting to speculate what his place would have been in history, with the typhoon of the Mutiny swirling about him. He should be considered one of the lucky incumbents of the post, without belittling his genuine abilities and vision in attempting to modernise India.

Even when Dalhousie was on his way to India, the regency of Rani Jindan, supported by the British under Charles Metcalfe, could not put out the hidden fires of intrigue and disgruntlement. Dissident elements had gathered around Diwan Mulraj in Multan. Dalhousie took over at Calcutta in January 1848. By April of that year Diwan Mulraj had revolted, and his revolt became a national one spreading across Punjab. Military committees of Sikh troops became important in the coalescing of dissidents, resulting in these committees becoming the makers of policy. The military could not be controlled and sent back to their barracks and camps. The influence of the British representative was resented and regarded with distrust, and the army was restive. Meanwhile, the British had been anticipating trouble in Punjab. At the Treaty of Lahore in 1846, a British resident had been established at Lahore. This was Sir Henry Lawrence who had developed considerable friendship and rapport with the traditional Sikh chiefs. However, his efforts to create a new Sikh state on modern, liberal tenets only succeeded in exciting suspicion as to the real intentions of the British. Lawrence's utilisation of Sikh troops to put down a revolt in Kashmir did not engender any confidence. His reform of the ruling system by which a regency council of eight Sikh chiefs with Lawrence himself presiding over it, and which replaced the regency of Rani Jindan, deepened suspicion.[130] His extending the stay of the British garrison in Lahore for eight more years, although done at the request of some Sikh chiefs, annoyed the military elements who wished for a return to Sikh

130. Ibid., p. 618.

management of the state instead of having Britishers usurping them. The humanitarian reforms of ending social customs like sati, female infanticide and cruel punishments, and the removal of certain unwelcome taxes were regarded by the military chiefs as gross interference by foreigners who had no business to be controlling the administration anyway. The despatch of two British officers to replace Diwan Mulraj, the Governor of Multan, became perhaps the last straw on the camel's back. The two British officers were murdered.[131] In April 1848, Mulraj revolted, and the revolt spread all over Punjab. The British delayed their reaction until after the monsoon and it was not until September 1848 that a large Sikh force under Sher Singh was sent to fight Mulraj. However, this force actually joined Mulraj, raising the revolt to far larger scales. Dalhousie was determined to put down the rising, and sent Lord Gough in command of forces which crossed the Ravi river on 16 November 1848.

The British were checked with heavy losses at the two battles of Ramnagar and Chillianwala, the British forces losing about 2600 men killed and wounded, and four guns.[132] But they managed to inflict a decisive defeat on the Sikh forces at Gujarat on the Chenab river, west of Jumna. The Sikh army was shattered beyond any hope of reorganisation and further fighting. The Sikh forces surrendered in detail by March 1849.[133] Dalhousie immediately annexed Punjab, abolishing the kingship and pensioning off Dalip Singh. A sidelight of this campaign and victory was the acquisition by the British of the Kohinoor diamond which today is a central ornament of the British crown. The Kohinoor diamond, one of the largest and

131. Bisheshwar Prasad, *Bondage and Freedom 1707 to 1947*, Vol. I, "Bondage, 1707-1858", p. 291. Also see Vincent A. Smith, *The Oxford History of India*, p. 618.

132. Vincent A. Smith, *The Oxford History of India*, p. 618.

133. Bisheshwar Prasad, *Bondage and Freedom 1707 to 1947*, Vol. I, "Bondage, 1707-1858", pp. 292, 293.

most splendid in the world was first given to Humayun by the family of the Raja of Gwalior when Humayun captured the fort in 1527. The Raja had himself died with Ibrahim Lodi on the field of Panipat in 1526. Humayun presented it to his father when Babar joined him at Agra. Babar merely gave it back to Humayun, though he idly calculated that the worth of the diamond could feed the population of the whole world for two-and-a-half days. Humayun, in the course of his wanderings during the period he had been driven out by Sher Shah Suri, gave it to Shah Jamasp of Persia.[134] The Shah, in turn gave it as a present to Nizam Shah in the Deccan, although how such a magnificent diamond, and under what circumstances, could be given away so casually as a present to someone who was separated by a whole sub-continent is a matter of wonder. From Nizam Shah, the Kohinoor seemed to have been passed to the Mughal emperor Shah Jahan who was a connoisseur and a devoted collector of precious gems. When Nadir Shah looted Delhi in 1739, the Kohinoor was included in the captured Mughal treasures which Nadir Shah took to Persia. It is said that Nadir Shah named the remarkable jewel as the Kohinoor, or "mountain of light". From Nadir Shah it went to his grandson, and from him to the ruling family in Kabul, the Ghilzars. When Maharaja Ranjit Singh captured Kabul, the Kohinoor went with him to Lahore where it stayed until Punjab was annexed by the British in 1849. When Sir John Lawrence took over the administration of Punjab as chief commissioner, the Kohinoor was given to him. He put it in his waistcoat pocket and forgot all about it for six weeks. Luckily, he found it there and managed to send it to Queen Victoria.[135] Soon, it found its place in the British Crown where it rests today. Dalip Singh, after being pensioned off, went to live in England as a country gentleman, and his descendants today

134. Bamber Gascoigne, *The Great Moghuls.*

135. Ibid.

have been making noises claiming that the Kohinoor should be returned to them as they are the rightful owners of the stone!

Dalhousie had no patience with the tender feelings of the rulers of the Indian states and introduced legislation in his council which was, in effect an active extension of the subsidiary alliance. He introduced the Doctrine of Lapse[136] by which if a ruler died without heirs, his state would automatically be annexed to the British territories. Hindu rulers who had no heirs would usually adopt a son from among their close relatives, and bring him up to be their heir. But this ancient practice was given short shrift by Dalhousie who first decreed that the heir should be approved of by the Governor General and later, in practice, annexed such states anyway. Also, he ruled that, if a state was badly administered, causing hardship and disaffection among the people, that state should be permanently annexed by the British.[137] During Bentinck's time such a situation had arisen in Mysore, but after taking over of the administration and running it through a Resident for 40 years, the administration was restored to the Maharaja well after 1858. These measures regarding states demonstrated the unilateral assumption of paramountcy of the Company administration over all the states which had not been sanctified by any treaty. Those states that did not fulfill the decrees of the Company, and with Dalhousie assuming (perhaps correctly) that British administration was far more enlightened and was for the good of the people, fell under the British one by one. Satara in 1848, Jaitpur and Sambalpur in 1849, Baghat in 1850, Udaipur in 1852, Jhansi in 1853 and Nagpur in 1854 were all annexed.[138] Baghat and Udaipur were restored by Lord Canning at a later date. But then annexations created considerable disaffection among the rulers and their nobles and henchmen,

136. Vincent A. Smith, *The Oxford History of India*, p. 658.
137. Ibid., p. 659.
138. Ibid.

often including the people as in the case of Nagpur. Oudh, and the Nizam's province of Berar were annexed under the "misgovernment" rule.[139]

Dalhousie also abolished titular rulers who had no control over the states they were supposed to rule. The Nawab of the Carnatic was reduced to the Prince of Arcot with a pension, and the Raja of Tanjore was abolished altogether. He also abolished the pensions of those princes and dignitaries who he thought did not properly fulfill the conditions of succession. The pension of the ex-Peshwa Baji Rao was denied to his adopted son Nana Sahib when Baji Rao died in 1853.

These measures, pushed through without consideration of local sentiments were some of the prime causes of spread of the Mutiny when it did breakout.

In civil government and reform, Dalhousie went ahead confidently and did contribute massively to ushering India into the modern age. Extensive expansion of irrigation, especially in Punjab and completion of the Ganges canal in 1853 were significant achievements.[140] He initiated a great road-building programme including the Grand Trunk road from Lahore to Peshawar.[141] Having already worked on the expansion of railways in Britain, he planned a network of railways for India which was designed to fulfil both strategic military and commercial needs. By the time he left India in 1854,[142] 200 miles of railway had been completed and brought into operation. He introduced telegraph services, building an 800 mile telegraph line from Calcutta to Agra which was commissioned in 1854. The telegraph lines were extended to Lahore and Peshawar by 1857, after the departure of Dalhousie. Dalhousie reformed the postal system by standardising the postage rate to half anna (or

139. Ibid.

140. K.M. Panickkar, *A Survey of Indian History*, p. 261.

141. Vincent A. Smith, *The Oxford History of India*, p. 657.

142. Bisheshwar Prasad, *Bondage and Freedom 1707 to 1947*, Vol. I, "Bondage, 1707-1858", p. 468.

6.25 paise) per letter to anywhere in India with stamps substituted for cash payments. In this he had for inspiration the system introduced by Sir Robert Peel in Britain.

Dalhousie spread the rise of high schools and colleges by the system of grant-in-aid. Provided local agencies or service minded people raised funds and started high schools and colleges, his government would provide a substantial share of the operating expenses every year. This encouragement increased schools and colleges enormously. Through his efforts, the universities of Calcutta, Bombay and Madras were finally established in 1857 although he was not present in India to see them. He also established an engineering college at Roorkee, then known as the Thomason College of Engineering which has developed into the University of Roorkee in the present day. He took steps for the conservation of forests, and even tried to improve the living conditions and administration of jails.[143]

In the development of India on modern lines, this versatile and energetic genius rammed through measures and implemented development programmes in six years which a less gifted individual would have taken a lifetime to achieve.

143. Vincent A. Smith, *The Oxford History of India*, p. 661.

8

Reasons for British Success

After the Norman conquest of Britain in 1066 A.D., the British people were largely confined to the British Isles except for fighting the French from time to time on the soil of France. English kings were allied by marriage to the kings of France and Spain, Portugal and Holland, Belgium and Burgundy, through themselves and their family members. Diplomatic relationships and war were quite common. But Britain was never again invaded. The late Winston Churchill half-humourously credited this unique distinction to the choppy and windy waters of the English Channel. But the British navy was no less responsible. The British had a long tradition of seamanship, from their Viking ancestors to the hardy and intrepid fisherfolk who sailed the North Sea, the English Channel and the north-eastern fringes of the Atlantic Ocean. The warm waters of the Gulf Stream from the shores of Central America brought a lot of fish to Britain and the British had learnt to exploit this resource to their advantage.

However, it was during the reign of Elizabeth I, the Virgin Queen, that British seafarers learnt to cross the oceans. Spain had shown the way. Columbus' expedition to find a sea route to India for its fabulous spices, its cloth and its gems, actually resulted in 1492 in his landing by mistake on the shores of America. Other Spaniards followed the Portuguese no less, and Spain and Portugal had established vast colonies in Central and South America. Their ships, escorted by fighting ships called

'Men-of-War' crossed and re-crossed the Atlantic Ocean at will, bringing gold and exotic produce and taking back soldiers and settlers to establish their conquest and work the land.

Queen Elizabeth's captains discovered an excellent means to participate in gathering the growing wealth from the newly discovered lands of America. With the encouragement and blessing of their remarkable Queen, they went forth in their ships towards the west, efficiently intercepted the Spanish galleons returning with gold, boarded them and transferred the riches to their own ships and high-tailed it for home. This became such a lucrative hobby that the rapid enrichment of Britain can really be dated from this period. Efforts by Philip of Spain to stop this traffic failed. First, he tried to marry Elizabeth but was rejected. Next, he tried to invade Britain, sending a large fleet of men-of-war with troops, but the British stopped the fleet at Plymouth Sound, defeated and scattered it. Ever since then the British navy had remained supreme on the seas. Neither the challenge of the French fleet during Napoleon's time, nor the German challenges of World War I, nor the German u-boat (submarine) challenge of World War II could beat the British navy.

It was through the means of this remarkable naval ability that Britain decided to send embassies and traders to India, in the wake of the Portuguese Vasco da Gama's discovery of a sea-route to India in 1498. It was Portugal which first came for trade in 1510 and commandeered the spice trade for nearly a century.[1] With their ships equipped with naval guns and boarding parties of marines, they easily displaced the Arab traders whose boats or dhows had not shown any change for 500 years. The British won a trading concession to establish a trading port and a "factory" at Surat on the west coast at the mouth of the Tapti river in 1612.[2]

1. Geoffrey Moorhouse, *India Britannica*, p. 28.
2. Ibid., p. 29.

The Mughal empire, four years into the reign of Jahangir, was at its height, confident in its own power, steeped in its own wealth and little inclined to waste much time on little trading posts. However, where the Portuguese initially and the English later, made an impact was their influence on the pilgrim traffic from the west coast and Gujarat to the port of Jeddah, and thence to Mecca and Madina. For over 300 years, Arab ships had monopolised and exploited this traffic. After the Portuguese came, for a hundred years, they controlled the traffic levying charges and imposts on the pilgrims at will. The Mughals had regarded the Portuguese unfavourably because of this, but at the same time the Portuguese could use their control of the seas to bargain for more concessions. The British, however, after displacing the Portuguese soon after they arrived, actually protected and facilitated the traffic. The Mughals and the Bahmani kings were beholden to the British for this signal service.

The Mughals knowing little of the importance of sea-power, and having neglected development of a navy, were unable to impose their will on the sea-powers. However, at this stage, there was little need for them to do so as there was no threat of enemy incursions from the sea, and had they decided to do so, they could presumably easily have dislodged these foreigners. Moreover, neither the Portuguese and certainly not the British were interested in conquest. They were only interested in trade.

In time, the British settlements organised themselves for protection against adventurous local potentates who tried to attack and sack the settlements just as they were wont to do against any prosperous neighbouring kings or chieftains. They fortified their settlements and trained their writers and factors in soldiery, as they did when Surat was attacked by Shivaji in 1664 and 1670, or when Madras was about to be attacked by Hyder Ali in 1779. The very fact that such civilian personnel agreed to be trained as soldiers without any extra compensation and that they actually fought at the walls of their settlement under severe threat by powerful rulers, illustrates the strange British character. There was no thought of surrender or escape. There was no fear in their minds as to what would happen to them had they lost. Most people fearing such consequences would have tried to insure their own survival either by escaping or by turning against their superior officers and handing over the factory to the attackers in return for promises by the attackers of safe conduct. The people within the walls of Bahamanbad and Alor and Multan betrayed their king Jaisimha to the Arabs in 714 A.D. Mir Jafar betrayed Siraj-ud-Doula to the British in 1757 A.D. Tipu's commanders betrayed him to the British in 1799 A.D. There are innumerable such instances in Indian history. However, the British stuck to their romantic loyalty to king and country and defended themselves unitedly and determinedly.

The funny British people, often petty and peevish, many times noble and generous, at all times loyal, brave and buccaneering, and still with many adventurous and engaging rogues and scoundrels in their ranks, were never understood, and often scorned by the other Europeans. Yet they have struck a strange rapport with the people of India. While their rank and file were hated and laughed at, their officers, their governors and their administrators were often liked, admired and imitated. Victor Jacquemont the French botanist who travelled extensively between Calcutta and Bombay had this to say about the British (as quoted in Geoffrey Moorhouse's book *India Britannica*):

"The English who inspire so much respect in the natives by their power, strength, wealth and morality (always true to their work, upright and just ninety-nine times out of a hundred) who... receive from them so many Asiatically servile demonstrations of respect and submission, the English are the only European people that do not take pleasure in these marks of respect. They esteem themselves too highly, they despise the coloured races too much to be flattered by their homage..."

Similarly, the Abbe Dubois, another Frenchman who spent thirty years in India, wrote in 1823 that: "the justice and prudence which the present rulers display in endeavouring to make these people less unhappy than they have been hitherto; the anxiety which they manifest in increasing their material comfort; and above all, the inviolable respect which they constantly show for the customs and religious beliefs of the country; and lastly the protection they afford to the weak as well as the strong...all these have contributed more to the consolidation of their power than even their victories and conquests" (quoted in *India Britannica* by Geoffrey Moorhouse).

These aspects of the British character helped them win the confidence of the people, so much so that people in India during these times trusted them rather than some of their own people who abused their trust and exploited them inhumanly for centuries.

In common with other European people like the French, the Portuguese and Spanish, the Germans and the Dutch, the British had developed their military drills, their technology in artillery and their use of gunpowder to sap and mine fort walls and their use of cavalry so that they enjoyed a far greater advantage over the forces of Indian states. But above and beyond that they had consciously practiced, preached and enforced the quality of discipline in their military units. The noted historian Vincent A. Smith says about discipline:

"An advantage that has been more justly stressed was that of military discipline. From the time of Alexander, the cult of discipline has given to men an often decisive advantage over superior numbers of brave but unregulated troops. The habit of obedience, the willingness to face dangers and suffer hardship to order, the power of restraint and the inner cohesion that discipline breeds provide a morale far superior to anything that personal or clan loyalty, the spirit of adventure or personal bravery can produce of themselves."[3]

The redcoats, as they were called because of the red coats of the British infantry, became famous all over the world. The thin red line advancing inexorably to the attack under heavy fire, and the unshakeable red square in defence, won many a battle against superior forces, very much more so in India. The successful defence of Arcot by Clive against the French in 1751, the advance of Major Kilpatrick at Plassey which contributed greatly to victory in the battle in 1757, Sir Eyre Coote's victory against Hyder Ali at Porto Novo in 1779, the victory won over Bhonsle's Mahrattas at Assaye in 1803, and the defeat of the Amirs of Sind at the battle of Meanee in 1843; all these demonstrated to the observer the superior value of discipline in winning battles.

To add to this superiority of British troops in military technique and discipline, should be mentioned the capacity of the British to train local levies, be they from Madras or Bombay or Calcutta. The Indian troops trained by the British and fighting for the British became equally effective and feared. The 'sepoy' advancing relentlessly with fixed bayonet, when even under heavy fire, threw the defenders first into confusion and then into panic. The British, the French, even Italian officers could train the Indian troops to such disciplined perfection and, of course, lead them into battle and wrest success regularly, often against far superior numbers. However, Indian kings, Indian generals, Indian officers, at this particular period of history could not do so. Nor did they attempt to. It was much easier to hire these foreign mercenaries and have them train, equip and fight these men against enemies. The Nizam of Hyderabad, Mahadji Scindia, the Gaekwad of Baroda, Maharaja Ranjit Singh of the Sikhs, even Tipu of Mysore hired foreign mercenaries to train their troops to employ correctly their

3. Vincent A. Smith, *The Oxford History of India*, pp. 447, 448.

artillery, and exploit correctly overall the characteristics of the infantry, the cavalry, and the artillery. While Indian kings understood, during this period, the value of having guns, cavalry and so on, and although they obtained them and incorporated them in their armies, they could not train their troops and lead them successfully. This is probably because they did not have the objective approach and had not subjected themselves to self-discipline. Their own methods of command and control were all too subjective and always inspired suspicion and fear. When checking subordinate princes or generals they would all too often either explode into spluttering rage, or exile them or have them killed by intrigue and devious means. These characteristics are probably as common today as they were in the 18th and 19th centuries. The British (and French) on the other hand could train any men, whether the Tamils or the Sikhs, the Bengali Brahmins or the Mahrattas, the converted Muslims of Mysore or the converted Andhras and Kannadigas of Hyderabad or Gulbarga and turn them into disciplined troops, steadfast under fire, undaunted in defence and irresistible in attack. The bulk of the armies of the company were Indian troops officered by the British but having a subordinate category of Indian officers through whom they administered the troops and commanded them in battle. The tradition of these Indian officers have been carried into the Indian army in the form of junior commissioned officers (and equivalent ranks in the navy and air force). This ability to train any men into first-class fighting troops and lead them into battle was one of the most important reasons for the success of British policy in India. Even officers of very senior rank, for example, the Governor General himself could march and live with the men, sharing their trials and austerities, and being seen by the men to share them. The Mughal and Mahratta commanders could also do the same, and often did so, but something was lacking. That something was obviously the failure to develop steadfast and committed leadership at levels of command of what today are called a 'section', a 'platoon', a 'company', a 'battalion', and a 'brigade'. The senior commanders, although often in the field, could not give up their luxuries and were accompanied by large tents, rugs, bolsters and beds; large retinues of personal servants; exotic food; personal families and so on, making their movement awkward and cumbersome. When Jahangir moved from Ajmer to Mandu (near Ujjain), his retinue took twelve hours to pass any one place.

The tradition of a liberal but practical education imparted to British nobility in the public schools and in Oxford and Cambridge undoubtedly developed the power of objective thought in the students. The stiff discipline in the British regiments, and the team games which first developed in the villages and which were fostered more methodically in the public schools were all not a little responsible to develop the British character. They could remain individualistic and yet could combine together when needed to confront and overcome enemies either in battle or in diplomacy. The present tendency in India to condemn everything British and to view them as evil men who cheated Indians and exploited them until they were liberated in 1947, is a sad example of Indians losing sight of the methods and techniques of the British in ruling (reasonably benevolently) countries from Canada to Australia, and from British Guiana to Hong Kong. They said that: "the battle of Waterloo was won on the playing fields of Eton". Waterloo was fought in 1814. In 1991 or so, when the chief guest at a school day function in a Hindu school, praised the games facilities in the school, and mentioned this harmless saying about Waterloo to illustrate how games playing developed leadership, the presiding officer, a senior priest invited for the occasion from Delhi, when his turn came to speak, literally burst out with fury and called such references as illustrative of the still "slavish" mindset prevalent among Indians in regard to the British. He recommended that the students forget all about this saying about Waterloo. Needless to say, the chief guest was greatly embarrassed and was hard pressed to keep both his countenance and his equanimity. The lack of restraint in the case of the presiding officer is a common trait among many others also.

This tendency to condemn everything British and encourage Indian languages without any discrimination is very common among people promoting the vernacular languages for the sake of strengthening the identity of the state, or of the majority of the people in the state. The denial of education in English almost completely in the villages, has deprived millions of bright children of sufficient exposure to English which is no longer merely the language of Britain, of our hated ex-rulers, but which is now a world language with a rich storehouse of world literature in the arts and science. Yet, the very same militant advocates of the banishment of English send their own children to the most expensive schools where the principal medium of instruction is English.

However, harking back to our analysis of the success enjoyed by the British in India, one has to take cognisance of the genuine desire of the British from the time of Lord Hastings in 1818, or even earlier to "improve" the Indian people, to "regenerate" their society, and to usher them into the "modern age of science and reason". The six hundred years of the pre-eminence of the education system in Oxford and Cambridge where free-thinking was allowed without fear or favour had resulted in, at all times, the existence of a nucleus of men who devoted their time to thought beyond their own limited personal requirements. Thus, it was that science and the arts, trade and commerce, the desire to explore new lands grew phenomenally in Britain. This phase grew at the same time with the growth of Reason in Europe. Emerging from the dark ages of superstition, fear and poverty, the Europeans started developing theoretical models of a better society. Fourier and St Simone in France, James and John Stuart Mill, father and son, in Britain, Hegel and later Marx, in Germany were prominent in bringing out their concept of a more egalitarian basis for the future of societies. This Utilitarian school was for introducing western education and laws immediately.

Meanwhile, in Britain certain Christian movements had taken the lead in fighting for humanitarian causes like the abolition of slavery in the United States, the betterment of living and working conditions of the workers caught up in the industrial revolution in Britain where seamstresses worked in dim light for 16 hours a day; where workers in factories were kept at their looms for 12 to 14 hours continuously; where workers were forced to buy bread from the factory-owned retail shops, such bread having a substantial component of talc mixed up with the wheat and so on.[4] These movements produced leaders like William Wilberforce who felt all Indians had to be converted to Christianity to liberate them from the "depths of superstition and fear into which they were sunk because of their own cruel religions". Such of these reformers who had some influence in ruling circles in Britain, were for starting a mass conversion programme of Indians into Christians and for moving Indians away from superstitions and ignorance, cruelty and indifference into the benevolent light of "Christian love and kindness". They believed that this was the best way to redeem and rescue Indians from their present plight and to usher them into the "modern age of science and reason" These were the Evangelicals or the Clapham sect.

The administrators and officers who had lived and worked in India for two or more decades and who had some understanding of the Indian people, whether Hindu, Muslim, Sikh or Jain, were against the introduction of radical reforms. They advocated caution as they realised the value of existing indigenous institutions in society and their strength. They understood the power of local religions, and the deeply

4. Karl Marx, *Capital*.

ingrained belief of the people in them, and that Indian religions had little to learn from the West. These "Orientalists" as they were called at the time, had read deeply into Eastern religions and philosophy, and had dealt with Indian people of all religions, castes, and from all economic and professional brackets. They felt that any changes introduced should not be such as to try and erase the in-built beliefs and traditions all at once. They believed that a society in existence for hundreds of years could only be modified with education over a number of years, combined with judicious introduction of reforms. They condemned such books as James Mill's *History of India* which criticised and ridiculed Indian religions and philosophies, as the work of a bigot. James Mill started writing his book in 1809 and completed and published it in 1817, but throughout his life, he had never set foot in India. The Orientalists realised the ethnic and caste and sub-caste variety of India, along with the variety of geography, customs and beliefs in the sub-continent and highlighted the folly of introducing uniform and hasty reforms.

For example, around this time, Colonel Stewart, a member of the Asiatic Society of India published and circulated a paper called "Vindications of the Hindus by a Bengal Officer", where he said that Hinduism hardly needed the ameliorating hand of Christianity to make its people form a civilised society. He also said: "Whenever I look around me, in the vast region of Hindu Mythology, I discover piety in the garb of allegory: and I see Morality, at every turn, blended with every tale; and as far as I can rely on my own judgement, it appears the most complete and ample system of Moral Allegory that the world has ever produced."[5]

Sir J. Malcolm, one of the well-known administrators of the period, writing in about 1832 had this to say: "Let us proceed

5. Geoffrey Moorhouse, *India Britannica*, p. 89.

on a course of gradual improvement, and when our rule ceases, as cease it must, (though probably at a remote period) as a natural consequence of our success in the diffusion of knowledge, we shall as a nation have the proud boast that we have preferred the civilisation to the continued subjection of India. When our power is gone, our name will be revered; for we shall leave a moral monument more noble and imperishable than the hand of man ever constructed."[6]

Also, Warren Hastings, for example, never believed that the British, or for that matter, any Europeans, held a monopoly of civilised values. He said that "the people of this country (India) do not require our aid to furnish them with a rule of conduct or a standard for their property." Hastings had learnt languages, Persian and Sanskrit being among them. He was steeped in knowledge of the people and their customs, and first introduced the system by which his judicial officers tried cases in the local language rather than in Persian, the court language of the Mughals.

This policy of gradual reform did not prevent Lord William Bentinck, genuine believer and advocate of this policy, from introducing some truly radical reforms. One was the abolition of sati, the ancient custom of the wife immolating herself on her husband's funeral pyre. The reaction from the people could hardly be called tumultuous or earth-shaking. The other major reform was of education where he decreed that the content of education should be western, that is, western science, western philosophy and literature, and that the medium of instruction should be English. However, this education would not be to the exclusion of Indian languages and Indian philosophy and arts. Realising that such an education was an advantage in obtaining employment in the administrative and judicial

6. Sir J. Malcolm in "Memoir on Central India", quoted by Smith, V.A. in *The Oxford History of India*, p. 580.

services of the Company, there was tremendous demand for seats in the educational institutions, and the sale of books in English multiplied enormously.

The remarkable feature of British administration from the time of Warren Hastings in 1772 to the end of the period of Lord Dalhousie in 1856, was a continuous interest on the part, not only of the Governor General and his officers, but also very much on the part of the British Government in London to "improve" the welfare of the people of India; to introduce a legal system which aimed at dispensation of justice according to the ancient beliefs, customs and practices of the people but tempered by "the universal laws of humanity". The British enforced law and order, dispensed justice, recast the education system so that world knowledge and culture became enmeshed with education, and devised a revenue system that was easily understood and adopted by the people because it built on old systems, and developed the country by large and widespread irrigation schemes, a reliable road network and the promotion of commerce. The exploitation of India by the Company and later, by many other commercial enterprises continued, but India experienced a regeneration, both physically and intellectually.

Therefore, the introduction of acceptable laws and their enforcement, the development of the country and the promotion of commerce, the resuscitation of intellectual life by a new and challenging system of education, and a benign, assured administration for the welfare of the people, were all important factors which ensured the acceptance of British power and the success of policies which could prolong British hegemony for another hundred years.[7] The Indian kings,

7. K.M. Panikkar, says in his *A Survey of Indian History*, Chapter 20, that "In short, from the point of view of actual administrative work, the British Government was one of the best in the world...", p. 261.

princes and chieftains who had been either dispossessed, or whose activities were closely monitored by British Residents in the states were dissatisfied and chafed at the increasing controls. But the vast majority of the common people, hitherto exploited, abused, ill-treated, neglected and overridden by every small commander of violent men were greatly happy at a predictable life in which they could work and derive the benefits of their work, in which they could plan a life for their families and progeny. No administration since that of the Mauryas and the Guptas, and to a great extent of the emperors Akbar and Jahangir, had so truly instituted a government which promoted the well-being of the common people. A system of government that could afford scope for the talents of the growing intelligentsia and of an intellectual elite, further enriched the people. British administration was regenerating India. Even the subsequent rise of national sentiments could not have been possible if British administration had followed the traditional pattern of systematic roughshod exploitation of the previous two centuries.

To summarise briefly, British successes in India which resulted in the small country of Britain capturing, dominating and ruling a great sub-continent and an ancient people, famous in Europe and Asia for its civilisation, its natural and created wealth, and for the bravery of its ruling classes were many. British domination of the sea around India enabled it to strike the Indian coastline anywhere at will. The steadfast courage and boldness of the Company officers and men, defending their territories successfully although so far away from their home island, enabled them to hold on to their factories, and later, to expand their influence over large territories. Their guile on the one hand, and their character on the other enabled them to play off the local powers against one other and, at the same time, win the confidence of the people they administered and, generally, the allies they supported. Their military drills and techniques combined with their discipline proved a deciding factor in the victories of their small forces against Indian forces many times their size. Their ability to train and fight Indian troops as major components in their armies, and to command the loyalty of such troops was one of the decisive factors in their successes. A humane tradition and a liberal education enabled their administrators and their officers to capture the minds of the people through enlightened government, which was in marked contrast to the rampaging hordes of the Mahrattas, or the plundering troops of Muslim potentates. Conquering British troops were rarely allowed to loot and rape the conquered peoples. Their non-interference in religious matters, and their freedom from religious bigotry disarmed any antagonistic feelings the ordinary people may have had. Their emphasis on the proper dispensation of justice through a judicial process won the people's support. Their urge to improve the well-being of the people by works of development like irrigation canals, roads, inland water transport or riverine communications, careful imposition and collection of taxes and reduction of impost barriers, revived the economy and promoted the enrichment of the common people. Their political ability and their military superiority enabled them to consolidate and stabilise their rule. Finally, the jealousies, quarrels and fratricidal wars among the more powerful Indian powers like the Mahrattas and the Sikhs, the Nizam and the Mysore rulers, namely Hyder Ali and Tipu Sultan enabled the British to play off those powers against each other, or the factions among them. The lassitude and lethargy, the vicious self-indulgence and ineptitude of the Rajputs, the Mughals, the Amirs of Sind, the Nawab of Oudh and sundry other Indian princes and chieftains during the period 1720 to 1850, rendered the British conquests easier. Thus, the British who came to India merely to trade, remained to rule.

9

The Mutiny and After

The Mutiny of 1857 and 1858 has been variously called the Sepoy Mutiny, the Great Indian Mutiny, the Mutiny, and so on. Marx has called it the first war of Indian independence. Veer Savarkar has called it the War of Indian independence. If one takes a narrow view, that the basic feature was the uprising of the sepoys of the British East India Company, against their British officers, and against the Government of the company, then, indeed it could be called as the Sepoy Mutiny. If one considers that the Mutiny encompassed a large number of units, in fact, almost all the Native Infantry battalions and regiments of the Bengal Presidency army, and caused restiveness and disaffection among many units of the Presidency armies of Bombay and Madras, and that it took more than one-and-a-half years for the uprising to be suppressed and for Indian units to be disbanded and re-created, then the term, the Great Indian Mutiny, would be justified. If, however, one takes into consideration the other aspects also in conjunction, namely, the involvement of various rajas, kings and chieftains in making common cause with the sepoys and fighting the British, and the general support of rural people mainly in Bengal, Oudh, Rohilkhand, Bundelkhand and in parts of Punjab, then the term, The War of Indian Independence may be appropriate. Although the western and southern parts of India were said to be untouched, there are evidences of disaffection in the north having communicated itself to the Bombay and Madras armies which were perhaps waiting to be sure before themselves joining. The uprising fell short of a war as there was no central leadership or central and effective co-ordination or central objective as for example, the defeat and expulsion of the British power from India as a whole, or even from north India. However, the duration of the uprising and the time taken to fully suppress it was more than 18 months, from March 1857 to October 1858. In fact, one of the leaders, the able Tantia Tope, was captured (he was betrayed) from hiding and hanged only in April 1859. In that sense also the term, war of independence, would be quite appropriate. All things considered, the most appropriate name could be: the Great Indian Uprising. In the interest of connectivity with many other histories of the war, especially those professional works which are so far universally accepted as authorities, it is convenient to merely call this great uprising as simply, the Mutiny. The articles of Karl Marx and Frederick Engels sent regularly during the period to *The New York Daily Tribune*, and published almost verbatim therein, have been compiled under the name, "The First War of Indian Independence, 1857-59." The book by V.D. (Veer) Savarkar, called *The War of Indian Independence* is another book which calls the uprising a war. The articles by Marx and Engels have the great merit that they were written during the Mutiny, their information being based on telegraphic dispatches by correspondents via telegraph from Calcutta to Vienna and London, and on private letters sent home by officers and other ranks serving with the front line British and Indian troops. Their information is as factual as could be under the circumstances of distance and means of communication, and the actual perceptions of the correspondents. But they contain almost a blow-by-blow account of the Mutiny and the operations to control, and later, to suppress it. They are contemporary and not based upon recollection of the participants well after the events. But while all the facts they got are presented, the ratiocinations of Marx and Engels, and their own predictions of further development of operations, suffer from their tendency to represent the British troops in a bad light, and from their subconscious yearning for the defeat and destruction of the British in India.

Savarkar's book was apparently written at a time (during the 1920s) when the freedom movement had gathered considerable momentum and when emotional hostility towards the British in India was at a very high level. While presenting the facts as he knew them, almost every second sentence ends with an exclamation mark indicating high praise for the mutineers and damnation for the British. His conclusions and assumptions lend themselves to be considered as written in a highly charged frame of mind, unlike that of an objective historian. Perhaps, Savarkar deliberately adopted such a style to inspire the freedom fighters of those days, especially those of the Hindu Mahasabha to which he belonged.

Other works in the realm of actual history are mostly written by British professional historians basing their histories on British official dispatches, and accounts of various parts and aspects of the Mutiny of actual participants. Sir Syed Ahmad Khan's book on causes of the Indian revolt is bound to be based on accounts of princes and chieftains actually affected by or whose forebears participated in the uprising. More recent books are by S.N. Sen and R.K. Mazumdar, both written in 1957. British historians tend to play down the strength and substance of the Mutiny over vast areas of India. Indian historians tend to bring out fresh material from Indian sources. But these various sources generally accept the facts of the events that took place, the causes of the Mutiny and its outbreak and its course, and the reasons for its petering out.

The main reason for the outbreak of the Mutiny was the change in the character of the interface between the Indian troops and their British officers.[1] Indian troops had been inducted as sepoys in their Presidency armies, trained by British officers and organised into companies and battalions of infantry, batteries and regiments of artillery and squadrons and regiments of cavalry. Also were trained companies of engineers for many duties but specially so for sapping and mining of fort walls and their demolition with gunpowder, for bursting open fort gates by explosives and for building improvised bridges and roads. Such troops, usually organised in so-called native units had taken part in the many wars of the East India Company and had become quite adept at the use of minor tactics, in the placement and use of artillery guns, and in employment of obstacles in defense lines, and in assault and breaching of fort walls. They had become excellent troops, and were disciplined in maintaining and using scientific tactics in attack and defense, and were generally feared by the motley crowds of the troops of Indian princes and chieftains who lost heart and fled at the slightest manifestation of a reverse somewhere on the battle field. This was often the case during this period of eclipse of Indian powers during the 18th and 19th centuries. Their British officers took care to learn a working degree of the common language of their troops, took interest in their personal concerns and joined them in recreation and celebrations. The troops felt they could trust their officers, identified with them and considered them as part of themselves in the units.

This rapport between the British officers and their Indian troops gradually gave way to a more formal attitude on the part of newly inducted British officers, whereby the Indian troops were generally left to themselves. Communication between officers and men became confined to whatever was actually necessary. The victories gained by the British over Indian

1. Vincent A. Smith, *The Oxford History of India*, p. 666.

princes and chieftains bred a sense of superiority among the British officers, especially in the junior ranks, in relation to their Indian troops. There was less understanding of, and more impatience with, the religious and societal concerns and obligations of the troops. According to Sita Ram Pande, a Brahmin soldier for over forty years since 1812 in the service of the company, as recounted in his memoirs, as quoted in Geoffrey Moorhouse's book *India Britannica*, the British officers had gradually become more aloof. He mentions that "The sahibs" often used to arrange dancing girls' (nautch girls) performances for the recreation of the regiment, and took part in games with their men. Later they stopped arranging such parties because their priest had said that it was wrong. He states that the "Padre sahibs" had been doing many things to estrange the officers from their men (presumably by introducing many restrictions in an evangelical or proselytising spirit). When Pande was a sepoy, his captain would invite some of the men over to his house from time to time and remained talking and eating with them almost the whole day. But forty years or more later, he found that generally many officers spoke to their men only when they had to do so and that the sepoys could see that such communication was irksome for them (the officers). One "sahib" told him that he never knew what to say to the sepoys. But when Pande was a young soldier, the "sahibs" always knew what to say, and how to say it.[2]

Local mutinies had occurred before. In 1806, there was a Mutiny at Vellore in the Madras Presidency because the British commanding officers had ordered that the men (mostly non-Brahmins and Muslims from Tamil and Telugu areas) should stop wearing caste marks or religious marks on their faces and should shave off their beards.[3] Although the Mutiny

2. Geoffrey Moorhouse, *India Britannica*, p. 109.
3. K.L. Srivastava, *The Revolt of 1857 in Central India-Malwa*, p. 80.

was put down, the order regarding caste marks and beards was rescinded. In 1824, there was a Mutiny of units of the Bengal army (in which the sepoys were mainly high-caste Brahmins and Kshatriyas) because they were ordered to go over salt water (the sea, called 'kala pani' or black water) which would have made them lose caste. The units were disbanded but the orders (to move to Rangoon by sea in the first Burma war) were cancelled. Later, four mutinies occurred in the Bengal army between 1843 and 1857. In Bengal and Oudh, the activities of the officers of the East India Company over the previous hundred years, especially since the battle of Plassey, had created a widespread and lurking antagonism among not only the nawabs, princes and chieftains and their dependents, but also among the vast majority of the rural population. The rampaging and domineering style of the company officers, who individually took advantage of the favourable terms of trade extracted by the Company for itself, trampled over the time-honoured practices of trade, taxation and agricultural cultivation in the region. The exemptions enjoyed by the Company in regard to duties payable to the Nawabs of Bengal and Oudh were demanded equally by individual British officers and tradesmen in their personal trading activities which benefited them hugely, whereas local Indian tradesmen were liable to pay all the duties. This even applied to the salt duty which was otherwise an important source of revenue for the Nawabs. The conversion of large areas of agricultural land from rice and cereal cultivation to the cultivation of indigo created famines in the 18th century. Not all the beneficial reforms of Warren Hastings, to some extent Lord Cornwallis, and Lord William Bentinck could neutralise the deep sense of wholesale exploitation felt by all sections of the people, except perhaps the urban people of Calcutta who benefited from the education policies of Lord Bentinck. The people were labouring under a feeling of disaffection which enabled the Mutiny to have a tacit support of the general population, when, in fact, it did breakout due to various other reasons.[4]

Causes of the Mutiny

The causes of the Mutiny should be considered under two different groups, although these groups of causes influenced each other. The developments that directly bore on the feelings of the sepoys and that, in fact, triggered the Mutiny should be in the first group. The extraneous causes that influenced the landed princes and zamindars (landholders) to make common cause with the sepoys and to exploit the Mutiny of the sepoys for their own ends, should belong in the second group.

The complex reasons which impinged directly on the sepoys and caused them to mutiny were many and apparently unrelated to other wider reasons. The gradual alienation of the sepoys of the Bengal army from their British officers was because the officers paid scant attention to the cultivation of the sepoys[5] and considered them merely as paid hirelings who could be commanded to do anything anytime. For the high-caste Brahmin and Kshatriya sepoys of the Bengal army who had become proficient soldiers under the selfsame British officers and their predecessors, this attitude bred a feeling of cynical evaluation of their officers in contrast to the friendly trust and comradely faith of old. The proficient soldier in any army in any country of the world is a proud man, proud of his own strength and of his skill as a soldier, proud of his mental toughness and physical toughness even under extremely adverse conditions. For him to be treated either plainly or covertly as an inferior being, available at beck and call would mean the very destruction of his personality and his self-respect,

4. Bisheshwar Prasad, *Bondage and Freedom 1707 to 1947*, Vol. I, "Bondage, 1707-1858", pp. 531, 532.

5. Geoffrey Moorhouse, *India Britannica*, p. 109.

cultivated under difficult conditions of service where he is often as good as, if not better, than his officer. When the platoon and company are involved in actual attack or defence or in long approach marches or tactical movements lasting many days or weeks over difficult country in trying climatic conditions, the men and their officers approach near equality. While a tough and competent officer will command the respect of his men and save his troops, the weak officer is often saved by his troops. This is the difference between a servant and a soldier. Although the servant may be monetarily better paid and have more comforts than a soldier, the soldier is a superior being who will rarely trade places with the servant, especially an Indian servant for whom the word 'servile' was probably specially invented.

The hundred years of regular victories of the British over Indian powers, often with far less troops but with superior discipline and superior military science, had unconsciously created a feeling of racial and civilisational superiority which, again probably unconsciously, manifested itself in many small signs in the dealings of British officers,[6] and perhaps even the government, with their troops. Hence the insensitivity to the signs of disaffection that existed, perhaps in many units of the army, and the neglect in timely recognition and removal of such disaffection. On the other hand, the Indian troops themselves felt proud and confident among themselves as important participants in the victories of the British over their Indian opponents.[7]

The recent policy of the company of recruiting soldiers of lower castes into the Bengal army probably added to the general feeling of discontent. Soldiers of lower castes had, from the early 18th century, been regularly recruited into the Madras and Bombay Presidency armies. Hence the decision of the

6. Vincent A. Smith, *The Oxford History of India*, p. 672.

7. Ibid., p. 666.

company administration to include soldiers of lower castes in the Bengal army without taking into consideration the deep-rooted feelings of caste differences created a sense of alienation among the older soldiers.[8]

The activities of the officious Protestant priests who truly believed that it was their Christian mission to convert Hindu and Muslim soldiers to what they were convinced was the true religion caused no small irritation. The priests failed to realise that the ancient beliefs and practices of the Hindus and the strong faith of the Muslims had sustained these peoples over centuries of hardship and turmoil.[9]

In this atmosphere of restiveness and rumblings, the British introduced the new Enfield rifle which had cartridges wrapped in greased paper which had to be bitten off before being loaded into the rifle. The rumours ran around that fat of cows and pigs were used for the greased paper, and many units refused to accept the cartridges. Some more sensitive officers of the higher command in Calcutta realised the folly and tried to convince the soldiers that wax was being used, although, in fact, the Woolwich Works in England had used beef fat in the initial stages which was discontinued once the opposition from India became known. Orders were even issued at some place to withdraw the cartridges, and for the soldiers to use whatever fat or oil they could get to slip the cartridges into the rifle.[10] But one might say that the fat was already in the fire. The single matter of the cartridges finally triggered the Mutiny.

On 22nd January 1857, incendiary fires occurred in the cantonments of Calcutta. On 25th February, the 19th Native Regiment mutinied at Berhampore, some miles north of Calcutta, the men objecting to the cartridges given to them.

8. Bisheshwar Prasad, *Bondage and Freedom 1707 to 1947*, Vol. I, "Bondage, 1707-1858", p. 542.
9. Ibid., p. 541.
10. Vincent A. Smith, *The Oxford History of India*, p. 667 (see footnote), p. 668.

The Regiment was disbanded in March. The 34th Native Infantry mutinied at Barrackpore and fought hand to hand with their officers. In April, incendiary fires occurred in several cantonments of the Bengal army, at Allahabad, Agra and Ambala. In the same month, men of the 3rd Regiment of Light Cavalry at Meerut mutinied and the offenders were jailed on 9th May. On 10th May, a Sunday, men of the 3rd Regiment along with three other regiments released their comrades from jail, shot their officers, and took off for Delhi 40 miles away.[11] The Mutiny had started!

The causes which alienated the Indian ruling classes and the peasantry, and thus enabled the mutineers to operate all over Bengal, Bihar and Oudh, and in other areas of North and Central India, were diverse and had been building up for some decades. From the time of Plassey, the Company and its officers enjoyed unfair advantage in trade as compared to the local tradesmen, in that they were exempted from paying duties to the Nawab at Murshidabad. With the threat of force always in the background, Company officers indulging in the 'country trade' often commandeered produce of the rural folk at lower prices. The Permanent Settlement of 1793 introduced by Lord Cornwallis alienated the village owners and tenure holders from the land and made it possible for the erstwhile tax collection officials to become owners. The subsidiary alliance system of Lord Wellesley broke the power of many rulers whose actions were, in effect, supervised by British Residents backed by Company forces maintained in their states at the Rulers' cost, ostensibly to protect them from any invaders from neighbouring states. The proliferation of missionary activity and the building of churches, introducing a strange new religion, heightened suspicion and distrust among the ordinary people in the villages and small towns. The penetration of

11. K. Marx and F. Engels, *The First Indian War of Independence 1857-59*, p. 41.

British reforms into the social life of ordinary people disrupted age-old social practices like sati or widow-burning and female infanticide during the time of Lord Bentinck. Likewise, the introduction of western education with its emphasis on European science, literature and on new legal concepts greatly reduced the importance of the Brahmin priests and Muslim mullahs who had hitherto had a firm grip on the minds of their adherents. The irrigation canals and trunk roads ended the isolation and self-sufficiency of the villages and seriously threatened the survival of the village cottage industries like spinning and weaving, iron-working, coppersmithy, goldsmithy, and so on.[12]

While the changes mentioned were reasonably spaced out, the reforms and changes introduced during the eight years of Lord Dalhousie's tenure as Governor General, from 1848 to 1856 saw many changes being rapidly introduced. The expansion of road activity and the building of railroads and introduction of smoke-belching steam engines, which also emitted sparks at night accompanied by unearthly noise, struck unease, not to say fear, in the minds of the common folk. Age-old beliefs encrusted with superstition gave rise to the feeling that the foreigners were in league with the devils. Rajas, nawabs, princes, chieftains and zamindars felt greatly threatened as even their rights to rule over their own lands were subject to close scrutiny and denial by Dalhousie and his lieutenants. If it was felt that a raja or nawab was not ruling his subjects according to the principles laid down by Aristotle and Plato, the raja or nawab could be dispossessed and the rulership taken over by the British. In this, Dalhousie's judgement was final. If a raja or nawab died without direct heirs, the rulership was to be taken over by the British. In this respect, the ancient practice of Hindu monarchies adopting an

12. Bisheshwar Prasad, *Bondage and Freedom 1707 to 1947*, Vol. I, "Bondage, 1707-1858", p. 530.

heir from among their close relatives, if they did not have direct heirs, was deliberately disregarded. This specifically happened in the case of the Rani of Jhansi whose husband adopted an heir before he died as he was issueless, for whom the Rani exercised her right of being regent as the heir was still a minor. All these measures, introduced and implemented with determination and vigour within a short span of eight years, precipitated dissatisfaction and discontent and were direct causes for the alarm and hostility of the general population.[13]

All in all, the seventy years before 1857 saw such rapid-fire changes as had not occurred for many centuries and upset the social balance that had existed with but minor disturbances.[14] The only major social disturbances had been at the times when Muslim rulers took it upon themselves to forcibly convert Hindus, but that was mostly well before the start of the Mughal era.

Development and Course of the Mutiny

At the time of the Meerut mutiny on 10th May 1857, the Bengal army had already been in a state of dissatisfaction for more than three months. Mutinous actions had been taking place at frequent intervals since 22nd January when incendiary fires had broken out in the cantonments of Calcutta, triggered off by the sepoys having to bite off the greased paper of the cartridges before loading into the musket. On 25th February, the 19th Native Regiment mutinied at Berhampore, about 170 kms north of Calcutta, the men objecting to the cartridges given to them. The Regiment was disbanded in March. At the end of March, the 34th Sepoy Regiment stationed at Barrackpore, a few miles up-river from Calcutta, allowed one of its men to advance with a loaded musket upon the parade ground, and after calling upon his comrades to mutiny,

13. Ibid., p. 530.

14. Ibid., p. 529.

attacked and wounded the Adjutant and Sergeant Major of his regiment. During the hand-to-hand fighting that then took place, many sepoys joined the fighting, attacking their officers with the butt end of their muskets, while hundreds of the other sepoys looked passively on. Subsequently, this regiment was disbanded. During April, there were incendiary fires in several cantonments of the Bengal army at Allahabad, Agra, Ambala and there was a mutiny of the 3rd Regiment of the Light Cavalry at Meerut. At the beginning of May there were signs of mutiny at Lucknow which was however, prevented by the promptitude of Sir Henry Lawrence. On 9th May, the mutineers of the 3rd Regiment Light Cavalry, were put in jail on their being sentenced to imprisonment.[15]

On the evening of 10th May, the following day, sepoys of the Light Cavalry the 11th and 20th Native Regiments, assembled on the parade ground, killed the officers trying to pacify them and released their comrades from jail.[16] It was evening of a Sunday, and the British part of the brigade consisting of one regiment of infantry and one of cavalry, and units of artillery, were able to concentrate only by nightfall and were unable to stop the three regiments of mutineers who took off for Delhi about 40 miles away. In Delhi, they were joined by the units of the Delhi garrison which consisted of the 38th, 54th, and 74th Regiments of Infantry and a company of Indian artillery. The British officers were attacked and killed and the Mughal emperor Bahadur Shah Zafar, who had been moved out to Mehrauli, was proclaimed emperor of all India. Meanwhile at Meerut, six companies of sappers and miners murdered their commanding officer, Major Frazer, on 15th of May and moved out to Delhi. Pursuit by the British 6th Dragoon Guards was unable to stop them although they inflicted 50 to 60 casualties

15. K. Marx and F. Engels, *The First Indian War of Independence 1857-59*, pp. 40-41.

16. Ibid.

(killed) on the mutineers. At Ferozepur in Punjab, the 57th and 45th Native Infantry Regiments mutinied but were put down by force by Sir John Lawrence. Still all the native troops there were in an openly mutinous state. On 19th May, troops at Calcutta tried unsuccessfully to take over possession of Fort William. Three British regiments arrived from England at Bombay and were despatched overland to Calcutta forthwith. Sepoy regiments, retaining their cohesion as regiments, were moving about Oudh and Bengal. The sudden turn of events in the first three weeks of May found the British desperately concentrating British troops wherever possible and wherever required. British troops under Lord Elgin and General Asburnham which were bound for China were stopped at Colombo and diverted to Calcutta.[17]

Although almost two-thirds of the Bengal army had mutinied, and were moving and camping as regular regiments, none of the Indian princes who could have benefited by assuming leadership of the Indian troops and defeating the British and working towards expelling them from India, were able enough, or prepared enough, to assume such leadership.[18] There was no genius available to exploit the situation. Bahadur Shah, the Mughal emperor was already over eighty years old and could only sympathise with the rebels. He could not muster, from among the princes of his household, anyone who could provide leadership to the rebels, nor could he evolve any plan or strategy for the rebels. Soon, local leaders manifested themselves notably in the person of Nana Sahib of Bithur, the son of the last Peshwa, who had been denied pension after the death of his father; the Rani of Jhansi whose regency of her dead husband's adopted son had not been recognised by Dalhousie; and Tantia Tope, Maharashtrian who was the one

17. Ibid., pp. 41-42.

18. Vincent A. Smith, *The Oxford History of India*, p. 668.

man who saw the possibility of defeating the British and dislodging them from India. However, the efforts of these leaders, and their influence was merely local.

The major development which engaged the maximum attention of the British was the entry of several regiments of rebels into Delhi and the subversion by them of the Delhi garrison, itself consisting of several regiments. Furthermore, mutineers from Rohilkhand and Oudh were daily making their way into Delhi crossing the Jumna by the Bridge of Boats east of Delhi. At this stage, the British were in no position to foresee what course the Mutiny would take, but were determined that Delhi, the seat of the Mughal emperors, should be recaptured from the rebels. Considering the prestige attached to the city, and the possible adverse reaction of the British Government and Parliament at home, it was imperative that Delhi was recaptured at the earliest.[19] British troops along with some native regiments were moved down from the north under General Anson and besieged Delhi, their main deployment being on the North Ridge, north-west of the citadel. But Anson's troop strength was only about 4,000 and were merely deployed to cut off the northern and western sides, but were too weak to attack. The walls of the citadel were seven miles long, and the rebels numbered 40,000. Soon Anson died of cholera and was succeeded by General Barnard who also died by 5th of July. General Reed who succeeded Barnard resigned due to ill-health. The command of the besieging force then devolved upon General Archdale Wilson.

The siege of Delhi lasted from early May until mid-September 1857, a period of four months. During these four months there were numerous sorties and sallies by the mutineers who attacked, sometimes after considerable preparation, and inflicted considerable casualties on the

19. K. Marx and F. Engels, *The First Indian War of Independence 1857-59*, pp. 64-65.

besiegers. But their lack of higher tactical knowledge and lack of leadership foredoomed their efforts to failure. The British stood fast and were periodically strengthened by new troops coming in from Ambala and Ferozepur, sent down by Sir John Lawrence. As hopes of strong leadership and defeat of the British receded, bands of mutineers started leaving Delhi. At the time of the fall of Delhi in September, only 13,000 mutineers were left in the city[20] whereas the British force had been built up to over 14,000 troops from the 4000 troops in May.

At Kanpur, a force of 200 Europeans under the command of General Wheeler, and having with them families of the British 32nd Foot were besieged by Nana Sahib of Bithur. On 28th June, Wheeler succeeded in extracting a promise from the Nana Sahib that the whole force along with the women and children would be given safe conduct by river boats to Allahabad down the Ganges if Kanpur were surrendered. After the surrender of the fortress, as the women and children and troops were in the process of embarking, Nana Sahib ordered his troops to fire on the fugitives and attack the troops and massacre them. Almost the whole lot of fugitives were killed. General Wheeler's young daughter was abducted and was traced years later when she was on her death bed as an old woman. A Muslim soldier had abducted her and married her, and ensured she could not reach back to her own people.[21] This particular episode of Nana Sahib going back on his word of safe conduct and ordering the killing of men, women and children who had trusted him has tarnished the name, not only of Nana Sahib but also of the mutineers as nothing else did in British and European eyes. Nana Sahib being a Maharashtrian should have remembered the tradition of his forebears, of Shivaji and the Mahratta commanders who always respected women and

20. Ibid., p. 111.

21. Geoffrey Moorhouse, *India Britannica*, pp. 110, 111.

children in all their great campaigns over the length and breadth of India.

General Wheeler died of his wounds, but Brigadier General Henry Havelock, coming up with a column of Europeans 1300 strong,[22] and joined by Major Renaud with another column fought battles with the mutineers on 3rd, 15th and 16th July and recaptured Kanpur. Nana Sahib was defeated and driven north of the Ganges and was pursued but managed to make good his escape first to Bithur and later, after the fall of Lucknow to Nepal where he died destitute.

Lucknow was overwhelmed by the mutineers except for the garrison of Europeans which fortified itself in the Lucknow Residency. A small column of British troops under Sir Henry Lawrence managed to penetrate through the besieging mutineers and joined the garrison in the Residency. However, the garrison was regularly subjected to shelling by the mutineers, but Sir Henry managed to strengthen the defences and reorganise and redeploy the small forces so that the Lucknow Residency was never overrun by the mutineers until it was relieved by Sir Colin Campbell. Sir Henry, however, was wounded in the leg, and died of his wounds on 4th July. But, as mentioned the garrison held out.[23]

Meanwhile, in north-western provinces of Bengal, i.e., in Oudh, in Rohilkhand and in parts of Punjab east of the Sutlej river, British forces were split up into small garrisons occupying important heights in a countryside teeming with mutineers and seething with revolt. In lower Bengal, there was partial insubordination in Mirzapur, Danapore and Patna. There was an unsuccessful attempt by local Brahmins to capture the city of Benares. In Punjab west of the Sutlej, Sir John Lawrence succeeded in keeping the Mutiny down forcibly, suppressing

22. K. Marx and F. Engels, *The First Indian War of Independence 1857-59*, p. 84.

23. Ibid.

CAPTURE OF DELHI
SEPTEMBER 1857

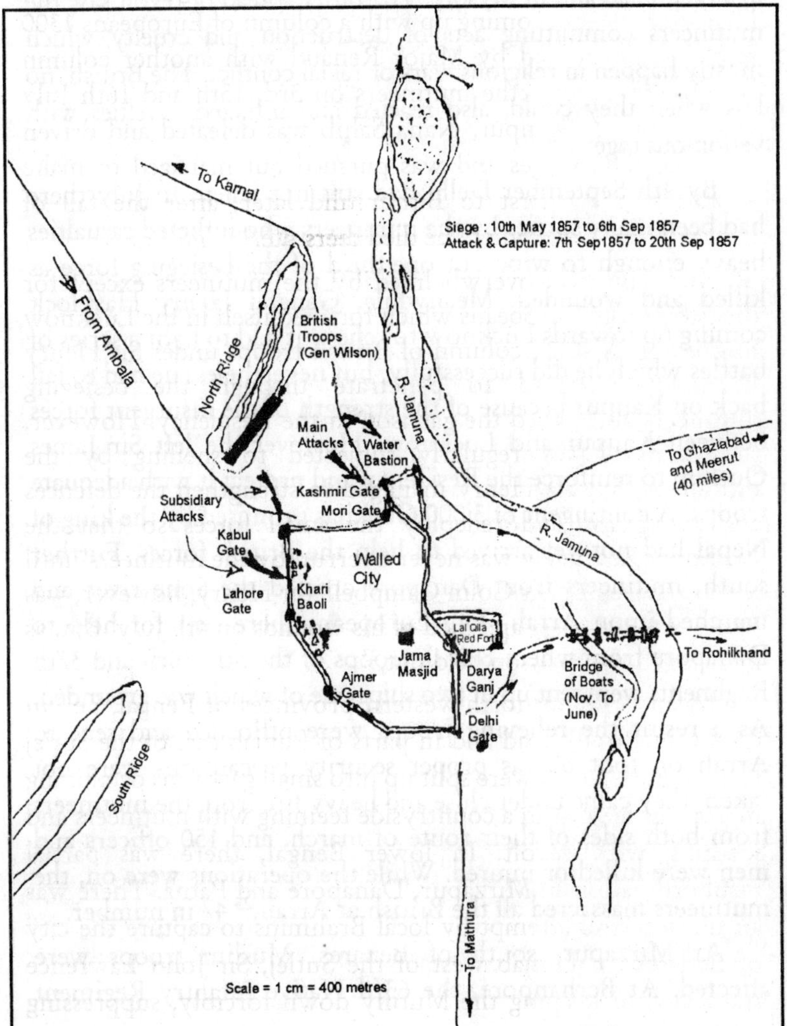

uprisings in Sialkot, Jhelum and Peshawar by strong action and instant retribution, often by hanging.[24] There were disturbances in Gujarat, at Pandharpur in Maharashtra, at Nagpur and Saugor, in Hyderabad and in Mysore. The bitter spread of revolt saw the mutineers committing acts of destruction and cruelty which mostly happen in religious wars or racial conflict. The British, no less when they could, also reacted and inflicted cruelties with venomous rage.

By 4th September Delhi had still not fallen. In July there had been many sorties by the mutineers who inflicted casualties heavy enough to wipe out one-third of the besieging force as killed and wounded. Meanwhile, General Henry Havelock coming up towards Lucknow to relieve it had to fight a series of battles which he did successfully, but nevertheless he had to fall back on Kanpur because of the strength of the insurgent forces between Kanpur and Lucknow. However, he left Sir James Outram to reinforce the Residency and protect it with adequate troops. A contingent of 3,000 Gurkhas promised by the king of Nepal had not yet arrived to help the British forces. Further south, mutineers from Danapore crossed the Sone river and marched upon Arrah. The Europeans there sent for help to Danapore from where British troops of the 5th, 10th and 37th Regiments were sent up in two ships one of which was grounded. As a result the relieving troops were offloaded and sent to Arrah on foot but as proper security precautions were not taken, they came under close and heavy fire from the mutineers from both sides of their route of march, and 150 officers and men were killed or injured. While the operations were on, the mutineers massacred all the British at Arrah,[25] 47 in number.

At Mirzapur, south of Benares, Muslim troops were affected. At Berhanpore, the 63rd Native Infantry Regiment

24. Ibid., p. 85.

25. Ibid., p. 97, a letter quoted from Bengal Gazetteer of 3rd August 1857.

was disarmed. The Governor General, Lord Canning felt compelled to disarm his own bodyguard.[26] That is, by September-October 1857, the whole province of Bengal was affected and the population was tacitly supportive of the mutineers. Further south-west, Holkar's troops were becoming unmanageable, but Scindia's 10,000 well-disciplined troops remained quiet. Scindia himself kept aloof and did not give any indication of either supporting the mutineers or the British. Sir Henry Havelock, marching 126 miles from Allahabad to recapture Kanpur, had to fight battles every day of the eight days he took to reach Kanpur.

The whole of North India was simmering and boiling with revolt. The aim of the war pursued by the British against Indian troops was the recapture of India[27] which was fully supported by the Government in Britain which sent trooploads of British regiments to the help of the beleaguered British in India. The British intended to re-establish and maintain British rule in India. As Delhi was the focal point of the mutineers because of the presence of the aged emperor Bahadur Shah, so was it one for the British whose prestige both at home and in Europe would have suffered badly were they unable to recapture Delhi within reasonable time. Brigadier General Nicholson joined General Wilson before Delhi with 4,000 troops, of whom about 1,300 were Europeans and the rest Punjabis of the 6th Regiment and some horse and foot from Multan. General Nicholson also brought with him a siege train and was joined by 3,000 Kashmiri troops[28] contributed by Raja Ranbir Singh, and his force finally concentrated before Delhi on 5th September.

The Capture of Delhi

Bahadur Shah Zafar, the 82-year-old Mughal emperor, was

26. Ibid., p. 97.
27. Ibid., p. 101.
28. Ibid., p. 111.

greatly inconvenienced by the influx of rebels into Delhi as his usually placid life was generally disrupted. While flattered that the rebels were supporting him to be restored to the power and glory of the old Mughals, and while hopeful that the hyperactive British would be defeated and forced to leave India, he resented the tumultuous activity of the rebels within the citadel, the firing and the sorties of the rebels, the cannonade of the British and the disturbed conditions. There were religious dissensions between Hindus and Muslims. There were quarrels between the old rebels and those arrived later from Rohilkhand and Agra. In spite of all these problems, the rebels withstood an 84-hour continuous bombardment by the British besieging force, and a further six-day cannonade.[29]

The British attack on Delhi started on 5th September 1857 after General Nicholson had joined General Wilson with his troops and siege train. The British force had deployed themselves on the North and South Ridges, on the north-west and west of Delhi respectively, and consisted in all of about 14,000 men, half of them Europeans. The rebels inside the citadel numbered about 13,000 men and had a large number of guns, muskets and reserves of ammunition from the Delhi magazine. Having withstood six days of bombardment, the rebels made two sorties on 10th and 11th September. On 12th September the British suffered a loss of 56 men, but on 13th September they succeeded in targetting and blowing up the ammunition magazine inside Delhi by cannonade. Meanwhile a British sapper officer along with three of his men, all sergeants, succeeded in sapping the walls and blowing open the Kashmir Gate. A second breach was made on the eastern side. The rebels were expecting attacks on the north-west and western wall. The British columns could then advance through the breaches and reach the Mori and Kabul Gates. But then, resistance of the

29. Ibid., p. 112.

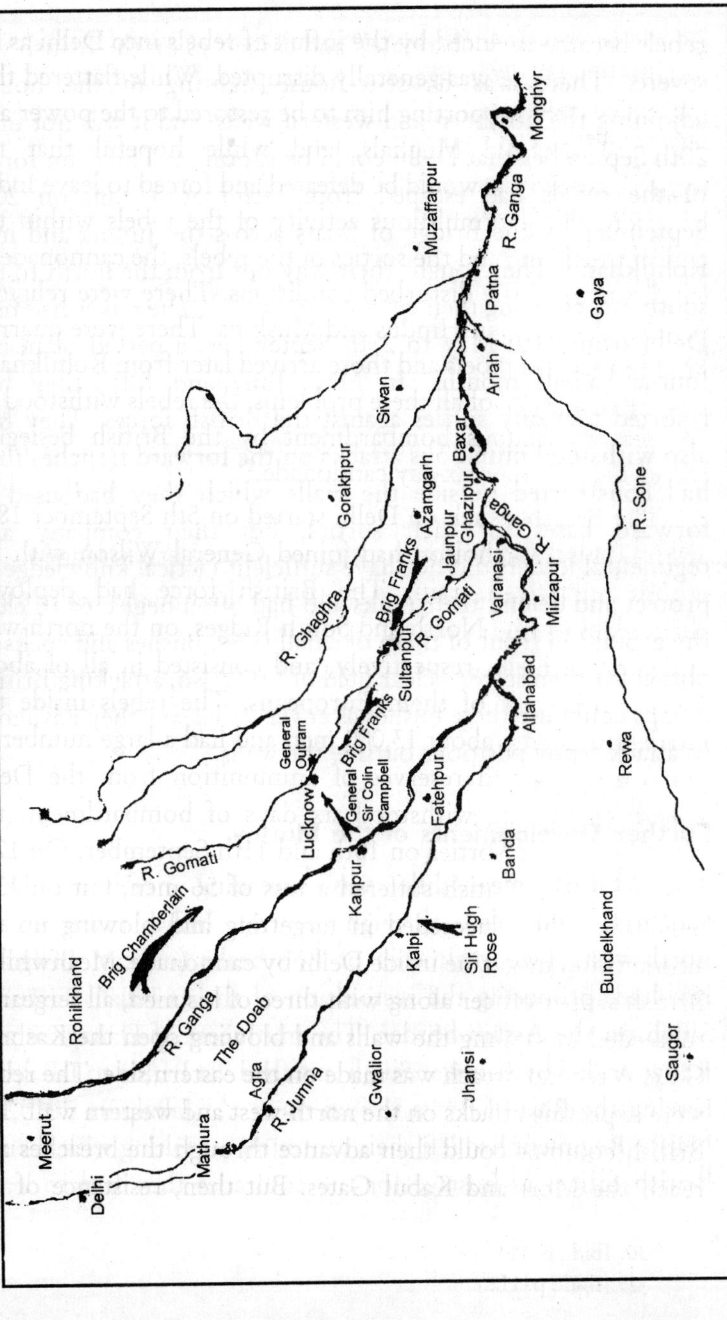

CAPTURE OF LUCKNOW, FEBRUARY-MARCH 1858

rebels became very obstinate[30] and casualties on the British side severe. There was house-to-house fighting in the houses adjoining the northern and western walls, and it was not until 20th September that Delhi could be captured. The main forces of the rebels had escaped from Delhi at 3 a.m. on 20th September by the Bridge of Boats across the Jumna and into Rohilkhand. They fought their way out from the north to the south-east covering their retreat very well.[31] The rebels had held Delhi from 11th May to 20th September, a period of nearly four-and-a-half months. In May, June and July, they had resorted to many sorties against the British forces. They had also withstood numerous attacks on the forward trenches they had constructed outside the walls which they had used as forward bases for their sorties, but their company and regimental leaders did not have sufficient tactical knowledge to protect and defend their ranks and had often neglected to clear the ground in front of them of small trees, bushes and rocks to obtain for themselves a clear field of fire. Also, attacking British troops could use these bushes as cover whenever they advanced to attack sepoy positions outside the walls.

Further Developments of the Mutiny

The Mutiny meanwhile was spreading north-east from Calcutta, and also through central India towards the north-west. Two regiments of Poorbeahs (or East Bengalis) revolted, proposing the restoration of the ex-Rajah Purandar Singh on the Assam border. The mutineers of Danapore and Rangpur, led by Kunwar Singh marched via Banda to Jabalpur, forcing the Raja of Rewa to join them. At Jabalpur, the 52nd Native Regiment had left their cantonments taking with them a British officer as hostage for the comrades they had to leave

30. Ibid., p. 113.
31. Ibid.

behind. The Gwalior mutineers crossed the Chambal river and camped between the river and Dholpur. The Jodhpur legion left and joined the rebel Rajah of Arwah about 90 miles south-west of Beawar. This combined force defeated a force sent by the Raja of Jodhpur, killing the General and Captain Monck Mason. But they were contained by a force under General G. St. P. Lawrence which came up from Nasirabad.[32] In Sind, where most of the European troops had left to reinforce the British at the many points of insurrection, there were attempts at mutiny at Hyderabad (Sind), Karachi and Shikarpur. Communication between Multan and Lahore was cut for eight days. Although 30,000 British troops with their equipment and weapons were sent by sea (round Cape of Good Hope) after 18th June, none arrived in India before October. In fact, 20,000 of these troops arrived only in November and December 1857.

General Windham with 2,000 troops was defeated before Kanpur by the rebels on 27th November, although the latter were poorly organised. The whole force retreated in disorder into the fort, the 88th Regiment and the 34th Regiment being the main troops. But by evening of 28th November, Sir Colin Campbell arrived, defeated the rebels, pursued them and defeated then again on 6th December. The rebels scattered and made their way mostly towards the Nepal border.

Relief and Capture of Lucknow

From June 1857, there were large forces of mutineers who captured Lucknow. The British garrison itself, with a large number of women and children, were forced to protect themselves within the fortified walls of the Lucknow Residency along with Sir Henry Lawrence, the Company appointed commissioner for Oudh. Lawrence dug trenches around the

32. Ibid.

Residency and strengthened the defences. By 1st July the Residency was totally isolated, with the besiegers frequently shelling the positions. Lawrence himself sustained wounds on his leg which soon deteriorated into tetanus and caused his death on 4th July. But the defenders, although having provisions only for about a month, held grimly on, and in fact, sustained themselves until relieved by Sir Henry Havlock on 25th September. Havelock had been attempting to fight his way from Kanpur to relieve Lucknow from July, after he had secured Kanpur. However, although he had to fight twelve pitched battles with the rebels, all of which were successful, he still could not penetrate into the Residency until 25th September. He then left Sir James Outram with a strong force to protect the Residency and himself hurried back to Kanpur where General Windham's garrison troops had been defeated by the rebels in the positions they had occupied defensively in front of the fort walls. Havelock hurried back and retrieved the situation, but could not embark on any offensive operations until the arrival of Sir Colin Campbell.

Lucknow continued to be besieged until Campbell effected the second relief of the Residency. Outram was now given 5000 troops and took up positions at Alambagh a few miles from Lucknow but was still too weak to attack Lucknow.[33] Outram was once again besieged, but held out until Campbell could return after defeating the Gwalior army of 20,000 men under Tantia Tope near Kalpi, some miles south-west of Kanpur. Campbell could return to Lucknow only on 1st March, 1858 when he could effect a junction with Outram's forces. He could now plan the capture of Lucknow.

While Sir James Outram remained at Lucknow, strengthened in November 1857 to a force of 5,000 troops entrenched at Alambagh, a few miles from the city, Sir Colin developed Kanpur as a base of operations for the capture of the

33. Ibid., p. 136.

city of Lucknow. He had already relieved the garrison in the Residency and sent all women and children from Lucknow and Kanpur to the safety of Allahabad, captured earlier and occupied by General Neill. Sir Colin sent to Calcutta for reinforcements and heavy guns, and made elaborate plans for the Lucknow operation. The number of troops, British and Indian, used for this operation exceeded any concentration previously carried out by the British in India.[34] Even in the first Afghan war, 1838-43, the entire force used did not exceed 20,000 of whom the majority were Indian. But for the Lucknow campaign, the British troops alone exceeded 20,000 to which should be added more than 12,000 Indian troops.

The main army, led by Sir Colin Campbell himself personally, consisted of three divisions of infantry, one of cavalry, and one of artillery and engineers (The division, as mentioned, of those times did not exceed about 5,000 to 6,000 men, and is not to be equated to the modern division which may amount to anything from 15,000 to 17,500 men depending upon the army organisation of the particular country). The first division of infantry under Outram consisted of five European battalions and one Indian battalion. The second and third divisions of infantry consisting of nine European and two Indian battalions in all, and the cavalry division commanded by Sir Hugh Rose consisting of three European regiments and five Indian regiments formed Campbell's main force which advanced north-east from Kanpur. This force also had the main portion of the artillery consisting of 48 field guns, siege trains and the engineers. A brigade under Brigadier Franks' advanced from Jaunpur north-west to Lucknow along the south bank of the Gomati river. Franks had under him three European battalions, two artillery batteries and some Indian troops and would form Campbell's right wing before Lucknow. Including Franks' brigade, Campbell's approaching force numbered

34. Ibid., p. 137.

20,000 Europeans and 10,000 Indians. Another 10,000 Gorkha troops under Jang Bahadur Rana were also to join Campbell, marching due west from Gorakhpur, but the timing of the arrival of this force, promised by Nepal was uncertain.[35] A strong column was also approaching from Saugor through Bundelkhand to Kalpi on the Ganges, the aim of which was to intercept and destroy any rebels who might escape through the gap between Campbell's and Franks' forces to reach the sanctuary of the hills of Bundelkhand. A force under Brigadier Chamberlain was also ordered to come from north-west, formed from the troops in Punjab and Delhi to prevent rebels escaping into Rohilkhand and the Terai. While all these columns were assigned their particular tasks, the actual troops to finally attack Lucknow amounted to the 20,000 British and 10,000 Indian troops of General Campbell and the 5,000 troops of General Outram.[36]

The rebels in and around Lucknow consisted of about 40,000 regular troops from the revolted battalions and about 1,00,000 or more local levies organised by the rebels.[37] While the regular troops had reliable armament and ammunition, the local levies were of far inferior training and had only their local matchlocks, spears and daggers which were more suited to close quarter battle. Hence, these local levies were virtually useless as, obviously, the British did not intend that they should engage in such close quarter battle until the rebels had been pounded and demoralised by heavy artillery fire. Apart from leadership at Company level, there was hardly any cohesion or unified plan among the rebel forces already disheartened by desertions and a sense of impending defeat and rout. Their most important leader, Nana Sahib, does not appear to have shown himself very much in rallying the rebel forces or infusing in them any sense of mission. It is remarkable that, in spite of such lack of

35. Ibid., pp. 137-138.

36. Ibid, p. 138.

37. Ibid, p. 139.

leadership, the rebel forces continued to occupy their positions and prepared themselves to fight. In fact, two columns of the rebel forces were despatched some time earlier in the direction of Allahabad and Jaunpur.

From 15th February 1858, Campbell's forces moved from Kanpur to Lucknow, reaching the latter city on 26th February, meeting no resistance en route. Meanwhile, the rebels launched desperate attacks on Outram's positions on 21st February and 24th February without any success. The rebel columns moving towards Allahabad and Jaunpur were met by Brigadier Franks at Sultanpur. He defeated both of them on the same day and tried to pursue them. These columns, however, joined up and confronted Franks together on the 23rd February, but were again defeated, losing 20 of their field guns and all their camp and baggage.[38]

Lucknow was on the south bank of the Gomati river, and to the south of the city there was a large irrigation canal. While Campbell's main force reached the canal on 2nd March, Brigadier Franks joined up on the right on 4th March. The rebels had thrown up strong entrenchments and defences between Lucknow and the canal and were preparing to resist. Campbell commenced his first attack on 3rd March, occupying the Dilkush Park. Artillery emplacements were constructed by the British for pounding the enemy positions beyond the canal. Also, Outram constructed two floating bridges across the Gomati and crossed his division of infantry, his 1,400 horses and 30 guns, taking position from where he could fire enfilade on the rebel positions along the canal, and on many fortified palaces to their rear. Outram also cut off all enemy communication with north-eastern Oudh. On 6th and 7th March, he was attacked by rebel forces, but succeeded in driving them off. On 8th March, he was again attacked but

38. Ibid., pp. 139-140.

could repulse the enemy.[39] Now the artillery batteries of the main British forces began their bombardment and were effectively supported by Outram's batteries which could pound the rebels from flank and rear. On 9th March, the 2nd division under General Sir E. Lugard stormed the Martiniere school area with its park, situated at the junction of the canal and river Gomati, and opposite Dilkush Park. On the 10th, the Bank House was taken, with Outram advancing up the river and bringing down enfilading fire on every successive position of the rebels. On 11th March, two highland battalions stormed the queen's palace, and Outram crossed back into the town over the two stone bridges over the Gomati which he had succeeded in capturing. On 13th March, the fortified Imambara was attacked and taken. The fighting was now well and truly within the city. The rebels left the Imambara and concentrated in the Kaiserbagh palace but were hotly pursued by the attackers. There was close and desperate hand to hand fighting, but by 3 p.m. on 14th March, the palace was in British hands. The loss of the Kaiserbagh ended organised resistance within the city, and the rebels got out of the city in strong bands. Still many remained behind to fight in the streets and in the houses, and from 15th to the 19th March, Campbell's troops were engaged in overcoming this desperate resistance. It was not until the 19th that the city was completely in Campbell's possession. About 50,000 rebels escaped, partly to Rohilkhand, some to the Doab and some south to Bundelkhand.[40] After the fall of Lucknow, the British had to fight forces in the Central Indian campaign.

Jhansi and Gwalior

The decision of the British Governor General Dalhousie not to

39. Ibid.
40. Ibid., pp. 140-141.

recognise the regency of the young Rani of Jhansi on behalf of the adopted son, a minor, of her dead husband who was issueless, caused tremendous dissatisfaction in the court of Jhansi. The widowed Rani on whom devolved the responsibility of regency until the adopted son grew up, felt that this cavalier disregard of one of the ancient practices of Hindu rajas amounted to an insult not to be brooked. With the support of her nobles she resolved to fight.

The fort of Jhansi, cunningly constructed by French engineers, consisted of three massive walls, one within the other, and the inner ramparts being successively higher than the outer one. From the innermost citadel, a subterranean tunnel existed for the escape of the besieged to a riverside some distance from the fort, should the latter be stormed and captured. The British besieged the fort, but the Mahratta rebel leader Tantia Tope arrived to relieve it but took no decisive action to attack the besiegers. He remained inert near the fort while deliberating the best course of action. However, as often in such situations the lack of action invites attack and defeat, Sir Hugh Rose attacked him in March 1858, drove him away and captured the fort.[41] However, Rani Laxmi Bai escaped with her ward, joined up with Tantia Tope but their combined forces were defeated at Kunch.[42] However, Tantia Tope and Rani Laxmi Bai went to Gwalior and won over the Scindia's troops. Tantia Tope with a force of 20,000 men seized Gwalior. The British had to fight two more battles before Gwalior could be captured. In one of these battles, the Rani of Jhansi was killed fighting. She was found lying on the battlefield in a soldier's uniform with a scimitar in her hand.

The defeat of Tantia Tope and the Rani of Jhansi, and the capture of Gwalior on 20th June 1858 brought the Mutiny to

41. Vincent A. Smith, *The Oxford History of India*, p. 670.

42. K.L. Srivastava, *The Revolt of 1857 in Central India-Malwa*, p. 108.

an end. Lord Canning proclaimed peace on 8th July 1858.[43] However, mopping up operations continued, but they were only against armed fugitive bands that had to survive by appropriating the food of the villagers. Hence, these armed bands themselves lost the support of the villagers who, in fact, ambushed them wherever possible to seize the money and jewellery these bands had looted in their flight from Lucknow and Gwalior. Tantia Tope, probably the best motivated and tactically able leader that the Mutiny produced, eluded capture until he was betrayed and captured in April 1859. He was tried and hanged for his supposed complicity in the massacre at Kanpur in June 1857.[44]

The Character of the Fighting and Reasons for the Failure of the Mutiny

These aspects have already been partly discussed earlier, but certain other important aspects emerge after the whole Mutiny is looked at in perspective. From May 1857, when the Mutiny was recognised to have broken out at Meerut, to June 1868 when Lucknow was captured, the sepoys showed tremendous courage at various times and an indomitable will to defeat the British. In their actions at Delhi, between 10th May and July 1857 they displayed competence in military tactics and adopted a policy of active defence (or offensive defence) by which they organised several sallies from the fort, attacking Wilson's troops on the North Ridge and causing appreciable casualties. They even established defensive trenches outside the walls which they used as firm bases for launching attacks on the British positions, with their field guns on the walls providing covering fire. During May and June 1857 they could well have launched full scale attacks, sustained over a period of days, and dislodged and driven away the British from their positions on the Ridge.

43. Vincent A. Smith, *The Oxford History of India*, p. 671.
44. Ibid.

However, they did not attempt to do so either due to divided counsel, or the lack of a dominating self-confident leader, or perhaps because their material resources in the forces of the guns and ammunition were not adequate for a full scale assault which could be sustained over a few days to push it to a successful conclusion. It could have been a combination of these factors. After the British were reinforced by troops from Ambala and Ferozepur, the opportunity may have passed, never to recur. The mutineers kept open their line of communications with Rohilkhand with the help of the Bridge of Boats in May and early June, and once again in early September with the monsoons having reduced in intensity. With confusion about overall objectives, lack of strong central leadership and internal dissensions between groups, many units left the fort and passed over to Rohilkhand and Oudh.[45] But they left as units, in possession of their weapons, their guns and their ammunition.

The sepoys seem to have expected British attacks on Delhi from the south and east, although how they came to this conclusion is not easily understood. The explanation seems to be that the north and western walls of the citadel of Delhi had a lot of civilian built-up area right upto the walls, whereas the areas within the walls on the south and east were relatively free and gave clear access to the Red Fort.[46] But when the British attacks did materialise in September on the north and west, the sepoys switched their troops to defend those sides. Ultimately, when the British entered through the breaches in the walls, the sepoys fought heroically in the streets and in the houses for four or five days[47] which demonstrated their hatred of the foe.

45. Ibid.

46. K. Marx, and F. Engels, *The First Indian War of Independence 1857-59*, in "The Capture of Delhi", pp. 121-123.

47. Bisheshwar Prasad, *Bondage and Freedom 1707 to 1947*, Vol. I, "Bondage, 1707-1858", p. 558.

General Windham who was in Kanpur in November 1857, being positioned there with over 2000 regular troops by Sir Colin Campbell who had proceeded to Lucknow for the second relief of the Residency there, was confronted by the rebels. They attacked General Windham's defensive positions outside the walls of Kanpur inflicting several casualties and forcing him to withdraw into the fort.[48] Sir Colin Campbell, and before him, General Havelock had to fight many pitched battles in their advance over the 125 miles from Kanpur to Lucknow. Rani Laxmi Bai's defence of the fort of Jhansi extended for over four days before she decided to escape and join Tantia Tope outside the walls.

In Sir Colin Campbell's Lucknow campaign, in spite of concentration around Lucknow of British and Indian forces numbering over 80,000 men, complete with heavy artillery and engineer support, it needed nearly 20 days of actual fighting before Lucknow could be captured. Out of these, the last five days were fully occupied with overcoming resistance of the rebels in the streets and houses of the old city. In spite of all precautions, 50,000 regular troops of the rebels escaped from the city and operated as guerrilla bands in Oudh, Rohilkhand and in the jungles of Bundelkhand and could be overcome only by June 1858. But in fighting as mobile columns, the rebels had not been very good fighters as evidenced by Brigadier Franks' victories at Sultanpur during his advance from Jaunpur to Lucknow in February, when he defeated the rebels who were several times his own numerical strength. But perhaps by that time, many of the rebels had felt that the days of the Mutiny were numbered, and that they should seek to escape while it was still possible for them to do so.

The various kings, princes and chieftains who had made common cause with the rebels had each their own particular

48. K. Marx and F. Engels, *The First Indian War of Independence 1857-59*, in "Windham's Defeat", pp. 130, 131.

motives and supported or withdrew their support in accordance with the denial or grant of their own requirements by the British.[49] In this, the British Agents and Residents in Oudh, Rohilkhand, Malwa, Bundelkhand and Rajputana played skilfully on the desires, hopes, feuds, greed and intrigues in the courts of these potentates and succeeded in dividing them and confusing them. It is, in fact astonishing how princes like Holkar, Scindia, Oudh, Mewar, Kashmir and so on, having sway over states larger than Italy or Holland or England, or even France could be manipulated by the diplomatic skill of a few army officers positioned individually at their courts supported by company forces of 1,000 or 2,000 regular troops.[50] To compound matters, the succession intrigues in favour of, or against, adopted sons as heirs in the courts of Holkar and Scindia, of Jhansi and Bhopal, had become chronically self-defeating, in which the British Residents took part enthusiastically. The lack of participation of Jayaji Rao Scindia of Gwalior and Tukoji Rao Holkar of Indore in supporting the rebels and leaders like the Nana Sahib of Bithur was not a small factor in the eventual defeat of the rebels.

On the other hand, the British officers from John Lawrence in Punjab to General Wilson and Nicholson at Delhi, or Generals Havelock and Campbell in Oudh, or Outram at Lucknow, displayed coolness and determination in meeting the initial threat of the rebels with small forces. They showed steadfast character coupled with military skills and ability in planning and executing the defeat, pursuit and destruction of the rebels as a fighting force at the various major centres of confrontation. A great boost to their confidence and morale was the support and preparedness of Lord Canning at Calcutta

49. Bisheshwar Prasad, *Bondage and Freedom 1707 to 1947*, Vol. I, "Bondage, 1707-1858", p. 570.

50. K.L. Srivastava, *The Revolt of 1857 in Central India and Malwa*, pp. 110, 100, etc.

and the British Government in London to help the British leaders in every way possible. But it is to the credit of such leaders in the field that they broke the Mutiny before supporting forces from England could join up and reinforce them.

After-Effects of the Mutiny

British officers and troops and administrators looked at Indians with new eyes during and after the Mutiny and were out to seek vengeance and humiliate Indians whenever and wherever possible. Captured rebels were tried by summary or Kangaroo courts and sentenced to be hanged. But before the sentence was executed, Hindus and Muslims were stuffed in their mouths with beef and pork to inflict on them what Britishers thought to be the ultimate humiliation and insult, that is, to defile their caste and their religion.[51] In Kanpur, captured rebels were made to lick the ground after Britishers urinated thereon. Their hatred of Indians and their desire for the most bloodthirsty vengeance became a paranoid obsession. Great cruelty and dastardly acts had been done on both sides,[52] chief among which were the Nana Sahib's orders for the massacre on 27th June 1857 of General Wheeler's men and of over 125 women and children who had surrendered at Kanpur on the basis of a promise of safe conduct, and of General Neill's actions on his capture of Allahabad. After capture of Arrah in Bihar by the rebels, every man in the British garrison there had been killed. In Peshawar and Punjab, John Lawrence executed by hanging hundreds of sepoys who showed signs of mutiny.

However, Lord Canning, the Governor General who had weathered the storm of the Mutiny throughout 1857 and upto

51. Bisheshwar Prasad, *Bondage and Freedom 1707 to 1947*, Vol. I, "Bondage, 1707-1858", p. 557. Also see Geoffrey Moorhouse, *India Britannica*, p. 114.
52. Vincent A. Smith, *The Oxford History of India*, p. 668.

July 1858 when he was able to declare peace, and who had by firm policies and effective support of his commanders in the field and of his political agents and governors provided steady, rock-like administration and leadership, now stepped in. He adopted a policy of healing the bitter wounds by restraining the violent vengeance-seekers. While disbanding affected units, he showed every mark of consideration to the Indian troops who had not mutinied but who had fought reliably alongside the British troops. He reduced the scale of punishment by allowing only those rebels to be hanged who were definitely proved to have committed cruel and criminal acts. While not withdrawing his proclamation for confiscation of the lands of those taluqdars of Oudh who could not furnish documentary proof of rights to the lands they held, he mitigated the effect by re-grant of confiscated lands to those taluqdars who were known to have been in undisputed possession of the lands for several years.[53] While his policy of healing was greatly resented, especially by those military and civil officers who had been in the actual battles, he held to it steadfastly and forced his officers to implement it as he desired. They scornfully called him "Clemency Canning" but this derisive epithet did in fact describe him accurately during this phase of his tenure.[54] He gradually restored good relations with the Mahratta and Rajput princes, and the Muslim nobility of Oudh, Bihar and Bengal. He rewarded those Sikh states which had remained aloof from the Mutiny, and the Maharaja of Kashmir who had provided troops to help the British. However, he restored British control of all the Indian states by maintaining Residents and troops in them at the cost of those states. By the time he left India in 1862, he had succeeded in large measure in reconciling the Indian people to British administration. In this he was ably supported by Sir John Lawrence.

53. Ibid., pp. 675, 676.

54. Ibid., p. 675.

By the Queen's proclamation of 1st November 1858, the East India Company was relieved of the administration of India, and India was brought under the direct administration of the British Government through a Secretary of State for India who was subordinate only to the Cabinet and to whom the Governor General of India was responsible for the government of the country. The Government of India Act of 1858, passed by the British Parliament, ushered in a whole new era for India with incalculable effects on the people of India.

The Mutiny exposed on a near-national scale the lack of unity among the ruling classes of India who were all too prone to magnify their individual grievances, their petty quarrels and feuds, to a degree where their satisfaction or solution assumed far greater importance than the creeping, inexorable domination of themselves by a foreign power represented in the country by a few thousand soldiers and administrators. Until November 1857, the British in India, inclusive of all sections, never numbered more than 40,000 heads. From November 1857 to March 1858, about 30,000 troops were sent out from England to help the East India Company control and suppress the Mutiny, but these reinforcements were neutralised by the death of soldiers in the fighting and by sickness and disease in the unaccustomed monsoon climate. Whether Hindus or Muslims, the princely and warrior families which normally provided the leadership were riven by intrigues for power and succession, for control of this or that border territory, or for the revenue of this or that district. The British, unified in their aims, closely controlled by their leadership both in India and Britain, actuated in their mental processes by reason, logic, cool calculation and overall patriotism, were able to easily manipulate the local kings, princes and chieftains by their diplomatic skills. They backed up these skills by their well-disciplined troops and their superior military knowledge and organisation, so much so that even their Indian troops trained by them were feared by all through the length and breadth of India. Although almost all the fighting classes of India in the service of Indian states were brave and motivated, and often held their lives of little account when actually committed to battle, they failed because of loose organisation, untutored leadership and lack of co-ordination. The British troops with their Indian auxiliaries were so much feared that soon the mere news of the approach of the "Sarkar's" troops made the troops of Indian states feel that the impending battle was already lost.

The British studied with genuine interest the character of the various princes. They studied at least in the form of a working knowledge, the religion, beliefs, superstitions and social practices of the Hindus and Muslims and made use of this knowledge like true rulers and administrators to influence and play upon the feelings of the princes, the villagers, the trades-people and the soldiers for their own advantage. This trait of theirs, combined with personal courage, pride in their nationhood, their sense of unity and their discipline enabled them to rule and dominate vast territories in North and Central America, in Africa, in West Asia, in India and in Australia with remarkable success.

On the other hand, the high priority given by Indian rulers and leaders to their personal interests, to their individual egos and their own '*izzat*' or honour and self-respect came in the way of unity even when they recognised the British as the single greatest threat to their own power and well-being. Even the great Mahratta people, united by religion, by culture and even by physical stock, failed to subjugate their personal desires in the interest of political and military unity and surrendered political power to the British. The desire for private gain or personal power, and the desire to score off their local rivals, became more important than forging a national unity to defeat and eject a foreign foe from their country.

These same tendencies, promoted by an individually

oriented religion, are heavily contributing to the subversion of Indian nationhood by being exploited by foreign business and national interests to dominate India's economy. This has its parallel now in the 'liberalisation' period of the Indian economy. Although the western industrial nations are not really interested in territorial conquest, they have a common policy to economically exploit the old colonies of which India is an attractive prospect because of its huge, over 1,000 million, population and its 250 million upswinging middle-class. The middle-class which provided the intellectual leadership for India in the 20th century, and was known for its austerity, its discipline and its strong moral values has become enamoured of the consumerist culture and has adopted as its status symbols the possession of luxurious houses, fast streamlined cars and a superficial western value system. It has therefore surrendered its leadership role. The commercial classes, especially the finance merchants, and the giant industrial houses have mortgaged the country's future by spiriting away their wealth and stashing it away in foreign banks where they do not have to pay the heavy taxes which India cannot do without imposing for the improvement in the social condition of the 500 million people near, or below, the poverty line. The powerful politicians and bureaucrats enter into virtually personal relations with Western multi-national companies to frame sleight-of-hand policies which commit the Government of India and governments of the states to anti-national policies which would only serve to drain away the wealth of India, created by her uniquely talented people, and to progressively impoverish the country. The attitudes of these politicians and bureaucrats are completely cynical and are particularly anti-social and anti-national in character, and are therefore near-criminal in nature when one considers that they have been fully educated and trained to have a national outlook and spirit, in contrast to the partial and diffuse nationalism of the early 19th century. This trend has to be arrested by once again creating a value system which had prevailed in large measure in the early and mid-20th century. The insidious influence of western consumerist culture should be counter-acted among the wealthy and middle classes who have been the principal gainers as a result of independence. It is they who have been principally responsible for a dilution of old value systems, and who have become the principal offenders in working to mortgage India to foreign national and financial interests.

This digression in the concluding chapter of this book is made to ponder over the question whether India has learnt any lessons from the Mutiny.

Bibliography

Bamber, Gascoigne, *The Great Moghals*, London: Jonathan Cape, 1971.

Basham, A.L., *The Wonder That Was India*, Calcutta: Rupa & Co, 1997.

Al-Beruni, *India*, Qeyamuddin Ahmed (ed.), New Delhi: National Book Trust, India, 1983.

Chaudhuri, Nirad C., *Clive of India*, Bombay: Jaico, 1978.

Chinnappa, N., *Pattolé Palamé*, Reprinted by Karnataka Kodava Sahitya Academy (in Kannada script), 1996.

Gibbs, Sir Hamilton A.R, *Mohammedanism: An Historical Survey*, The New American Library, 1953.

Griffiths, Sir Percival, *The British Impact on India*, London: MacDonald & Co., 1952.

Gupta, Rajni Kant, *The Military Traits of Tantya Tope*, New Delhi: S. Chand & Co., 1987.

The History and Culture of the Indian People (Fourth Edition), Mumbai: Bharatiya Vidya Bhavan, 1988.

Lawrence, T.E., *The Seven Pillars of Wisdom*, New York: Dell Publishing Co., 1967.

Marx, K., and Engels, F., *The First Indian War of Independence, 1857-1859*, Moscow: Foreign Languages Publishing House, 1959.

Majumdar, R.C., *Ancient India*, Delhi: Motilal Banarsidass, 1994.

Moorhouse, Geoffrey, *India Britannica*, London: Harvill Press, 1983.

Nehru, Jawaharlal, *The Discovery of India*, London: Meridian Books, 1960.

Panikkar, K.M., *A Survey of Indian History*, Bombay: The National Informations and Publications Ltd., 1947.

Prasad, Bisheshwar, *Bondage and Freedom 1707 to 1947*, 2 Vols, New Delhi: Rajesh Publications, 1979.

Row, B. Suryanarayana, *A History of Vijayanagara: The Never to be Forgotten Empire*, New Delhi: Asian Educational Services, Reprinted 1998.

Shaman, Hwui Li, *The Life of Hiuen Tsang*, translated by Samuel Beal, New Delhi: Asian Educational Services, Reprint 1997.

Smith, Vincent A., *The Oxford History of India*, New Delhi: Oxford University Press, Reprinted 1997.

Srivastava, Kushalilal, *The Revolt of 1857 in Central India - Malwa*, New Delhi: Allied Publishers, 1966.

Thapa, Netra B., *A Short History of Nepal*, Kathmandu: Ratna Pustak Bhandar, 1981.

Tolstoy, Count Leo N., *War and Peace*, translated by Constance Garnett, The Modern Library, New York, Random House Inc.

Index